GETTING OPEN

Winner of the Indiana Center for the Book's 2007 Best in Indiana Award for Nonfiction

---

"Before there could be five black starters, there had to be one. ... Bill Garrett was the first black basketball player in the prestigious Big Ten." —*Booklist*

"To the average aspiring Michael Jordan or LeBron James, Bill Garrett is a far more important figure [than Jackie Robinson], a now nearly forgotten hero who used his considerable talent, brains, and character to open the door of opportunity for black players. ... [This] is a story of endurance, perseverance, and achievement on a par with any in the history of desegregation." —*Washington Times*

"One of the most engaging sports stories I have ever read." —*Indianapolis Monthly*

"A great basketball book, rich with Hoosier lore and on-court drama, ... [it is] also the story of the handful of trailblazers, black and white, who pushed back against the full institutional weight of segregation at the height of the Jim Crow era." —*Indiana Alumni Magazine*

"Beyond the racial overtones that help define the time and place in the book, its greater context includes the present. For a country at a crucial turning point in its social consciousness, *Getting Open* offers a quiet but necessary reminder of certain essential values that might be within our reach." —*Washington Post*

"This meticulously researched book sets basketball in its context, a world likely to be alien to many readers: an Indiana with the Klan and segregation; the postwar Indiana University, with its influx of veterans and very separate life of black students; but a world that black veterans and Jackie Robinson were changing."

—*Baltimore Sun*

"Character-rich and thoroughly revealing of its times . . . and the characters alone make it worth the while. Faburn DeFrantz . . . an early civil right giant whose deft influence cracked open the door to IU for Garrett. . . . Nate Kaufman, the son of a Polish Jew [who] became one of Garrett's most stalwart supporters . . . IU President Herman Wells, a giant in his own right. Legendary basketball coach Branch McCracken, the reluctant integrationist . . . Phil Buck, Gene Ring, and Bill Tosheff, white Indiana teammates whose ready acceptance of Garrett was . . . remarkable for its time." —*Ft. Wayne Journal-Gazette*

"Much more than a dry retelling of Garrett's biography—the Grahams have come up with a story that reads more like a novel [and] transports the ready from the dusty streets of Shelbyville on the wrong side of the tracks in the 1940's, through the pains of integration at IU to taking over the reins at Crispus Attucks and leading them to the state title in racially-charged Indianapolis in the late '50's." —Washington [IN] *Times-Herald*

"Bill Garrett did more than break through basketball's racial barrier. [He] changed the course of sports history."

—Johnson County [IN] *Daily Journal*

"*Getting Open* doesn't end with a rah rah feel good ending, like *Glory Road*, where the upshot is a glorious victory. . . . But every African American basketball player who has since followed should be eternally grateful to the person who blazed the trail." —*Peegs Inside Indiana*

"A terrific read, covering a wealth of interesting subjects and personalities." —Angelo Pizzo, writer/producer of *Hoosiers*

"Not just entertaining—informative, provocative, and a worthy tribute to an epic figure." —Bob Hammel, past president of the U.S. Basketball Writers Association and the National Sportscasters and Sportswriters Association

"That rare bird: a sports book that even the reader who doesn't care much for sports will devour." —*Indiana Alumni Magazine*

GETTING OPEN

The Unknown Story of Bill Garrett and the Integration of College Basketball

Tom Graham and **Rachel Graham Cody**

INDIANA UNIVERSITY PRESS
BLOOMINGTON & INDIANAPOLIS

This book is a publication of

Indiana University Press
601 North Morton Street
Bloomington, IN 47404-3797 USA

http://iupress.indiana.edu

Telephone orders	800-842-6796
Fax orders	812-855-7931
Orders by e-mail	iuporder@indiana.edu

© 2006 by Rachel Graham Cody and Tom Graham
Originally published by Atria Books, an Imprint of Simon & Schuster Inc.
Indiana University Press paperback edition 2008

The paper used in this publication meets the minimum requirements of American
National Standard for Information Sciences—Permanence of Paper for Printed
Library Materials, ANSI Z39.48-1984.

Manufactured in the United States of America

Library of Congress Cataloging-in-Publication Data

Graham, Tom.
Getting open : the unknown story of Bill Garrett and the integration of
college basketball / Tom Graham, Rachel Graham Cody.
p. cm.
Originally published: New York : Atria Books, 2006.
Includes bibliographical references and index.
ISBN 978-0-253-22046-2 (pbk. : alk. paper) 1. Garrett, Bill, 1929–1974.
2. Basketball players—Indiana—Biography. 3. Basketball—Indiana—
Shelbyville—History. 4. Discrimination in sports—Indiana—
History. 5. Indiana Hoosiers (Basketball team)—History.
I. Cody, Rachel. II. Title.
GV884.G375C63 2008
796.323092—dc22
[B]
2008028559

1 2 3 4 5   13 12 11 10 09 08

Contents

Well, what happens now to Bill Garrett, Emerson Johnson and Marshall Murray? After the medals and trophies have been stored away, what then? Was it all just moonglow?

Was all the celebrating merely a moment of brotherhood in an eternity of intolerance?

THE INDIANAPOLIS RECORDER
APRIL 12, 1947

Lake
Michigan

MICHIGAN

CHICAGO

MICHIGAN CITY

EAST CHICAGO

FORT WAYNE

Wabash River

MARION

Michigan Road

ILLINOIS

LAFAYETTE

MUNCIE

ANDERSON

OHIO

INDIANAPOLIS

SHELBYVILLE

MARTINSVILLE

TERRE HAUTE

COLUMBUS

BLOOMINGTON

CINCINNATI

INDIANA

MADISON

KENTUCKY

JEFFERSONVILLE

EVANSVILLE

LOUISVILLE

Ohio River

Prologue

ON A SPRING DAY WARM ENOUGH TO HINT AT THE HUMID
summer to come, the Harlem Globetrotters landed in Indianapolis. It
was April 19, 1951, halfway through the second annual "World Series
of Basketball," a Globetrotter-sponsored cross-country series of games
between the Trotters and the college All-Americans—one of the best
pro teams against the best amateurs. The Globetrotters were the most
popular sports act in the world; their series with the All-Americans
was drawing record crowds across the country, and Indianapolis was
no exception. On that Monday night fourteen thousand people
turned out, still, more than fifty years later, the largest crowd ever to
see an athletic event at the Indiana State Fairgrounds Coliseum.

My family arrived early, and by the time the lights dimmed we
were settled in our seats high up on one side of the vast Coliseum.
We joined in the polite drizzle of applause as the first nine All-
Americans, all of them white, were introduced in perfunctory succession. At some point my mother, who believed she could foresee
the outcomes of horse races and basketball games, stage-whispered
proudly, "He's gonna be last." And indeed, with only one player left,
the emcee paused and the crowd quieted. When he started up again,
his voice was a little deeper, his cadence a little slower. "And now
. . . ladies and gentlemen . . . here is *everybody's* All-American. . . . In
1947 he led Shelbyville High School to the . . ." That was as far as he
got before fourteen thousand fans were on their feet, blocking my
view, their cheers drowning out everything else as Bill Garrett, the
lone black All-American, stepped into the spotlight and trotted to
center court. I was eight years old, and I thought nothing in life
would ever make me as proud as I was at that moment, hearing all
those people—from all over the state—cheering the man who had

been my, my family's, and my town's hero for as long as I could remember.

If anyone had been looking for a civil rights breakthrough in the years immediately following World War II, Indiana probably would not have been on their list. Often called "the most southern state in the North," Indiana had a sorry history of race relations and was hostile to change. The Ku Klux Klan had controlled the state in the 1920s. In 1930 Indiana had been the site of a double lynching, one of the last north of the Mason-Dixon Line. And through the 1940s a patchwork of segregation blanketed the state.

But the war changed things, even in Indiana. In the years after 1945, all over the country, blacks emboldened by their wartime experiences and unwilling to return to the status quo were putting quiet pressure on institutions ripe for integration. One was the armed forces, another was major league baseball, and a third was college basketball—which from Pennsylvania to Oregon was as segregated as swimming pools, neighborhoods, and churches.

The key to integrating college basketball was to break the gentleman's agreement barring blacks from the teams of the Big Ten athletic conference.* Stretching across the Midwest from Ohio to Iowa, the Big Ten was at the center of the country's industrial and psychological heartland—the place where "real Americans" set the tone of the nation, many believed. Big Ten universities were in or near major urban centers such as Chicago, Detroit, and Minneapolis. Some claimed a whiff of elite status, such as Northwestern and the University of Michigan, and a few, like Wisconsin and Minnesota, were keepers of their states' progressive traditions. Several were in states that produced outstanding black high school basketball players year after year, such as Indiana, Ohio, and Illinois. As long as the Big Ten's gentleman's agreement held, others could hide behind it, and if it fell, others would be next in line.

Indiana in the 1940s had neither urban centers nor a progressive tradition; it was considered by many the sticks of the Midwest—its capital derided as "Indy-no-place." But in the summer of 1947, as

---

*The Big Ten was called the "Big Nine" from 1946, when the University of Chicago withdrew, until 1950, when Michigan State joined. For simplicity, it is called the Big Ten throughout this book.

Jackie Robinson was integrating major league baseball, Indiana had four things that existed in combination nowhere else: a pervasive basketball tradition; a leader of the largest black YMCA in the world who was pushing sports as a wedge for integration; a state university president of boundless determination and finesse; and a teenager who was, as nearly as any civil rights pioneer has ever been, the right person for his role and his time.

In hindsight, it is easy to see that the Big Ten's gentleman's agreement was doomed and that basketball, along with other facets of American life, eventually would be integrated. But we didn't know that at the time. Events usually look inevitable only after the fact. Like the emcee, the mostly white crowd at the Coliseum in 1951 knew there was something special about Bill Garrett's presence among the college All-Americans, and we cheered harder because of it. But it would be a long time before we would fully understand what we were cheering so hard for.

PART ONE

1

October 15, 1943

INDIAN SUMMER CAME LATE TO SHELBYVILLE, A WELCOME respite in hard times. The war in Europe and the Pacific was taking the lives of American soldiers at a rate of more than six thousand a month—some of them local boys drafted straight out of high school—and though the conflict was starting to turn in the Allies' favor, the end was not yet in sight and the outcome was still uncertain.

Fear for the boys at war hung over the small Indiana town like a gray net. Families traced their loved ones' movements with stickpins and crayons on giant maps spread across kitchen tables and tried to guess where their soldiers might be headed next. Starred flags dotted windows all over town, blue for a family member in military service, gold for a son or father who would not return. A few days earlier, a fight had broken out at Walt's Bar & Grille when a farmer had boasted of high wartime grain prices, saying, "This is the best year I've ever had," and a mechanic, with a son overseas, had responded with a right cross.

There were also wartime shortages: gasoline, coffee, sugar, and most other staples were rationed. But shortages did not bring dread of the next news bulletin, and making do with little was nothing new to a population that had just come through the Great Depression. In Shelbyville, as throughout the country, people were accustomed to low expectations and were told to be grateful for any job, eat what was put in front of them, wear what they had, and not whine or make trouble. Irving Berlin had captured the prevailing mood in song: "This is the army, Mr. Jones! No private rooms or telephones!"

On this warm day almost two years into the war, in the shops and offices on Shelbyville's public square, men too old to be soldiers rolled up the sleeves of their white dress shirts and loosened their short, broad ties. Everywhere radios played low in the background, the surface calm belying ears and nerves alert for news. In neat frame houses along side streets women dusted and ironed to the click and rattle of electric fans, hurrying to finish and freshen up before their men came home to have their supper, listen to Gabriel Heatter deliver the day's news with feeling ("There's good neeeews tonight!"), and sit on the porch swing to read the *Shelbyville Democrat*.

In other times and other states people might call a sunny fall day like this a football afternoon, but in Indiana's high schools it was the first day of basketball tryouts, and war or no war, few high school boys across the state could think of anything else.

At Shelbyville High School, a three-story redbrick rectangle in the town's south end, 560 boys and girls fidgeted in their homerooms waiting for the 3:20 bell. In one of those rooms five boys, the school's entire contingent of black freshmen, sat across the back row. Nearest the window Bill Garrett leaned back, stretched his arms, brought his hands together, right thumb against open left palm, and squeezed off an imaginary one-hander, his right wrist flopping forward on the follow-through. On the cusp of being hand-some, three months shy of his fifteenth birthday, copper-skinned and wiry with a long rectangle of a face, Garrett had hands that belied his impassive expression: he couldn't wait to get onto the court. Turning his head right, he held his pose and arched his eye-brows at his friend, Emerson Johnson, as if to say, "It's almost time."

If Emmie was excited about the start of basketball season, he didn't show it. Johnson had a sly wit, but he spoke rarely and almost never smiled. To his right Marshall Murray was struggling to keep open his wide, saucer eyes, which had earned him the nickname "Goo Goo," after the song about a cartoon character: "Barney Google (With the Goo Goo Googly Eyes)." As the bell rang, Garrett and John-son surrounded Murray and lifted him up, Garrett with one hand, Johnson with two. "Come on," Bill said, "let's play ball."

The three paused on the high school's wide front steps as students swirled around them, some rushing away to farm chores or after-school jobs, others stopping to flirt or gossip. Freshman tryouts wouldn't start for a few hours, and they had time to kill, but Garrett and his two friends knew they were not welcome at a lot of places uptown. On Bill's nod, they made their way through the crowd, turned their backs on Shelbyville High, and started walking east toward their old school.

Booker T. Washington Elementary School sat by itself off Harrison, Shelbyville's four-lane main street, a half-mile south of the public square on an island of land in the crook where Harrison bent sharply east, crossed the railroad track, and headed south out of town. Built in 1870 to separate black grade-schoolers from white, the building had been condemned by the State Board of Health in 1914.* In 1930, the editors of the *Indianapolis Recorder,* Indiana's largest-circulation black newspaper, had demanded improvements, calling Booker T. "that old, ugly, dilapidated building where our children have to be housed." A subsequent WPA project had stuccoed and whitewashed the walls, which were now a light gray, but little else had changed. For six grades and thirty children, Booker T. had two classrooms, two teachers, no lunchroom, and, alone among Shelbyville's schools, no gym. Every recess, regardless of weather, was spent outdoors.

One thing Booker T. had was an outdoor basketball court, one of the few in town, a patch of dusty ground with two usually netless goals near the railroad track behind the school. Bill Garrett had grown up playing there, his life tuned to the thud and ping of a dog-eared basketball bouncing on packed dirt. He played basketball all summer and after school, shoveling snow off the court in winter, often taking on older boys and grown men, some of them semipros on teams that barnstormed around central Indiana, who played rough and gave him no breaks. As he did, Garrett did not pretend to be the local high school star of the moment or imagine the home-

---

*Before 1869 there had been no public schooling for black children in Indiana. Required to offer public education to blacks after 1870, communities could choose whether their schools would be integrated or segregated. Shelbyville schools were segregated through the sixth grade until 1949, when the state legislature mandated integration.

town crowd cheering his name. Raised on Shelbyville's sidelines, he played basketball because he loved it and because there was nothing else for him to do.

Approaching Booker T., Garrett, Johnson, and Murray could see Tom Sadler and Carl "Jelly" Brown, home on leave from the Navy, playing one-on-one. Four years earlier, in the fall of 1939, Sadler and Brown had been the first black students to play varsity sports at Shelbyville High School, Sadler in football, Brown in basketball. The boys watched from the sidelines until Sadler, with a wave of his hand, said, "I got Bill," and Brown responded, "I got Goo Goo." Johnson, still small enough to be mistaken for a grade-schooler, picked up the extra ball and headed off to shoot by himself, as Sadler tossed Garrett a bounce pass and said with a chuckle, "OK, little man, show Jelly what you got."

Garrett was posted up, with his back to Brown, who stood between him and the basket. Sadler was still chuckling as Garrett feinted to his right with the ball, Brown went with the fake, and in one smooth motion Garrett swung his left foot backward and pivoted 180 degrees—leaving Brown off-balance and behind him. With one dribble Garrett was directly under the basket. Leaping off his right foot, he reached out to the far side of the basket with his left hand and softly laid the ball backhand against the backboard so that it fell through the rim: a perfect spin move and reverse layup.

"Damn!" Sadler whistled.

Two possessions later Brown waited under the basket for a rebound, using his larger body to block Garrett out, keeping Bill behind him and away from the basket. This time Garrett leaped from behind Brown, reached over him, and gracefully picked off the ball as it left the rim.

"Damn!" Sadler said a little louder.

Brown raised his eyebrows and said softly, "Guess we been away a while, Tom."

By the time Loren Hemingway got to Shelbyville High School's Paul Cross Gym, the narrow basement dressing room assigned to freshmen was packed with ninth-grade boys horsing around, snapping jockstraps and towels. Hank, as friends had called him back in

Franklin, didn't know any of them beyond a nod. A few months earlier his family had moved to Shelbyville from Franklin, a smaller town fourteen miles west. His father had taken a job managing Shelbyville's first supermarket, and even if the family could have afforded a car for the commute, wartime gasoline rationing would have made it impossible. Polite and shy, Hemingway had spent the summer exploring the new town with his younger brother, carrying his mother to Saint Joseph Catholic Church on the handlebars of the boys' shared bicycle, and waiting for basketball season.

Big-boned, still awkward, and barefoot, Hemingway edged around the clumps of boys in the dressing room and headed upstairs holding his worn sneakers in one hand. The shoes had been a parting gift from Tim Campbell, Franklin's head basketball coach. Twenty years earlier, when he had a swagger and a black mustache, Campbell had been Shelbyville's first real basketball coach, but now he was on the downside of his career. Campbell had found his rising ninth-grade basketball star sitting on the steps of Franklin's gym distraught over his family's impending move. For a long moment coach and young player had sat silently, until Campbell rose and slipped inside the gym without a word, returning with an old shoe box. Kneeling to face Hemingway, Campbell set the box beside him and said gently, "It'll be OK, son, once you get to Shelbyville and go out for basketball."

After almost three hours of tryouts by sixty-plus boys, the gym was as humid as an Indiana July, and it smelled of fresh sweat. The playing floor was a few feet shy of the maximum regulation length, with a small dead spot under one basket where the ball refused to bounce, but in other ways it was one of the better gyms in the state, and to Hank Hemingway it looked bigger and the court more brightly polished than any he had seen before. The goals at each end had black rims and gray-tinted retractable glass backboards suspended from the ceiling. Twenty-four rows of worn, backless, dark wood bleachers rose at steep angles up each side, framing the playing floor. Ten more rows filled each end, and in the four corners little "crow's nests" of seats were wedged above broad entrances. Thirty-five hundred men, women, and children—one-third of Shelbyville's population—crowded into these stands at every home game.

Hemingway had thought he was early and was surprised to see a few boys already on the floor shooting around and warming up. He recognized Bill Garrett, shooting by himself at the nearest basket. Until now, Garrett had looked to Hemingway like a gawky freshman, but on the court he had an easy grace and unforced air of confidence that commanded attention. In Franklin, Hemingway would have joined Garrett on the court immediately, but in Shelbyville, Hemingway was new, and he was shy and white and not sure what to do next. He stood staring longer than he realized until Garrett looked over and tossed him a bounce pass. "Hey, man," he asked, his voice as easy as his shots, "wanna shoot with me?"

2

The Way Things Are

BABE RUTH PASSED THROUGH SHELBYVILLE, AND ABE LINCOLN
and Al Capone and everyone else who ever moved by rail or road
between Chicago and Cincinnati in the days before interstates. The
train was the James Whitcomb Riley. Named for the "Hoosier Poet"
from nearby Greenfield, it whistled and chugged through town every
evening just after bedtime. The road was the Michigan Road. Built
in the 1830s to slice the length of Indiana diagonally—connecting
the Great Lakes steamer port of Michigan City with the Ohio River
paddle-wheeler landing at Madison—it ran through Shelbyville two-
thirds of the way down. By train the town was a blur in the night, by
car another slow spot on the Michigan Road—a bridge, two stop-
lights, a left turn, another stoplight, and on past the cornfields to the
next town like it, two hundred miles down from Chicago, another
ninety to go before "Cincinnatah," as the locals called it.

It was like thousands of other small midwestern towns, only more
so: almost at the center of the state; its population of eleven thousand
average for an Indiana county seat; astride the population median
between the East and West coasts. In just about every way Shelbyville
hit, as journalist John Bartlow Martin wrote of Indiana as a whole,
"the mean that is sometimes golden, sometimes only mean."

Indianapolis was only twenty-five miles away in a ten-o'clock
direction, but a trip to "the City" was not easy. A century earlier a
frustrated traveler had declared the Michigan Road "impassable,

hardly jackassable," and though pavement had replaced mud, the road was still narrow, its curves were deadly, and the drive to the City took the better part of an hour. Indianapolis was for a trip—the Indy 500 qualifications in May, the state fair in August, a show at one of the ornate movie theaters, or a medical problem that stumped a local GP—but it was not part of the day-to-day life of the town.

Shelbyville's public square, with a small fountain at its center instead of the traditional courthouse, hummed with business every day of the working week and overflowed on Saturdays, when farmers came to town for their supplies, stores stayed open late into the night, and everyone turned out to see and be seen. On one side of the square the four-story, limestone Shelby Hotel, its entrance shaded by a four-poster balcony, was picturesque but plain: "Shelby Hotel pants," local men joked about tight-fitting trousers, "no ball room." South of the square the banks, shoe stores, dress shops, and movie theaters, where kids under twelve could get in for twelve cents, were practically all locally owned, managed, and staffed. Even the modest factories were owned by local tycoons and manned by nonunion workers.

Shelbyville was the market town for Shelby County, and it drew on the surrounding farms that were its economic engine, smelling of corn dust from the grain elevators on late summer days and pumpkinlike sweetness from the canning factories on fall evenings. Thousands of years earlier glaciers had passed through without stopping, pressing Shelby County flat. With nothing to block the horizon, cold winter winds swept down unhindered from north central Canada, and the summer thunderstorms' purple clouds and lightning could be seen for miles, long before the first waves of rain came shushing across the cornfields. In both town and country the predominant sound was stillness, broken regularly by working sounds: the elevators' metallic rasp, the tow chains' clank, the hiss and huff of a steam engine on a siding. Shelbyville moved to the measured pace of people who knew where they belonged, and their limits. Striving was frowned on, "don't work too hard" a common good-bye.

This part of Indiana had once been almost all woods. The white oaks, black walnuts, and sycamores had supplied a thriving furniture industry before they were all cut down. Now the loam nurtured by millennia of fallen leaves, dead trees, and varmint droppings gave

Shelby County some of the richest farmland in the world. Year after year, the "International Corn King" came from Shelby County or someplace nearby. All over the county families made decent livings on farms of 80, 120, 160 acres—their dimensions neatly reflecting the original survey of the Northwest Territory—fathers and sons milking cows and baling hay while mothers and daughters raised chickens, cooked, and canned. Few farmers held second, city jobs, and few city folk braved the dusty gravel roads to live in the country. No self-respecting farm family would ever say they were *from* Shelbyville, that den of city-slicker ways and easy office work; they were from Boggstown, Ray's Crossing, Fairland, Flat Rock, or one of the other small farming communities that dotted the county.

It was in this rural territory that Shelbyville's favorite native son, Charles Major, set his second novel, *The Bears of Blue River*. Published in 1901, the book tells a story of life on the Indiana frontier in the 1820s; the ever-present dangers settlers faced amid Shelby County's dense woods; and fourteen-year-old Balser Brent's fear and excitement in confronting with his muzzle-loader a succession of increasingly menacing bears. East Coast critics dismissed the book, but in Indiana teachers and parents read *The Bears of Blue River* to children from the moment it appeared in print, and soon people all over the state knew the tale of the most ferocious bear Balser encountered: "the fire bear," whose phosphorus-covered fur glowed gold in the moonlight.

Shortly after Major's book swept Indiana, Shelbyville found a new source of pride. This one would last a hundred years and called on the town to adopt a nickname—one with a local connection and a connotation of combative courage. For the people of Shelbyville the choice was a no-brainer. They called their high school basketball team "the Golden Bears."

Shelbyville High School first played competitive basketball in 1908 at the Bijou roller rink. There, on the second floor of a warehouse, a couple of hundred spectators stood with their toes practically in-bounds to watch players in black wool tank tops and gold knee-length leather shorts shoot underhand, often arching court-length shots over low rafters. In 1917 Shelbyville's team captain was a long-shooting guard named Paul Cross, son of the pastor of the West Street Methodist Church. When the United States entered World War I, Reverend Cross was at the forefront of those speaking out for young men to answer the call of duty. Paul signed up with the first wave of local recruits. That August, a crowd of thousands turned out to see Shelby County's first volunteers march to the depot to board a troop train and head off for a few months' training before shipping out to France.

On Memorial Day, 1918, Reverend Cross spoke out against workers striking during wartime, telling a crowd gathered on the square for the Sunday holiday: "With a heart just as full of father-love, and just as weighted with anxiety as any heart in this audience, I would rather *my* son should fill a soldier's grave yonder in France in the defense of righteous principles than to fill a fine bullet-proof job here at home with neither inclination nor desire for aught other than selfish personal interests." Two weeks later, on another Sunday afternoon, a telegram arrived at the West Street parsonage. Paul Cross had been killed in the Lorraine Sector of France on June 5, 1918, the first Shelby County boy to die in the Great War. The town that had waited anxiously to hear which of its sons would be lost first, and quickly let the Cross family know that "the great sympathetic heart of the community bleeds with theirs," as the *Shelbyville Republican* put it. Flags were lowered to half-staff, and that evening churches all over town held impromptu memorial services.

Reverend Cross asked the Methodist authorities for a transfer and moved with his family to Sullivan, in the western part of the state. It was too painful to stay in Shelbyville, and they needed a fresh start. But they wanted their son to be remembered in his town, so in 1919 the Cross family conceived and funded the annual Paul Cross Award, which would quickly become the best-known honor the town bestowed, symbolizing qualities the people of Shelbyville wanted most to see in themselves. The award was given each year to the Shelbyville High School basketball player who "ranks the highest in athletic ability and skill, and in sportsmanship; in studentship and interest in school work; in loyalty to the best interests of the school; and who is clean, honorable and self-controlled in his personal habits; in short, to that player who is at once a student, an athlete, and a gentleman."

Then it all happened so fast—the Great War, the Depression, and the Second World War—that in the 1940s signs of "the old days" were still all around Shelbyville: in the two blacksmith shops, the ice plant, the horse-drawn wagon Compton's Dairy used for making home deliveries of milk in glass bottles, and in the outhouses—"Eleanor Roosevelts" many called them—tucked behind houses and tipped over by teenagers on Halloween. Most people over thirty knew how to crank a Model T so it wouldn't break their arm if it kicked back. To them, history was Grandma's time or Great-grandpa's. It was known firsthand and felt in the gut. The people of Shelbyville believed to their bones in American progress, for they had lived it.

But not all had lived it the same way.

Less than two decades before Bill Garrett and Hank Hemingway met on the basketball court at Shelbyville High School, the Ku Klux Klan had dominated Indiana, claiming between three hundred thousand and a million members—one-quarter to one-third of all the state's white, Protestant, native-born men.* It had taken hold in early 1922, with crosses burning in lonely country fields. Within a few months the crosses had moved to town squares, many Protestant ministers were promoting the Klan from their pulpits, and soon "monster rallies" of up to one hundred thousand robed Klansmen were taking place throughout the state. In the elections of November 1924, candidates publicly supported by the Klan were elected governor, mayor of Indianapolis, to most seats in the Indiana congressional delegation, to a majority of the seats in the state legislature, and to almost all other top positions in the state government. D. C. Stephenson, the state Klan leader, was boasting publicly, *"I am the law in Indiana!"*

Indiana had a long history of unhappy race relations. The state's early settlers were hardscrabble whites from the hills of Kentucky, Tennessee, and North Carolina, too poor to own slaves and unable to make a living competing against slave labor. To them, blacks were rivals for jobs, for land, and for next-to-last place in the social pecking

---

*In some communities membership was as high as fifty percent. Exact membership numbers are impossible to verify. At its height, the Klan said it had 500,000 members; historian Leonard Moore offers a "conservative" estimate of 300,000.

order, a prejudice they passed on to their descendants. For much of the nineteenth century, state law had barred blacks from public schools, the state militia, testifying against whites in court, marrying whites (a ban not removed until 1969, making Indiana the last northern state to do so), and, at one point, from settling in the state at all. In Reconstruction's wake, as black migrants poured up the Michigan Road—giving Indianapolis in 1900 a higher per capita black population than New York, Chicago, or any other northern city except Kansas City—many Indiana communities reacted with hostility.

Directly north of Shelbyville, in Hancock County, signs warned residents not to help black migrants, and those who did suffered retaliation: a barn burned down, a horse's throat cut. Riverboat captains plying the Ohio learned to discipline black crew members by threatening to put them ashore at Jeffersonville or other Indiana river towns with reputations for violence. Lynchings were common enough that, by the 1890s, the governor of Georgia, which led the country in lynchings, was citing Indiana's record in defense of his own state. "Sundown towns" sprang up—places where no black dared linger, some with signs at their outskirts, "Nigger, don't let the sun set on you here."

David Curtis Stephenson, a pudgy, itinerant salesman in his early thirties from Texas, with blond hair, hard eyes, and a politician's ready smile, seized on Indiana's streak of intolerance to transform the Indiana Klan from a marketing gimmick into the most powerful political force in the state in less than three years. Starting in 1922, Stephenson brought in Texas "bond daddies" and Florida real-estate hucksters to promote the Klan, promising them part of his own cuts on ten-dollar membership fees and on the sales of white robes, hoods, and pointed hats. Claiming to stand for Prohibition, small-town family values, and the racial and ethnic purity of native-born white Protestants, the Indiana Klan was in reality a power trip and money machine for Stephenson, a twice-divorced heavy drinker. In his thirty-six months as Indiana's Grand Dragon, "Steve," as cronies called him, pocketed between two and five million dollars—equal to about twenty million to fifty million dollars today.

Calling himself "the country's foremost mass psychologist," Stephenson tapped into white Protestant Hoosiers' fear of a post–World War I world gone chaotic: immigrants and blacks competing for jobs; jazz and bathtub gin percolating down from Chicago and up from Cincinnati and Louisville; a collapse of farm prices and the ever-present longing to feel connected over the empty stretches that separated Hoosier farms and towns. Just as high school basket-ball—also hitting its stride in the early 1920s—gave Indiana communities tradition and pride expressed in energy and ritual, Stephenson gave them klaverns, klavalcades, konklaves, and kloranic orders—a goofy fraternity at once slapstick and menacing. In Shelby County, a Klan-sympathizing country preacher reportedly set fire to his own church in order to blame the deed on the Catholics—and inspired a mob to burn down St. Vincent Catholic Church. A crowd in northern Indiana, brought to fever pitch by a Klan speaker's claim that the pope was on his way from Rome to take over America, stopped a train near Fort Wayne and demanded its lone passenger, a frightened ladies corset salesman, *prove* he was not the pontiff.

Railing against Jews, blacks, Communists, pacifists, evolutionists, foreigners, feminists, and "bootlegging Catholic democrats," the Klan seemed unstoppable for a little while. But in March 1925—as the national Klan leadership was moving to expel him for "conduct unbe-coming to a Klansman"—Stephenson kidnapped and brutally raped Madge Oberholtzer, a twenty-eight-year-old Indianapolis woman. A month later, after trying to kill herself by ingesting bichloride of mer-cury tablets, Oberholtzer died of blood poisoning related to infected bite wounds Stephenson had inflicted on her breasts.

Stephenson bragged that no Indiana jury would convict him, but as the details came out Hoosiers were appalled. Convicted of second-degree murder, Stephenson was sentenced to life in prison and served thirty-one years. Klan membership immediately plummeted, and association with Stephenson and the Klan became political poison.* By 1929, within a decade of its fiery arrival, the Klan was gone as an organized force in Indiana.

---

*The Klan's chosen governor, Ed Jackson, refused to pardon Stephenson. When the *Indianapolis Times* launched an investigation into Klan corruption, Stephenson cooper-ated, hoping to shorten his sentence and exact revenge, pointing investigators to reams of evidence against politicians he had bribed. By 1928, the *Times* had won a Pulitzer Prize for its coverage of the Stephenson debacle. Governor Jackson, Indianapolis mayor, John Duvall, six members of the Indianapolis city council, virtually the entire city administration, the Republican state chairman, judges, and many other officials were impeached, indicted, or forced to resign.

But bigotry in Indiana ran too deep to be discredited by a single crime, no matter how sordid. The Klan's messenger failed, not its message. On the night of August 7, 1930, a white mob from all over north central Indiana dragged three black teenage boys—accused of killing a white man and assaulting his female companion—from their jail cells and beat them in the public square of Marion, Indiana, sixty miles north of Shelbyville. They strung up two of the teenagers, Abe Smith and Tom Shipp, from a tree on the Marion courthouse lawn, and a crowd of thousands posed for pictures beneath their dangling corpses. The third boy, James Cameron, was spared at the last moment by what he later claimed was divine intervention and others remembered as a man's voice proclaiming Cameron's innocence. The murders of Shipp and Smith would be the last lynchings in Indiana and among the last anywhere north of the Mason-Dixon Line.

Born April 4, 1929, the second of Laura and Leon Garrett's five children and the first to survive infancy, Bill Garrett grew up in a world that had changed little since his great-grandparents had trudged with their eleven children up the Michigan Road from Kentucky searching for work, housing, and a little more freedom. What they found in Shelbyville was an attitude best expressed by a local newspaper editor who, urging whites to contribute money for the building of Booker T., had written, "These people can't help being colored among us."

The racial violence that plagued other Indiana communities had largely passed by Shelbyville. The town's only lynching victim had been a white ne'er-do-well, Charlie Hawkins, who was strung up in 1891 for shooting the town marshal. Prominent black speakers such as Frederick Douglass and George Washington Carver had been well received at the city's opera house (after speaking before an integrated crowd in nearby Richmond, Douglass had barely escaped with his life). And though the editor of the *Shelby Democrat* had railed against an impending "Ebon onslaught," when a ragged group of seventeen starving men, women, and children had stumbled into town during one of the harshest winters on record, they had been fed, clothed, and housed at public expense.

But charity was one thing, full acceptance another. There was no mistaking the fact that Shelbyville was a segregated town. Like all the town's black children, Bill Garrett attended Booker T. The public swimming pool was closed to him, except on Tuesday mornings just before it was cleaned. On hot summer days, Bill and his friends swam instead in Little Blue River, behind the county fairgrounds, near the spot where they hosed down the elephants when the circus came to town. Since his family would not have felt welcome at most white churches, Garrett missed most of the church-run summer camps and enrichment programs. He could not belong to "the Rec," the town's teen center. When he could scrape up pocket change for a Saturday double feature at the Strand, Garrett and his friends had to sit in the balcony. One day a week was "Negro Day" at Kennedy Park, when Garrett and others who won footraces received ribbons with "Colored" stamped on them.

Few blacks could get bank loans, which put home ownership out of reach for most. Practically all blacks in Shelbyville lived in a sixteen-block mixed neighborhood, where the Garrett family rented their house. Almost the only employment open to black women was domestic work; most black men were laborers, and since there were few standard wage scales they were often paid less than their white counterparts. Black customers could not try on clothing at most of the town's shops, black visitors could not stay at the local hotels, and blacks could not get sit-down service at Shelbyville's restaurants.

Cut off from much of the life in Shelbyville, the black community linked up with a network of black communities throughout the state that gave both adults and children a wider circle of reference and identity. The Garretts, like blacks all over the state, read the *Indianapolis Recorder,* which few whites knew existed. Together with the leaders of the Second Baptist Church, Booker T.'s longtime principal, Walter Fort, established a summer enrichment program for black children. After the Rec, the segregated teen center opened in 1943, Fort started one for black teens at Booker T. Every spring, Fort, a fine artist and calligrapher, meticulously hand-lettered diplomas for his graduating sixth graders, knowing it might be the only such certificate some would ever receive. Under Fort's direction Booker T. was a bulwark against segregation's daily insults, providing its students a sense of dignity and belonging as well as a solid education. To Shelbyville's black community he was "Professor Fort," and by the 1940s even some white parents, seeing him on the street, whispered to their children, "There goes Mr. Fort," as if the governor himself were passing by.

In all this, there were no signs saying "Colored" or "Whites Only." There was very little explicit enforcement, and most day-to-day interactions between blacks and whites were polite and respectful. Segregation was the crazy uncle in the attic, the unspoken code of conduct, just "the way things are." "Nobody said directly, 'You can't go there,'" said Bill Garrett's younger sister, Mildred Powell, "you just knew."

Tacit acceptance of "the way things are" served a purpose—albeit a different one—for whites and for blacks. It enabled whites to keep the status quo without acknowledging responsibility for it and without having to commit or witness overt meanness. And it helped black parents to ease a bit the sting for their children—as they learned the implicit boundaries and unspoken limits of their world—by teaching them that segregation and discrimination were "just the way things are."

If Bill Garrett chafed against the restrictions on his life, he never said so. He was raised to succeed in this world, not challenge it. His mother, Laura Belle O'Bannon Garrett, had taught Bill and his younger siblings, Jim, Mildred, and Laura Mae, to read before they started school. Despite the family's limited means, she filled their rented homes with books and newspapers, took them on trips to Indianapolis and the Cincinnati Zoo, and spent time talking candidly with them about anything and everything. "If you got sense enough to ask," Laura told them often, "you got sense enough to hear the answer." Segregation, she told them, was the way things were—but it was never an excuse to do less than their best.

Laura Garrett was her own best example. Tall, with wide, high cheekbones, auburn hair, hazel eyes, and the same grit and determination that had propelled her grandparents north, Laura was a woman, her white lawyer recalled, who made you want to sit up straighter when she entered a room." At a time when few black girls continued school beyond the sixth grade, and despite the death of her father when she was eleven, Laura graduated from Shelbyville

High School with honors in 1924, tenth in her class of seventy-six. But in 1924, with the Klan on the upswing, there were few jobs for black women, even honors graduates, so Laura worked as a domestic, cleaning houses for well-to-do whites, as her mother and grandmother had done before her, and threw herself into volunteer activities. She helped neighbors with their taxes, taught Sunday school, organized black history lectures at the Second Baptist Church, and registered voters for the state Republican Party. When Republican Ralph Gates became governor in 1944, Laura got her reward: a clerical job at the state Auto Licensing Bureau in Indianapolis. It required an hour's commute each way by bus, leaving Bill to bring in coal for the family's stove every morning and to watch over Jim, Mildred, and Laura Mae in the afternoons, but it was better than anything available to black women in Shelbyville and a step up for the Garrett family.

As Laura thrived, her husband faded as a factor in their family's life. Known as "Pokey," Leon Garrett had come to Shelbyville from northern Kentucky in the early 1920s. He had been aiming for Indianapolis but stopped short, more comfortable with the unspoken rhythms and rules of small-town life. Working a series of factory jobs, Leon was a steady provider but a wispy presence to his family, often sitting silently for long evenings. "Nothing about him stood out, nothing at all," a coworker remembered.

Named William Leon for his father, Bill was closest to his mother and absorbed her lessons. Mellow on the surface, at his core he was always a fierce competitor. From a young age, Garrett entered every competition he could, often crossing Shelbyville's color line to do so. He learned early that once he was present and ready to play few white adults would exclude him. By ten, he was the town's grade school marbles champion and regularly won footraces at Kennedy Park. He became the town's teen tennis champion at thirteen, despite never having played before and the organizers' efforts to give him the slip by telling him the wrong time for the final match. He played a year of football on the high school freshman team, and with his outward nonchalance and deceptive quickness he might have been a great wide receiver. But in Indiana football was a minor sport. The best athletes concentrated on basketball.

Basketball in the 1940s was tailor-made for Bill Garrett. He was only six-two, but that was about average for a high school center of his time. Agile players taller than six-four were rare in an era when people were shorter, summer basketball leagues were strictly prohibited, and total-immersion basketball camps were nonexistent. It was a different game then. The jump shot—graceful, quick, and accurate—remained the experiment of a few. With most players still gravity-bound, the game was less fluid and shooting percentages were lower; one field goal in three was the mark of a hot-shooting team. Zone defenses, in which players guard areas of the floor instead of particular opponents, were rare at the high school level, and aggressive physical defense—overplaying to keep the player being guarded from getting the ball, and using a weight advantage to push an opponent out of position—would almost always get the defender called for a foul.

Garrett learned to use these limits on his defenders to his advantage. A natural center, he played best posted up, with his back to the basket, ten to fifteen feet from the basket at one side of the narrow free-throw lane (then only six feet wide, compared with twelve feet today). Few who guarded him ever solved the dilemma: Play him close, chest-to-back, and with a quick first move he would spin around the defender for a reverse layup, as he had done to Jelly Brown on the court behind Booker T. Lay off him, sagging back to prevent him from using his quick spin move, and he would nail a one-hander, or even a turn-around jump shot—leaping with his back to the basket, spinning in the air and releasing a soft one-hander—a rare sight in the 1940s.

He had a striking instinct for being in the right place on the court at the right time. He was almost always the fastest player on the floor, an advantage enhanced by his deceptively casual style. At the high school level he could play all five positions, and he often did so in the same game—on successive possessions, even—controlling the game like a pro among amateurs. And he played poker-faced—sweet-faced, almost. Bob Collins, a columnist and sports editor of the *Indianapolis Star,* would describe him as "the silent assassin" because, Collins often said, "Garrett will kill you on the court before you even notice."

After their meeting in Paul Cross Gym, Bill Garrett and Hank Hemingway had become fast friends and the stars of the best freshman basketball team Shelbyville had ever had. Along with Emmie

Johnson and Marshall Murray, they played pickup games behind Booker T. and hung out at Garrett's house, sharing lemonade and cookies Laura Garrett made them, playing cards, and listening to the radio. By the end of the season, Garrett and Hemingway were both over six feet and were ready for varsity play the next year. Soon adults were greeting Garrett on the street, shaking his hand, and discussing last week's game. Grade schoolers, tossing rubber balls against door sills, pretended to be him. And for the first time since Jelly Brown, many black adults and students began to attend Shelbyville High School basketball games.

Garrett had reached this point on natural talent—speed, coordination, and feel for the game—not special effort. Walter Fort had taught him to play organized basketball on the outdoor court behind Booker T. His freshman coach, Ray Hinshaw, had drilled him on basketball fundamentals—screening and blocking out, staying between the player he was guarding and the basket, looking for the open teammate, not "telegraphing" his passes, playing under control—all season long on winter nights in empty Paul Cross Gym. Arthur "Doc" Barnett, Shelbyville's interim head basketball coach during World War II, had hoped moving Garrett up to the varsity in his sophomore year—playing against tougher competition and in front of bigger crowds—would draw from him greater intensity. But none of his early coaches had been able to fully get inside his head—to make him want to practice and play every minute as hard as he could, not because it was needed to win but because it was the only way to develop fully his extraordinary gift for basketball.

In part, it was a problem of motivation; Garrett did not feel responsible for upholding Shelbyville's basketball tradition, and he could not see a future for himself in basketball beyond high school. Also, appearances were deceptive. Garrett's easy grace could make it look as if he was dogging it when he wasn't. His run had the gentle rhythm of a lope; his style was economical and unadorned and he never huffed or grimaced. Additionally, he played with the pain of inflamed arches, a condition that bothered him off and on throughout his career. Sometimes, too, Garrett's detachment was just the shrug of a gifted teenager getting by on superior talent.

In November 1945, at the start of basketball season in Garrett's junior year of high school, Ray Hinshaw sat in the bleachers of Paul

Cross Gym with his freshman players, waiting for the varsity to finish its practice. Small but tough, a former Shelbyville football player, Hinshaw believed in the basics—in sports, in school, and in life. Watching Garrett spin around a teammate for a clean reverse layup, Hinshaw said aloud, as if to himself, "That boy could be a tremendous basketball player if he ever puts his mind to it."

3

Frank's Office

IN THE FALL OF 1945, HEAD BASKETBALL COACH FRANK BARNES
returned to Shelbyville after three years as a captain in the Army Air
Corps, part of it with a B-29 group in wartime India and China. Gruff
and acerbic, Barnes was the polar opposite of Doc Barnett, the interim
coach, in personality and coaching style, and the town was not at all
sure which coach it liked better.

Barnes was an out-of-towner, the son of a banker from north central Indiana. He was in his early forties, older than most high school
coaches, and stocky, with salt-and-pepper hair parted down the middle. He had no roots in town; he had been in Shelbyville only two
years—the 1940–41 and 1941–42 basketball seasons—before heading
off to war, leaving no children or family to remind the town of his
absence. All the time Barnes was away, Shelbyville fans had carried
the painful memory of how his last season had ended: his 1942 team
had been picked to win the state tournament but instead was beaten
by their archrival, nearby Columbus, in the tournament's opening
round. During Barnes's absence, Doc Barnett's teams had enjoyed
three strong seasons; Bill Garrett, Hank Hemingway, and other promising young players were coming along, and the people of Shelbyville
had grown used to thinking of Doc as the town's basketball coach.

Doc Barnett was a local man, tall, gracious, and genial, the son of
a respected country doctor. Barnett was also a former Shelbyville
High School basketball star and University of Michigan baseball

pitcher who, twenty-five years later, could still outshoot his teenage players in free-throw practice. Doc considered himself an educator, a science teacher, more than a basketball coach.

In contrast, coaching basketball was Frank Barnes's life. Barnes spent his days in the gym, presiding casually over a few physical education classes and holding court at his desk in the varsity basketball dressing room, known to all as "Frank's Office." His players hung out there at lunchtime and listened to Barnes's management style as he dealt with rival coaches and unreliable equipment salesmen on the telephone ("I think you're a *goddamn liar*, and I'm not gonna do business with you anymore"). Hanging up, Barnes would tell his players, "Boys, business is business, and friendship's friendship, and the two have nothing in common."

During preseason tryouts Barnes was gentle with the many whose hopes exceeded their talent and had no chance of making the team. But when practices began, Barnes was relentlessly demanding of his players and a master of motivational mind games. Early in the season Barnes pitted his players against each other one-on-one, and then walked among the pairs telling one, "If *you* don't score, you're running laps!" and then the other, "If you *let him* score, you're running laps!" Whenever a player gave less than his best, Barnes was in his face, and if the player sulked or talked back Barnes would challenge him, "Come on in my office, big boy. We'll lock the door, and whoever comes out is the boss." No one had ever taken him up on that offer.

His players loved him for his rough intensity, his firm and clear example, his ability to take it as well as dish it out. One winter, a group of players taped rancid jockstraps and socks onto a hidden surface under Barnes's desk, which was next to a radiator, and watched for days as Barnes opened windows, sprayed air-fresheners, and searched for the source of the foul air. When Barnes finally discovered the problem, as the desk was being removed from the dressing room, he laughed long and hard—and then bit the ringleader's ear until the boy screamed for mercy. On the bench Barnes elbowed Doc Barnett repeatedly, leaving the assistant coach's ribs sore all season. To adult fans he met on the street Barnes could be cordial and charming, but he often ended these conversations with an anecdote that set up his parting punch line, "If I have to choose between being liked and being respected, I'd rather be respected."

A lot of Shelbyville's adult fans had lost sight of the upside of Barnes's strong character during the years he was away at war. In the fall of 1945, when Barnes returned, Shelbyville still considered him an outsider and on probation.

A rocky relationship with local fans was nothing new to Frank Barnes. He was in his twentieth year of coaching when he came to Shelbyville in the fall of 1940 from the Ohio River town of Jeffersonville. It had been a lateral career move at best, for Jeffersonville was twice Shelbyville's size, but Barnes's years there had not been happy ones. He had taken the job at Jeffersonville in 1935 under spectacularly notorious circumstances: his predecessor, Hunk Francis, had just been run out of town—despite an undefeated, top-ranked season—for inexplicably sitting propped up, head on his chest, passed out, the entire day and night of the state championship in Indianapolis, leading to the upset defeat of his heavily favored Jeffersonville team. Rumors flew that Francis had been drugged, possibly by mob-connected gamblers who worked the boats along the Ohio River.

During his five years at Jeffersonville, Barnes was never able to beat rival New Albany in the first round of the state tournament, and by 1940 the fans were hanging him in effigy and planting "For Sale" signs in his front yard. Barnes took the hint and headed north to Shelbyville, where two years later his strong 1942 team suffered an unsettlingly similar first-round tournament loss to rival Columbus, in the last season before Barnes went off to war leaving angry Shelbyville fans with an unhappy memory of him.

The whim of the fans had plenty to do with an Indiana high school basketball coach's career. New coaches came to town with three-year contracts, if they were lucky. They became full-time faculty members, some teaching math or history or other academic subjects, but most, like Barnes, teaching physical education or driver training, tasks that did not compete for their time and energy with coaching varsity basketball, which everyone understood was their reason for being in town. If they hoped to renew their contracts and keep their career paths intact they were expected to win, especially against nearby rivals in the early rounds of the state tournament.

When Barnes left for the war in 1942, he had one year remaining on his original three-year Shelbyville contract. When he returned, the school board had given him an extra year. Thus Barnes found himself, in the fall of 1945, with two years to win over skeptical fans or start again somewhere new. He thrived on the pressure. A feisty original in a town that valued conformity, Barnes played to the contrast, in part by delivering colorful aphorisms in the sing-song cadence of a country preacher. He liked to tell his players, "I hate Columbus; I hate anybody *from* Columbus; I hate anybody who *likes* anybody from Columbus!" Of opponents, he would say, "I hatecha till I beatcha." And to his players, whom Barnes, childless himself, fiercely defended off the court, the coach declared, "I can give you hell, but nobody else can."

And he did give them hell, especially Bill Garrett. Barnes had a great coach's gift for making players believe they could do more than they had ever before thought possible. He quickly saw that Garrett's talent ran much deeper than the teenager bothered to show. For a coach under pressure to win, Garrett's untapped abilities held tantalizing promise. But more than that, Barnes hated to see potential unrealized by lack of effort. He sometimes ended speeches to athletic banquets and local service clubs with a favorite homily, "Perfection? Naw, that you'll never see. A champion only tries to be." In Garrett, Barnes saw something exceptional: rare basketball gifts combined with a preternaturally focused will to win.

Intent on tapping into the fierce competitiveness he saw beneath Garrett's mellow exterior, Barnes demanded the teen's strongest effort in every practice and every game, regardless of whether it was needed to win. If he didn't get it, Barnes ordered extra laps and tongue-lashed Garrett as he ran them, goading Bill to see that the effort would be worth it, even if the rewards were not self-evident in 1945. The effect was encouraging. That 1945–46 season, Garrett's junior year, he was the second-leading scorer in the nine-team South Central Conference and—always identified as Shelbyville's "Negro star"—he began attracting statewide press attention as one of Indiana's best high school players.

But again Barnes's 1946 team lost to Columbus in the state tournament's sectional round, and the loss was even more humiliating than the one four years earlier. In the final quarter of the tense game, as the Shelbyville cheerleaders led the home fans in a popular chant against the visiting Columbus Bulldogs—"We want dog meat!"—Columbus fans had chucked scores of hot dogs across the gym floor into the Shelbyville section. Just as bad, the refereeing had been outrageous. Every man, woman, and child in Shelbyville was convinced that late in the game Garrett, guarding Columbus's leading scorer, Bob Welmer, had swiped at the ball and missed, but that Welmer had nevertheless dropped the ball, leading a referee to call Garrett's fifth and final foul. With Garrett out, Columbus had gone on to beat Shelbyville and win the sectional, leaving Frank Barnes with two strikes against him and one year to go on his contract.

Shelbyville's 1946 basketball season closed with the school's spring awards ceremony. It was a day full of promise, the first peacetime spring in five years, and the crowd included students, faculty, parents, and many members of the community. The guest speaker was Branch McCracken, the head basketball coach at Indiana University, who had recently returned from his own three years of military service. In his speech McCracken touted the future of IU basketball and described the qualities he looked for in a player besides talent: intelligence, discipline, good attitude. The IU coach and the rest of the Shelbyville audience then watched as Reverend S. J. Cross presented the Paul Cross Award to Bill Garrett, a seventeen-year-old junior, for best meeting the criteria the Cross family had defined twenty-seven years earlier: that the recipient be "a student, an athlete, and a gentleman."

4

The Black Bears

WHEN PRACTICE BEGAN IN NOVEMBER 1946 FOR FRANK Barnes's make-or-break season, the coach had only four returning varsity lettermen: Bill Garrett, Hank Hemingway, Emerson Johnson, and Bill Breck. Even after a growth spurt, Johnson, who had been a substitute the year before, was only five-eight and 135 pounds, too small to get his long two-hand set shot to the basket without his feet leaving the floor. But Johnson was a quick streak shooter, and when his set shot was working it spread defenses and opened the middle for Garrett's spin moves. Breck, only slightly bigger than Johnson at five-nine and 145 pounds, was the son of the Shelbyville High School principal. Of the four, he was the only one who had grown up following Shelbyville High School basketball, attending home games with his family and state championships in Indianapolis with his father, a rare treat for a boy in Shelbyville. Sandy-haired, wiry, and confident, Breck was a floor leader and defensive ball hawk.

With Garrett at center, Hemingway at one forward, and Johnson and Breck at the guards, Barnes needed to find a fifth starter, a forward with some size. There was an obvious choice. Marshall Murray was six-two, the same as Garrett and Hemingway, strong and quick, a senior who had played with the other four off and on for years. But Murray's game needed work. Barnes and Doc Barnett, now the assistant coach, spent hours practicing plays with him, marking his positions on the basketball court with tape and walking him from one spot to the other. An extraordinary effort went into preparing him to be the fifth starter, but the coaches were confident Marshall was worth it.

In reuniting Garrett, Hemingway, Johnson, Breck, and Murray as the all-senior starting five for Shelbyville's 1946–47 season, Frank Barnes was doing something no other Indiana high school basketball coach—and few, if any, basketball coaches at any level nationwide—had ever done: make three black players regular starters on the basketball team of a predominantly white school.*

It shocked some in Shelbyville, but that could not have surprised the coach. Barnes had received hate mail for playing Jelly Brown and Tom Sadler in 1940–41, as had Doc Barnett when he continued to use black players during the war years. After Shelbyville's first game of the 1946–47 season—a win at home—a few adult fans started a whispering campaign against Barnes's use of three black starters, with one local trying to drum up support to run Barnes out of town.

To both the black and the white players, the talk was adult nonsense. They horsed around, played euchre and gin rummy, and listened to the radio together at each other's houses. Their camaraderie was easy, though much went unsaid. The white players, having been taught that it was polite to ignore race discrimination, didn't think consciously about the differences between their lives and those of their black teammates. They were baffled by the controversy. "Hell, they're the three best!" Walt Wintin, a white varsity reserve, had replied when his sister alluded to it. And the black players had been raised not to complain. "White kids saw we weren't at the pool or wherever and thought we didn't want to be there," Jim Garrett, Bill's younger brother, explained years later. "We wanted to be there, but there were just some places we knew we couldn't go."

The Shelbyville team flouted convention together once, when early in the 1946–47 season, at Bill Breck's urging, the players sat together downstairs for a pregame movie at the Strand. As a gesture it had been a success; no one complained, and they had watched the

---

*Sports historian John Behee would find the same action remarkable when taken by a few major universities seventeen years later: "In the early 60's some university coaches were brave enough to name three or more black athletes to their starting five. Dave Strack named three at Michigan in 1964. At first, it was shocking and repulsive to many whites."

movie undisturbed. But the experience had seemed to make Garrett, Johnson, and Murray deeply uncomfortable, as if segregation were their shame. They never went to a movie as a team again.

Frank Barnes also ignored the chatter. The coach had made it his business to know his town. He teed off at the country club with Shelbyville's best-connected citizens, rented an apartment from the mayor, and saw to it that Paul Cross Gym's lower rows displayed the town's elite at home games. Barnes stood his ground, and the fan uprising sank after Shelbyville opened the season with four decisive wins, including an eleven-point home victory over traditional power Muncie Central, and a ranking of second in the state by United Press International.

But the short-lived fan revolt had one enduring result: the 1947 Shelbyville Golden Bears became known, first at home and then throughout Indiana, as "the Black Bears." White adults in Shelbyville had started the nickname as a thoughtless joke, and from there it quickly spread, taking on more sting after opposing fans picked it up and used it derisively. On game days many local newspapers carried head shots of the opponent's starting five. With those three dark faces showing up in newspapers all over central Indiana, it didn't take long for the Shelbyville team to become known not only as "the Black Bears" but also as "Shelbyville's colored team," "Crispus Attucks" (Indianapolis's segregated, all-black high school), "the Jigaboo Boys," and worse.

On the road, at all-white towns like Martinsville, where the parents of Shelbyville's black players refused to travel, and throughout the state, Garrett got elbows to his ribs, kicks to his shins, and shoulders to his chest while fans near the floor poked him with pens, pulled on his shorts, and tried to trip him, believing referees would not call them for it and hoping to rattle Garrett or provoke a fight. It never worked. Raised by his mother and his community to deflect the discrimination around him, Garrett ignored harassment on the court and just played harder. In the 1946–47 season he displayed a flash of anger only once, at Columbus, when he stalked toward an opponent before teammates and better judgment turned him around.

Barnes, who had never coached a black player before coming to Shelbyville, compensated with his gift for pithy aphorisms. During rough games on the road Barnes told Garrett, Johnson, and Murray not to react to taunting because "it's what they want you to do." And sometimes, leaning closer and dropping his voice, his tone pleading, Barnes warned, "Boys, don't mess with shit; you'll just get it all over you."

Shelbyville's strong 4–0 start was followed by two losses to highly ranked teams, Columbus and Lafayette Jefferson. Furious over the defeat and anticipating a rematch with Columbus early in the state tournament, Barnes painted the score of the loss—Columbus 42, Shelbyville 33—in large letters on the dressing room's floor directly in front of the door where the players would have to step over it every time they left. After the hard-fought game against Lafayette Jeff, which Shelbyville lost by two points on a last-second shot, the visiting coach, Marion Crawley, let himself into Frank's Office and had a quiet word with Barnes. Crawley was a decade younger than Barnes, but already he stood among the top Indiana high school coaches, having won back-to-back state championships at Washington, Indiana, in 1941 and 1942. Washington was a town about Shelbyville's size, and Crawley's teams there had also been taunted for having black players. Standing in the Shelbyville dressing room, in front of a large sign by the door that asked, "WHO WANTS TO BE A GOOD LOSER?" and facing the sweaty, downcast players slumped in front of their lockers, Crawley said simply, "Boys, I don't know which team it was, but the state champions played here tonight."

Two weeks later, the Golden Bears traveled to Indianapolis for their last game before the 1946 year-end break. The game was at Shortridge, the city's oldest, most academically advantaged and affluent public high school, which could trace its roots to the beginning of free public education in Indiana in 1853. But the rest of the state looked down on Shortridge and other Indianapolis high schools, for they couldn't play much basketball. No Indianapolis high school had won a state championship, and only one, Tech, had ever made it to the final game. Unlike one-team towns such as Shelbyville and Columbus, the capital city had few defined communities whose faces were their high school basketball team. Not all the best athletes went out for basketball in Indianapolis, and even fewer of the best coaches wanted to work there, for the city school administration paid basketball coaches poorly compared to their counterparts around the state. To the small-town kids who came as visitors to play in them, most Indianapolis high school gyms were embarrassments, with wood backboards, bad lighting, and scuffed floors.

The Shelbyville players went to Shortridge overconfident, wearing new road uniforms that had arrived that day. Barnes had placed the order a year earlier, for gold uniforms with black detailing, but as the country returned to peacetime production basketball uniforms were not a priority, and the coach was given the choice of waiting indefinitely or taking whatever was available. He chose potluck, and the road uniforms that had arrived were bright red with white numbers and lettering. They came with long red-and-white-striped socks, which would not stay up. Two days earlier, Barnes's order for new basketball shoes had also arrived: black leather high-tops with thin rubber soles, looking for all the world like the kind boxers wore.

The first Shelbyville player on the floor was Louie Bower, a junior reserve, whose feet flew out from under him on his first step, landing him flat on his butt. Shortridge's floor was slick with baubles and confetti strewn about from a dance the night before. Mortified in their new red uniforms, tugging at their striped socks, and sliding on the littered floor in their strange new shoes, the Bears played abysmally and lost to a weaker team from the basketball backwater of Indianapolis.

Ten days later Shelbyville closed the 1946 half of their season with an 8–3 won-lost record. They had dropped from the state's top twenty rankings, they were being taunted and harassed by opponents, and sportswriters were discounting them as a "one-man team." But by a growing consensus that one man, Bill Garrett, was one of the best players in Indiana, along with the state's tallest player—a six-ten, 225-pound redhead from Terre Haute named Clyde Lovellette.

5

January 3, 1947

BILL GARRETT CLEANLY SLAPPED THE BALL OUT OF CLYDE
Lovellette's hands and into the third row of seats, but the senior ref-
eree didn't see it that way. From across the floor and behind the play
Earl Townsend whistled Garrett's fifth foul, overruling a no-call by
the official closer to the play. With five minutes left in the game and
Shelbyville leading by one point, Garrett was out of the game.

Garrett left the floor as calmly as he had stepped onto it, but
thirty-three hundred Shelbyville fans were not so cool. Before the last
note from Townsend's whistle had died, the hometown fans were on
their feet, filling the overheated gym with furious boos, screaming
angry threats at the referee, and pelting the playing floor with
crushed cups and wadded up programs. Again Townsend blew his
whistle, this time to warn school officials about the Shelbyville
crowd. With that, the local fans had had enough. From the darkened
bleachers, red-faced men began pushing their way down the narrow
aisles toward the floor.

It wasn't easy. Paul Cross Gym had been standing room only all
night, with fans packed into the aisles and jammed so close to the
floor that visiting players had to elbow the crowd back from the sidelines in order to take the ball out of bounds. Waiting for play to
resume, Clyde Lovellette looked into the stands and saw men his
father's age taking off their jackets, rolling up their sleeves, wrapping
handkerchiefs around their hands—getting ready to fight. A giant

seventeen-year-old who didn't frighten easily, Lovellette had never been so scared of a crowd getting out of control and, though he would become a college Player of the Year and longtime NBA All-Star, he would never be so afraid of a crowd again. The Shelbyville fans, he thought, were coming after him and his teammates.

Earl Townsend knew better. A former high school and college basketball standout now in his early thirties, with a long chin and a full head of wavy hair, Townsend saw the men gathering around the floor and heard shouts of "Get the ref!" He knew these fans weren't bluffing. Townsend found Shelbyville High School principal J. W. O. Breck at the scorer's bench and demanded Breck call for state police reinforcements, screaming, "You're responsible for security!"

It was a wonder the crowd was there at all. January 3, 1947, had dawned cold and icy on Shelbyville and the rest of central Indiana. The winter's worst storm had blown across the region overnight, the day's temperatures never topped five degrees, and by evening state police were warning people to stay home and off the snow-covered roads. But an important high school game was not to be missed. On this frigid Friday night, as for every other home game, thirty-five hundred fans packed every seat in Paul Cross Gym. Two hundred of them, from visiting Terre Haute, one hundred miles away, had driven or ridden school buses over slick two-lane roads to fill the seats allotted to visitors, and many more Terre Haute fans had tried and failed to get tickets.

Fans arrived early, filling Paul Cross to cramped capacity a half hour before the tip-off. There was a ritual buildup in that last half hour, anticipated and repeated to the letter every game, when the junior varsity teams left the floor and the crowd fell silent for a dramatic moment before the Golden Bears, resplendent in their white warm-ups, took the floor as the band struck up a bastardized version of Indiana University's fight song, adults cheering, students singing along. For a couple of hours in Paul Cross Gym, life was not tedious or ambiguous or conflicted. Winning was joy, losing was agony. Against the cold, gray winter background, basketball games were an experience of emotional purity like nothing else in life.

In Shelbyville there had been special excitement and anticipation for the Terre Haute Garfield game. It fell on the last weekend of the Christmas vacation, the first Friday of the new year and the beginning of the basketball season's second half, and it offered a chance for the Golden Bears to regain statewide recognition. All through the first half of the season, the Indiana press had been comparing Lovellette and Garrett as two of the best centers in the state. Terre Haute Garfield was unbeaten, highly ranked, coached by a Shelbyville native (Coach Willard Kehrt had played for Shelbyville and later for Indiana University in the early 1930s), and led by the state's tallest player, Lovellette, and one of the state's leading scorers, Ronnie Bland. To the people of Shelbyville, Terre Haute, with its population of sixty thousand, was a big city and Garfield a big school, though in truth Garfield, one of six Terre Haute high schools, had a smaller enrollment than Shelbyville High. Like Muncie Central, Columbus, and Lafayette Jefferson before, Terre Haute Garfield was another test against a top-ranked team, this one led by a giant and coached by a local basketball hero.

It was a common practice for the two opposing coaches, when scheduling a big game, to handpick the referees and then schedule the game around their availability. Frank Barnes and Willard Kehrt thought they had signed up two of the state's best. Earl Townsend was an up-and-coming trial lawyer and part-time sports announcer who had refereed college games in the Big Ten during the war. Don Veller, the newly appointed physical education director and head football coach at nearby Hanover College, would go on to be head football and golf coach at Florida State University.

When the Terre Haute team arrived in Shelbyville, Barnes met their bus as a special courtesy to Kehrt. Returning to the Shelbyville dressing room, Barnes told his team that a swaggering Ronnie Bland, Terre Haute's high-scoring forward, had asked a lot of snide questions about "this guy Garrett." "Is he really so good?" "What's *his* scoring average?" "He's only six-two, isn't he?" Barnes, who was not above stretching a story to motivate his players, stood in the middle of the dressing room and worked himself and his team into a rage over Bland's supposed arrogance and Garfield's assumed overconfidence, and by the time the coach finished the Bears didn't even want Terre Haute on their floor.

They played that way. For three quarters the game was a rough, see-saw battle, with Garrett's quickness offsetting Lovellette's size. By the end of the third quarter Shelbyville held a small lead, 35–32. Garrett and the other players had been too focused on the game to notice the unusually ugly anger that had been building among the Shelbyville crowd. It had started as soon as Terre Haute took the floor for warm-ups, cocky city boys in their flashy purple uniforms. Lovellette's towering height alone seemed an unfair advantage and his bright red hair made him an easy target for catcalls. Then, struggling for a loose ball early in the second half, Lovellette had knocked Hank Hemingway momentarily senseless with a stray elbow between the eyes. But more than anything as fouls piled up on Bill Garrett and Marshall Murray, the mostly white Shelbyville crowd concluded that Earl Townsend was making calls against Shelbyville's black players in favor of Terre Haute, whose players were all white. More than fifty years later Townsend would vehemently deny making racially motivated calls, claiming he appeared the villain because Veller, the other referee, "never blew his whistle." But many who were there saw it otherwise. In an unusually pointed allusion, *Shelbyville Democrat* sports editor Bill Holtel, in the next day's paper, wrote that "Townsend . . . certainly had one of the 'blackest' nights of his officiating career in the foul-calling department."

With Garrett sitting out the last five minutes, Terre Haute took over the game and won, 52–44. The instant the blank shot from the timekeeper's starter pistol sounded, signaling the end of the game, "it looked like someone pulled a giant drain at the center of the floor and sucked fans out onto it," one player remembered. Spring-loaded with anger, Shelbyville men and a few women swarmed the floor, pushing, shoving, throwing fists and anything else they could get their hands on. Police fought their way through the mob to Townsend and Veller, formed a cordon around them, and led them to the referees' basement dressing room.

Willard Kehrt corralled his Terre Haute team and hustled them off the floor. In the safety of the visitors' dressing room, the door guarded by state police, Kehrt told the boys they could relax; the crowd was after Townsend, not them. In near silence, the Garfield players showered, dressed, and waited, staring at the walls and each other for more than an hour. Finally, two state policemen walked them to their bus, which they were relieved to find intact. Knots of men loitered between the gym's door and the bus, muttering and glaring at the players, but they did nothing more than spit on the ground as the Terre Haute players and coaches set off for the long trip home through the snow.

Below Frank's Office, Earl Townsend waited. One end of the narrow room had frosted daylight windows, high on the inside wall and low to the ground outdoors. As Garrett and Hemingway stood on tiptoe to watch from their dressing room windows directly above, a large knot of men, their breath forming clouds around them, banged sticks against the exterior of Townsend's windows while others leaned against the building's brick walls, picking their teeth with pocket knives. A police cruiser pulled up to rescue Townsend, but as soon as the policemen disappeared inside, some of the loitering men let the air out of its tires. Finally, Doc Barnett led Townsend through a basement labyrinth and out a side door to his car. Shaken, unshowered, and under a heavy police escort, Townsend sped up the Michigan Road toward the safety of Indianapolis.

The Shelbyville players were the last to leave. They were excited by the riot and disappointed by their loss. Terre Haute remained unbeaten, the untoppled Goliath to their hamstrung David. Hanging around the dressing room, many of the players swore they would beat Terre Haute if the two teams ever met again. With a forced chuckle and unsmiling eyes, Frank Barnes, still seething and pacing, told his team, "Maybe we'll see them again, boys. Maybe we'll see them again."

6

Hoosier Hysteria

THAT WEEKEND, AS THE ICE MELTED AND THE SIDEWALKS turned to slush, Indiana buzzed with talk of the "Townsend incident," as the Shelbyville–Terre Haute game quickly came to be called. Radio roundups of the Friday night games had picked up the story immediately. Saturday's papers played up the riotous crowd and the need for police intervention, and soon sports columns, editorials, and radio hosts around the state were condemning the Shelbyville fans' "unsportsmanlike behavior." None of these accounts mentioned race. To most readers and listeners, the Shelbyville crowd sounded like sore losers and rowdies.

As the story built, white Shelbyville's rage at Earl Townsend soon mingled with fear. Rumors flew that Townsend would file formal "charges" with the Indiana High School Athletic Association. Sportswriters and radio hosts were calling for the IHSAA to make an example of Shelbyville by suspending the Golden Bears for the rest of the season. By Sunday evening, the realization was hitting Shelbyville that their best basketball team ever might be barred from the state tournament.

Bill Garrett had more personal reasons to be worried. A basketball scholarship was his only chance for college and a future beyond Shelbyville. With virtually no blacks in college basketball, Garrett had little chance of getting a basketball scholarship under the best of circumstances, and no chance if his team was barred from the state tournament and its attendant publicity. But Garrett wasn't thinking about college, a scholarship, or a basketball future. Almost all the college players were white, and the radio broadcasts of their games were solemn play-by-plays without much color commentary. The Harlem Globetrotters and the New York Rens, both innovative all-black professional teams, played far away; the nearby pros were makeshift white teams with names like the Indianapolis Kautskys and the Anderson Duffy Packers that usually played before small crowds in borrowed gyms. With his family, Garrett listened to Joe Louis's fights on the radio, went to Negro League baseball games in Indianapolis, and read the buzz about Jackie Robinson signing with the Brooklyn Dodger organization without anticipating its significance. ("We were glad for Robinson because we had seen him play," Jim Garrett said, "but at the time it wasn't much of a big deal to us.") Bill and his friends had cheered when Indiana University's football team, with several black players, won the Big Ten in the fall of 1945, his junior year in high school. But studies and competitive sports beyond high school all seemed far away, part of another world to which Garrett did not belong. "All any of us thought about at that point was making it out of high school," his brother, Jim, recalled.

Protected by adolescent bravado, the rest of the team largely ignored the fallout from the riot. The day after the Terre Haute game, Bill, Emmie, Marshall, and Hank shoveled slush off the court at Booker T. and shot around. That night, joined by student manager Jack Worland, they played cards and listened to the radio in the front room at Emmie's house. In different ways they all felt a sense of injustice, but they couldn't talk about it across the black-white divide. All they could do was grumble that they would have beaten Terre Haute if Bill had not fouled out, and that they would do so if the teams ever met again.

On Monday morning Earl Townsend, indignant over the riot but not wanting to punish players for adults' behavior, told the newspapers he would not file a complaint with the IHSAA. But whatever relief Shelbyville felt was short-lived; the next day the commissioner's office announced that the IHSAA was pursuing its own investigation.

By the 1940s basketball had become America's most popular amateur sport—played in more high schools than football, baseball, and tennis combined—and Indiana was the game's acknowledged epicenter. Magazines like *Time, Life,* the *Saturday Evening Post, Collier's,* and *Sport* constantly reminded the rest of the country that every Hoosier boy had a basketball goal on the side of his barn or garage and that every crossroads high school had a team that carried the pride of its community. All over the country, college teams built winning traditions on the backs of former Indiana high school players and coaches. The "Sweet Sixteen" and "Final Four" were Indiana high school innovations; today's NCAA Tournament—the annual national college basketball championship that generates "March Madness" from coast to coast—is the Indiana high school state tournament of the 1940s gone national. Even Chuck Taylors, the Converse basketball shoes worn by practically every basketball player from the early 1930s to the late 1960s, were named for an all-state forward from Columbus. Hoosier boys started younger, focused on basketball more seriously, were better coached, and faced consistently tougher competition than their counterparts in other states. "The first time the kids lift their hands, they find a basketball in them," one Indianapolis fan told *Collier's.* "It may be a dirty trick, but it sure turns out some swell forwards."

Indiana basketball's unlikely Johnny Appleseed was Nicholas McKay, a Presbyterian minister from England who in the summer of 1892 took over as head of the YMCA in Crawfordsville, a college town fifty miles northwest of Indianapolis. McKay wanted to start a physical education program at the Crawfordsville Y, and to prepare, signed up for a course to be given in the fall of 1892 at the International YMCA Training School in Springfield, Massachusetts.* The course was run by a thirty-one-year-old Canadian named James Naismith. Less than a year earlier, in the winter of 1891–92, Naismith had invented a way to break up the boredom of wintertime calisthenics by nailing up open containers at each end of his Y gym, dividing his students into two groups and tossing a soccer ball into their midst. For goals, Naismith had asked the custodian to fetch boxes, but the best the man could provide was peach baskets, so Naismith called his game "basket ball."

The next year, McKay brought basketball straight from Naismith to the Crawfordsville Y, where he set about adding refinements. He

---

*The school is now Springfield College.

had a blacksmith forge iron hoops to which he sewed coffee sacks, and he then nailed the new goals to the railing of the running track that circled above his gym, located on the second floor of a tavern. A few months later, on March 16, 1894, the Lafayette Y came to town to play the Crawfordsville Y in the first organized basketball game in Indiana. Spectators lined the track above the floor. There was no dribbling. Everything in the room was in-bounds—the fans, the track, the walls, the red-hot potbellied stove in one corner. Fans reached through the railing to swat away Lafayette shots and to guide those of Crawfordsville toward the basket, the first hint of a need for backboards. Within months, Indiana boys were playing basketball anywhere they could nail up a hoop.

Played well, no other game requires such a combination of individual and team discipline by so many players in such a small and congested space. "You don't play against opponents," coach Bob Knight would tell his Indiana University basketball players a century after the Lafayette and Crawfordsville Ys first squared off. "You play against the game of basketball." But it was easy for one or two kids to shoot around with a rag-stuffed sock or inflated pig's bladder, and high schools too poor or too small to field football or baseball teams, could afford basketball. It could even be played in the brutal Hoosier winters, and was, by players wearing gloves and hats in haymows after it got too cold to shoot outside.

In Indiana, basketball was "a sport for the lonely," filling a need for activity and connection in that brief gray lull that settled on farming communities between December and early March. The state had no big, dominating cities offering too many distractions and had too little cohesion for earnest civic pride to be invested in high school basketball teams. In the early decades of the twentieth century, as basketball spread, Indianapolis had fewer than 350,000 residents and no other Indiana town topped 100,000. Nor did Indiana have any major league sports teams or state university football traditions—no Chicago Cubs or Cincinnati Reds, no Ohio State Buckeyes or Michigan Wolverines—to soak up attention and dollars.

In a time of bad roads and no television, high school was the highest level of basketball most Hoosiers ever saw. Their high school basketball teams became the faces isolated communities presented to the outside world. The games provided not only a respite from winter's bleakness but also a source of local bragging rights and a medium for common memory. To most Hoosiers, high schools did not field basketball teams, or win championships, *towns* did, and when a town won the state, or went far in the early rounds of the state tournament, or just beat a bigger town, its citizens would dine out on the glory for years to come.

James Naismith thought he had invented a gentlemanly source of winter exercise. He made the goals ten feet high, and horizontal, so players would have to gently arch their shots instead of hurling them. He prohibited running with the ball to encourage passing and teamwork. He made any significant contact between opposing players a foul and hoped the close proximity of players, officials, and fans would inhibit roughness or cheating and promote good sportsmanship. To Naismith, who had trained for the ministry before turning to athletics, basketball was another pulpit for preaching the virtues of "muscular Christianity" popular in the late nineteenth century. The game, he wrote, was intended to be a "laboratory for moral development."

In reality, early basketball games were often physically brutal. By the turn of the century, even President Theodore Roosevelt, who had cultivated his own Rough Rider reputation, worried about the unregulated violence of the sport some were calling "indoor football." As interurban commuter trains helped spread organized basketball across Indiana, Hoosier high school basketball teams collided in barns, church halls, warehouses, wire cages, outdoor driveways, and any other marginally available space, often under "local rules" known only to the home team and in front of crowds so unruly that many referees packed revolvers.

In 1903, the state teachers association stepped in to make school authorities responsible for their high school basketball teams by creating the Indiana High School Athletic Association. A decade later, the IHSAA found its J. Edgar Hoover: Arthur Trester—six-four, clean-shaven and high-collared, his strong jaw jutting outward with the proud, straitlaced look of the Victorian educator he was—took over the association and ran it until his death thirty-one years later.

Between 1913 and 1944, Trester knit Indiana high school basketball so tightly together that Boonville, in the far southwest corner of the state, knew it was playing by the same rules and standards as

Angola, 330 miles away in the far northeast corner; so tightly that L. V. Phillips, the IHSAA commissioner who succeeded Trester, could say with complete sincerity, "Two things hold this state together: the legislature and basketball, and it seems that basketball sometimes does the better job." Trester's office in Indianapolis was "the state's woodshed." To those who violated the rules and then complained of their punishment, Trester had a retort, "The rules are clear, the penalties severe."

It worked. From the 1920s onward, from November through February, Tuesday and Friday nights in Indiana were reserved for boys' high school basketball. On those nights stores were closed, schools held no other functions, and adults didn't meet to play bridge or to attend their lodge, church, or PTA meetings. Even college teams learned to play on Mondays and Saturdays if they hoped to draw crowds. As Indianapolis sportswriter Bill Fox, Jr., who coined the phrase "Hoosier Hysteria" in the 1930s, told the *Saturday Evening Post,* "High school gymnasiums are our nightclubs."

The highlight of the basketball season—and of the year in Indiana—was the high school state tournament held every year from late February to late March, after the end of the regular season. When Arthur Trester took charge of the IHSAA in 1913, the state tournament was in its third year and had thirty-eight participating high school teams, playing before twelve hundred spectators over a couple of days at Indiana University in Bloomington. When Trester died, still on the job in September 1944, all 778 Indiana high schools participated in the four-week tournament, in open competition in which the smallest school could hope to upset the largest, and the championship game was played before fifteen thousand frenzied fans and a three-state radio audience of some two million. By 1947, total live attendance at all rounds of the Indiana high school basketball state tournament was nearly 1.25 million—more than the total attendance at the 1947 World Series, Rose Bowl, Orange Bowl, Cotton Bowl, Sugar Bowl, Indianapolis 500, Kentucky Derby, NCAA and NIT college basketball championships, professional football and basketball championships, U.S. Professional Tennis Singles Championship final, Notre Dame–Army football game, and the Joe Louis–Joe Walcott heavyweight title fight *combined.* This, in a state with fewer than four million people.

Hoosier Hysteria, however, was not always for everyone. For almost forty years, from its creation in 1903 until August 1942, the IHSAA refused membership to Indiana's segregated all-black public high schools and the state's Catholic schools, and barred both black and Catholic schools from participation in the state tournament. In the face of repeated appeals by black leaders, Arthur Trester clung to his peculiar position: segregated black high schools did not meet a criterion for IHSAA membership because they were "not publicly open to all." It did not seem to matter that Indiana's segregated, all-white high schools were similarly closed or that blacks had long fought the restrictive schooling.

The IHSAA's transparent excuses for excluding segregated black schools added insult to the difficulties the struggling schools were already facing in trying to offer basketball programs. Few had gyms. All had a hard time finding opponents, often playing games as far away as St. Louis and Lexington, Kentucky, riding old buses and packing their food. When the regular season ended and the rest of the state fixated on the state tournament, black players in the segregated high schools, their classmates, and their communities could read in newspapers about the Hoosier Hysteria from which they were barred. All over Indiana, the state tournament was a geography lesson for fans who learned from the sports pages to pinpoint Young America, Rising Sun, and Prairie Creek, but who hardly knew that Indianapolis Crispus Attucks, Gary Roosevelt, or Evansville Lincoln—the state's three largest all-black high schools—existed.

In late 1941, black Republican state legislator Robert Brokenburr finally got the best of Arthur Trester. For decades, Indiana politicians had coveted the state tournament's revenues and the patronage possibilities of controlling the distribution of tournament tickets. Brokenburr introduced legislation to empower the state government to take over the IHSAA at a moment when support for such a move was running high. It passed the Indiana State Senate 130 to 3, before mysteriously dying in the House. But a deal was cooking behind the scenes. At the end of December 1941, two weeks after Pearl Harbor, with strong support from local sports editors, most notably the *Indianapolis Star*'s Blaine Patton, the IHSAA Athletic Council voted to admit black and Catholic high schools effective August 1, 1942, and to allow them to participate in the 1943 state basketball tournament.

•   •   •

IHSAA commissioner L. V. Phillips was a big, friendly, outgoing man respected for his open mind as well as for his adherence to the rules. Even so, Shelbyville fans had good reason to fear that the IHSAA would judge harshly their attack on a referee. It didn't help that throughout central Indiana—especially in Indianapolis—students were chanting "Remember Earl Townsend!" whenever referees made unfavorable calls. For three weeks, while the IHSAA gathered reports from Shelbyville's principal Breck and coach Barnes, from Terre Haute coach Willard Kehrt, and from referees Earl Townsend and Don Veller, Shelbyville fans held their breath.

In the last week of January 1947, Phillips issued the IHSAA's report. Characterizing the atmosphere at Paul Cross Gym on January 3, as a free-for-all fight, and adding that—"according to statements by referee Veller and Coach Kehrt of Terre Haute Garfield"—Earl Townsend had done "a competent job in very difficult circumstances," the IHSAA's report strongly condemned the Shelbyville fans' reaction. But in the end, Phillips spared the team and the town. The Golden Bears would be allowed to play in the state tournament because only adult fans, not students or players, were involved in the riot; because Shelbyville's civic leaders had promised to improve fan behavior; and because principal Breck, a member-elect of the IHSAA Board of Control, had taken immediate corrective actions. The IHSAA let Shelbyville off with a warning—that any future disturbance would result in suspension—and an admonition: In the future, Frank Barnes must stay seated and not egg on angry fans.

Shelbyville heaved an enormous collective sigh of relief. But resentment of Earl Townsend did not dissipate. In the years to come it grew with each retelling of the story, which eventually became part of the town's oral history. Earl Townsend soon stopped refereeing high school basketball games. He became the first television broadcaster of the Indianapolis 500, the author of a book on archaeology, and one of Indiana's top trial lawyers. But for the rest of his career, whenever he tried cases in the courts of Shelbyville, opposing lawyers never failed to remind the local jury, "Now Mr. Townsend, I'm sure you remember, is a *very* well-known basketball referee."

7

Golden Again

AFTER THE LOSS TO TERRE HAUTE THE GOLDEN BEARS WON twice, but then in mid-January they lost again, this time to a much weaker team in a horribly played game at nearby Rushville. For the first and only time all season, the referees had noticed Emmie Johnson's habit of shuffling his feet together before releasing his two-hand set shot, and they had called him repeatedly for traveling. Rattled by the referees and by their own expectations of an easy win, the team was out of sync all night before losing 52–44.

In the dressing room the players showered and dressed in silence. They knew better than to speak in Frank Barnes's presence after a blown game, and they were embarrassed and confused. This defeat put their won-lost record at 10–5 and dropped them from the state's top twenty teams for good. They were playing far below their ability with the state tournament only a month away. Outside, still mute, the five senior starters took their usual places in Barnes's Buick: Breck at shotgun; Johnson, the radio man, in the front middle; and in the back, Garrett on the left, Murray in the middle, and Hemingway on the right. Emmie knew better than to touch the radio, and the car was silent for the eighteen-mile trip home. Barnes did not tell them what he had discovered, nor what he had in mind. Pulling up alongside Paul Cross Gym a few minutes after 10:30, Barnes got out first, walked to Barnett's open window, and told the six reserves, "You boys go on home." To his seniors, now standing outside his car, he said curtly, "You come inside."

A few hours earlier, the final game of the county tournament had been played to a full house at Paul Cross. The gym was still warm and humid, and it smelled of fresh popcorn, with crepe paper in school colors and empty paper cups strewn across the bleachers. Barnes unlocked the door and directed the five stiff and tired seniors to the varsity dressing room. They were standing in a semicircle when student managers Jack Worland and Gene Shadley set the wood chest holding the Bears' dark-gold road uniforms in the middle of the floor, directly in front of them. Worland opened the trunk as Barnes stood in front of it, slowly looking each player full in the face. Before they left Rushville, the coach had stood in the parking lot, brooding and perplexed over his team's inability to play consistently. As the managers carried out the chest holding the uniforms, Barnes had stopped them, opened the lid, stuck his hand inside, and then said to no one in particular, "Just as I thought." Now, standing in Paul Cross Gym's semidark dressing room with the hour getting late, he told his senior starters: "Boys, those uniforms aren't wet. We're gonna get 'em wet."

They ran drills. They ran sprints. They scrimmaged two-on-two and three-on-two. Two-and-a-half hours later, as the clock ticked past 1:00 A.M., and their uniforms were soaked through, Barnes still wasn't done with them. He sat them down in the dressing room and stood glaring, the clarity of his will silently screaming, "Don't you see? *I* want you to be your best more than you do." Quietly, Barnes asked, "Does anyone have anything to say?" The white players felt guilty and remorseful, thinking they had let down not just their coach but their school and town. The black players were mad, mad at the referees' traveling calls, mad at losing in front of a crowd of white strangers to a rinky-dink team they would have chewed up on the court at Booker T., mad at Frank Barnes and his demands, at the late hour, at their fatigue—and at themselves for being intimidated, for deferring too much, for not seizing control of games as they knew they could. Thirty years later, Barnes would call this the defining moment for his team and for himself as a coach. But at the time, after a long silence Emmie Johnson said simply, "Let's just tell the man we're sorry. I want to go home."

Led by Garrett, Johnson, and Murray, the Bears won their next five games decisively, ending their regular season by humiliating

Indianapolis Tech, the largest high school in the state, by a score of 57–36.

Despite their strong finish, the Golden Bears' won-lost record was 15–5, the same as the previous year. At the season's end, UPI ranked Shelbyville twenty-first out of the 781 teams in the state—not bad, but not a contender for the state championship either. UPI ranked East Chicago Washington first and still-unbeaten Terre Haute Garfield second. Most sportswriters were picking Marion Crawley's Lafayette Jefferson to win the tournament. Even the *Shelbyville Democrat's* sports editor, Bill Holtel, could only bring himself to predict that the Golden Bears would reach the Final Four and lose there to Lafayette Jeff. In all of Indiana only one reporter, a writer for the *Indianapolis News'* International News Bureau named Jack Estell, picked Shelbyville, his alma mater, to win the state.

But the Golden Bears had strengths not apparent on paper. They had a rare degree of cohesion: Garrett, Johnson, and Murray had played basketball together all their lives. All five starters were seniors. They had faced a tough schedule and knew they could compete with the best in the state. They had worked through low points and peaked at the right time.

They also had something to prove. For Garrett, Johnson, and Murray, in particular, the loss to Terre Haute Garfield had come to symbolize the whole season of name-calling and meanness, and they wanted to play Terre Haute again even if they had to go all the way through the tournament to do so. Though Barnes seethed for a rematch, he never mentioned Terre Haute by name. Terre Haute was "them," and everyone, players and fans, knew who "they" were. During the whole second half of the season, student pep rallies regularly ended with a cheerleader shouting into a megaphone, "You *know* who'll be waiting at the end!"

The town also wanted revenge but didn't expect to get it. Early in the season, the taunts of opposing fans had drawn heated rejoinders by Shelbyville's adults, but those were just part of the game, the kind of ritual shouting matches that frequently took place between opposing fans. The loss to Terre Haute at midseason had been a turning point. With a perceived injustice played out on their home floor, the people of Shelbyville closed ranks with an "us against them" mindset that lasted beyond game nights and pervaded the daily chatter.

But the Shelbyville fans were also realists, nurtured on low expectations. To meet Terre Haute again, the Golden Bears would first have to get to the Final Four. Only one Shelbyville team had ever done that, and few fans really expected it to happen now.

The state tournament had a tight structure that built drama over four successive weekends. The first round was the sectionals, 64 mostly county-based playoffs of 10 to 15 teams each held from Thursday through Saturday at the end of February. The following Saturday, the 64 sectional winners competed in regionals at 16 sites around the state. The Saturday after that the 16 regional winners—the "Sweet Sixteen"—met in four semifinals. And on the fourth Saturday the four semifinal winners—the Final Four—"went to the State." Held at Butler Fieldhouse in Indianapolis, the State followed the format of the previous three Saturdays: four teams, two games in the afternoon, and the championship game at night. With 781 teams competing, to win the 1947 Indiana State Championship a team had to win ten straight tournament games—the last eight consisting of two-a-day wins on four successive Saturdays—against increasingly tough competition.

A couple of days before the sectionals began, the IHSAA commissioner and two board members drew the entry forms of each school from a box to match up teams for competition. The results were relayed periodically, like election tallies, to pool reporters waiting next door. Wire services—recognizing this was the only news in the state that day—stopped all other operations in Indianapolis, and almost every radio station in the state interrupted its regular programming to announce the pairings as they became available.

The sectionals began on Thursday evening, February 27. From then until late Saturday night, all over the state the only real business that got done was at simple restaurants near the gyms. There would be no school anywhere in Indiana on Friday, so students could attend the afternoon games. Adults went to work but spent most of the day hovering near radios calling out scores, guessing future results, and celebrating or bemoaning their team's latest game. By Saturday night, the nearly eight hundred teams that started the tournament would be pared down to sixty-four, and almost a million people would turn out to watch from every corner of the state.

Shelbyville was matched against Mt. Auburn, a small county

school, in the first game of the tournament on Thursday night. Shelbyville versus Mt. Auburn was the ugly side of the open tournament, in which the strongest teams often played painfully one-sided games against small, rural schools in the early rounds. As expected, Shelbyville dominated Mt. Auburn from the start, taking a 16–1 lead in the first quarter and winning, 60–20. Midway through the game, a Shelbyville cheerleader led one of the standard chants, "Go back! Go back! Go back to the woods! You haven't, you haven't, you haven't got the goods!" Done with mindless innocence, it stung. Mt. Auburn fans shook their heads and waved their hands in disgust, too courteous to respond with the chant the county students privately aimed at Shelbyville, "Shelby, Shelby, thinks they're it. SH for Shelby; IT for it." The following night, a Friday, Shelbyville easily beat Waldron, a community of eight hundred, 53–24, to set up the big game with Columbus on Saturday afternoon.

Overnight Friday a storm dumped three inches of snow from Kansas to Ohio, and again the state police warned Hoosiers to stay off the roads, but on Saturday every one of the sixty-four gyms hosting a tournament game was filled to capacity. In Shelbyville, a crowd of thirty-five hundred filled Paul Cross for the grudge match against rival Columbus, the second of two afternoon games to determine who would play that night for the sectional title. Hundreds who could not get tickets crowded into the National Guard armory downtown, and hundreds more packed the Morristown High School gym, ten miles north, to listen via makeshift "broadcasts" consisting of frequent telephone calls from Paul Cross Gym, amplified for the remote audiences by loudspeakers. Twenty-five miles south, fifteen hundred fans assembled in Columbus for a similar broadcast.

Bartholomew County, where Columbus was the county seat, had only three high schools, so the IHSAA sent Columbus High and its two county schools to the Shelbyville sectional. Every year, if they survived the first couple of games against smaller schools, the two county seat towns had to compete against each other, and only one could advance to the regional round of the tournament. People of Columbus howled about having to drive twenty-five miles to play at hated Shelbyville, and they demanded to host the sectional in alternate years. People of Shelbyville laughed scornfully at the thought of playing in Columbus's "crackerbox" Pearl Street Gym, which seated *only* twenty-two hundred, and petitioned the IHSAA to get Columbus out of their sectional entirely.

The rivalry was visceral. Fights in or outside the gym were commonplace. Cars parked near Paul Cross bearing Columbus tags regularly turned up with broken windows or flat tires. Cars with Shelbyville tags were sometimes harassed by Columbus police. In truth, by the late 1940s the competition between the towns was becoming unbalanced. Columbus was twice Shelbyville's size, and its population was growing while Shelbyville's remained stagnant. Columbus's leading company, Cummins, had a visionary CEO who was turning his town into an international showcase of modern architecture, "the Athens of the prairie." Columbus was pulling away, and the people of Shelbyville felt it more than they wanted to admit.

In the final UPI poll, Columbus ranked sixteenth in the state, compared with Shelbyville's ranking of twenty-first. Their players were taller, they had won the previous year, and on paper the all-white Bulldogs from the bigger, more progressive town were slight favorites to win the sectional. But on the court the Golden Bears played with an intensity that froze their rivals. Believing Shelbyville to be a one-man team, Columbus sagged around Bill Garrett, leaving Emerson Johnson open to hit from the outside. When Columbus defenders came out to guard Johnson, Garrett moved freely under the basket, spinning for reverse layups and tipping in missed shots. At the end of the first quarter, Shelbyville led 18–8. By the half, Shelbyville's lead was 33–12, and the fans listening by phone hookup at the Columbus gym began drifting away. The final score was 48–36. In the traffic heading away from Paul Cross Gym, exultant Shelbyville fans made a sport of following cars with Columbus license tags, honking vigorously.

That night the Golden Bears ran up the score on another smaller school, Franklin Township, 56–23, to win the sectional. They had now won nine straight games, the last seven of them by an average of twenty-five points, since the late-night practice following their loss to Rushville. They were past Columbus and on their way to the regional at Greensburg, twenty miles south down the Michigan Road, the following Saturday.

The week before the regionals, the flu hit Shelbyville. On Friday, twenty-two Shelbyville high school students too ill to make the trip to Greensburg gave up their tickets to the game. The school administration immediately organized a lottery to apportion the extra tickets among hundreds of clamoring fans, and the post office made special deliveries late into Friday night to get the lucky winners their tickets. The next day, hundreds again crowded into the Shelbyville armory, overflowing into the street where additional loudspeakers were set up, to hear the jury-rigged long-distance telephone "broadcast" directly from Greensburg's Memorial Gym.

All week Bill Garrett had been too sick with the flu to practice. At the pregame meal on Saturday morning he was still feeling so poorly that Frank Barnes asked Bill Tindall, a local physician who served as the team doctor, to determine whether Garrett could even make the trip to Greensburg. Tindall cleared Garrett to travel but insisted on accompanying the team and checking Garrett immediately before, and at the half of, the afternoon game.

Shelbyville's first regional opponent was Madison, a picturesque town of seven thousand on the Ohio River, with segregated high schools and a strong basketball tradition at its white one. After Tindall cleared Garrett to play the first half, the Madison players came out taunting—hurling racial slurs, shin-kicks, and elbows at Garrett, Johnson, and Murray and delivering the worst physical and verbal abuse the Shelbyville team had taken all season. The attacks threw the Golden Bears off their game. Johnson couldn't hit at first, and the others were out of sync, standing around waiting for Garrett to take over. But whoever told the Madison players that abuse could rile Garrett was wrong. Playing poker-faced, limping on sore arches, and getting his throat swabbed at the half, Garrett dominated the game at both ends of the floor, scoring twenty-nine of Shelbyville's forty-four points to lead his team to an ugly 44–37 win. Johnson and Murray found their range in the second half and hit just enough outside shots to take some of the defensive pressure off Garrett. Together, Garrett, Johnson, and Murray accounted for forty-one of Shelbyville's forty-four points and outscored the entire Madison team. That night Johnson took over, scoring eighteen points as the Bears crushed North Vernon, 55–23, to win the regional.

After the game, Madison coach Ray Eddy, who would lead his team to the 1950 state championship and go on to be the head basketball coach at Purdue University, visited the celebration in the Shelbyville locker room. Congratulating Emmie Johnson on his hot out-side shooting against North Vernon, Eddy asked, "Why didn't you do that to us?" Perhaps remembering the taunts from Eddy's players that afternoon, Johnson looked levelly at the coach and answered, "Well, sir, I guess I just can't hit in the daytime."

On the way home from Greensburg, with Johnson working the radio in Barnes's Buick, the five seniors heard that Lafayette Jefferson was out of the tournament, upset 39–38 by Rossville in the final game of the Lafayette regional. A gasp went through the car, and then Barnes broke the silence with a chuckle, "Well, I guess it must be us." All season they had remembered Marion Crawley's words in Frank's Office after their last-second loss to Lafayette, "The state champions played here tonight." As they made their way up the Michigan Road, the chant of the Shelbyville fans, as the players had cut down the nets and posed for pictures, rang louder in their ears, "Butler Fieldhouse, here we come!"

Winning the regional brought statewide attention back to Shel-byville. Sportswriters around Indiana grudgingly favored the Bears to win at Indianapolis, considered by many the weakest of the four semi-finals. For much of the Indiana press, the label of bad sportsmanship that had started with the Townsend incident had settled into a stereo-type: "Rowdy fans." Between the lines, this meant "colored team; rowdy fans." On the Wednesday before the semifinals, a big headline across the sports page of the *Indianapolis Times,* over a picture of the team, declared, "Shelbyville Is the Big, Bad Boy of Local Tourney," with the subheadline, "Crowd's Sympathy Undoubtedly to Be Against Strong Bruins." One exception was the *Indianapolis Recorder.* After Cris-pus Attucks, Indianapolis's segregated black high school, had lost in their sectional, the *Recorder* spoke for blacks all over Indiana when it headlined, "CAHS Tigers Out, Many Fans Turn Eyes to Shelbyville."

It had been twelve years since a Shelbyville team had made it to the Sweet Sixteen, and the town had a hard time getting used to the favorite's role. Even the players' parents had doubts, as reserve guard Louie Bower's told him, "You've done well to get this far, now don't be disappointed if you don't go any farther." "Nobody really thought we would go farther," Bower remembered. "But when we got to the semifinals, people stopped calling us the 'Black Bears'; we were the Golden Bears again."

•   •   •

On Saturday morning, March 15, thirty-five hundred Shelbyville fans drove twenty-five miles up the Michigan Road for the Indianapolis semifinal at Butler Fieldhouse. Technically a college arena, the Fieldhouse was in reality a shrine to Indiana high school basketball, for which it was built. In 1926, Arthur Trester, tired of playing the tournament finals in the state fairgrounds cow barn, committed the IHSAA to pay a hundred thousand dollars for a decade's advance rent on a new home for the Indiana high school state championship, just as Butler University was moving to a new campus nearby. By that happy coincidence, in 1928, Butler, then a small liberal arts college with a thousand students, found itself with the biggest and most beautiful basketball fieldhouse in the country.* The place so powerfully represented the pinnacle of Indiana high school basketball that just its name—Butler Fieldhouse—brought excitement to players and fans all over the state. Seating just under fifteen thousand, with a long, barreled roof, tall arched windows at either end, and side-court grandstands running far up and back to the ends of the long building, the Fieldhouse was for decades the largest arena in the country built specifically for basketball at *any* level. Renamed Hinkle Fieldhouse, for Butler's longtime coach, it is today the oldest major college basketball arena still in use.

The Shelbyville boys had seen the size of Butler Fieldhouse when they had practiced there a few days before the semifinals. But it had been empty then, and nothing had prepared them for what lay ahead as they walked up the ramp from their basement dressing room for their first semifinal game. As the players reached the corner of the basketball court, they heard the Shelbyville fans cheer, but the sound was muffled by the distance and echoed around in that cavernous

---

*Two years later, the North Central Association of Colleges and Secondary Schools briefly dropped Butler from its approved list, citing the cost of Butler's new athletic facilities and the reduction of the university's endowment. In response, Hilton U. Brown, chairman of Butler's board of trustees, issued a statement that said, in part, "I would call attention to the reason for the businessmen of the city building this plant and leasing it to the college. The high schools of the state, which I believe are under the influence of the association, as are the colleges, needed a place in which to play their yearly tournament. Reasonable rent is required, and the plant in due time ought to pay for itself."

interior. The Golden Bears were playing the first afternoon game, and almost a half hour of warm-ups remained before it began, but already more than ten thousand fans were in their seats, and the Fieldhouse was filling fast. A line of radio broadcasters, with big white call letters on their microphones, sat along the front row. Sunlight streamed in through the tall, vertical windows that stretched high above the third tier of grandstands, silhouetting the fans on the west side. The glass backboards were at first hard to find against a sea of faces.

Perhaps intimidated by the crowd, as a team Shelbyville did not play well in their afternoon game against Clinton, a small town west of Indianapolis. Hank Hemingway was hobbling on a knee he had injured in the regional. Emmie Johnson again could not hit in daytime and scored only four points. The only one not bothered by the scale of Butler Fieldhouse was Bill Garrett. In a near-repeat of his performance the week before against Madison, Garrett scored twenty-seven points, carrying the Bears to a 48–39 win. After dressing and downing box lunches, the team headed off to rest a few hours at the Riley Hotel.

In the week leading up to the semifinals, Doc Barnett had called most of Indianapolis's well-known hotels, looking for a place where the team could rest between games. Although Indiana law had barred discrimination in public accommodations since 1869, Indianapolis's major hotels, like most of its restaurants, theaters, and hospitals, refused to accept black customers. Just a month before the 1947 semifinal, the National Council of Church Women had canceled plans to hold its annual convention and fiftieth-anniversary celebration in Indianapolis because, the chairwoman wrote, "not one hotel in Indianapolis would receive our guests for the reason that some of them did not have white skin." In his calls, Barnett had made a point of telling each hotel that Shelbyville had black players, and in most conversations he had been rebuffed immediately. Finally, a manager at the Riley said it would be all right if the team was not staying overnight, did not linger in public areas, and would be gone by early evening.

It was after three o'clock when the three Shelbyville cars pulled up at the hotel's driveway. A uniformed doorman reached for the door of Barnes's Buick—and then flinched before opening it. Oblivious,

Barnes led the group inside and announced to the front desk clerk, "We're the Shelbyville team." The clerk, a tall, middle-aged man, leaned forward, looked over the group, said, "Just a minute, sir," and left. A moment later the manager appeared. "Is that your team?" he asked, gesturing toward the players, who had drifted into the lobby, some sitting around on couches, others joking in small groups.

"Yes, it is. Why?" Barnes was starting to sense a problem.

The manager lowered his voice and leaned across the counter. "I'm afraid *they* can't stay here," he almost whispered, nodding toward Garrett, Johnson, and Murray, standing at the far end of one couch, watching.

"What do you mean *they* can't stay here?" Barnes thundered, his eyes widening, face starting to redden. "We made a reservation for the Shelbyville team."

"I'm sorry, sir, we don't take Negroes."

Doc Barnett tried to reason. "When I made the reservation, I said there were Negroes on our team, and the person I talked to said it was all right. We're playing in the semifinal championship game tonight, and we've only got a few hours to rest."

"I'm sorry. There must have been a mistake," the manager replied. "I've got strict instructions. I can't even let them stay in the lobby like this."

Barnes turned crimson and glared at the manager a long minute. He was exhausted, protective of his players, and naturally combative, but he did not want to upset his team and he needed to get them off their feet. All season he had watched Garrett, Johnson, and Murray face taunts and insults, and all season he had pleaded with them, "Don't mess with shit; you'll just get it all over you." And now they were watching him.

Barnett was standing close, almost leaning on Barnes, and once again at a moment of stress the coach elbowed Barnett in the ribs, and this time Barnes stepped aside. Doc looked the manager in the eye and said evenly, "We've obviously got a problem here. What can we do?"

The manager's face relaxed slightly. "There's a rooming house off the parking lot behind us I can send them to."

"What about our five-o'clock meal?"

"You can all have it together—in a private room in the basement—if you want to."

Barnett looked at Barnes, and then at Malcolm Clay, Shelbyville's junior varsity coach standing nearby, and then back at Barnes. Barnes, his face drained of color, nodded slightly. Barnett turned back to the manager. "Will you call the rooming house?"

The manager nodded and disappeared. Most of the players had drifted into the gift shop where they were reading magazines, pointing out pictures, and laughing. Only Garrett, Johnson, and Murray, each in his white letter sweater with a big, gold S on the front, stood in the middle of the lobby, not speaking, staring at Barnes, Barnett, and Clay.

The manager returned and said quietly, "They've got room," and wrote an address on a slip of paper. Barnett told Malcolm Clay, "You get the others to their rooms." And then he and Barnes turned toward their three best players. They stopped face-to-face, the coaches unable to meet their gaze, the players impassive. Before anyone could speak, Garrett said softly, "It's OK, Mr. Barnes."

It broke the tension. Garrett, Johnson, and Murray appeared to take their rejection in stride, and not to be very surprised by it. But Frank Barnes was not used to being treated this way. As they walked together out of the hotel Barnes vented, "Those goddamn sons-of-bitches! They never told us that! They took our money and pull that shit! I'm sorry, boys. The best thing you can do now is show you're bigger than them. Get some rest, and come back and give a good account of yourselves tonight. You mess with stuff like that, you just get it all over you."

A few hours later the team ate their pregame meal together in one of the hotel's basement conference rooms. By now the white players knew that Garrett, Johnson, and Murray had been barred from staying with them. The trio reassured their teammates that it was better at "the annex," because they had a phonograph player and some records in their room. But privately, they told Barnes they couldn't stay there because it was "too wild." Saturday night was starting.

Barnes dragged out the meal as long as he could, going over the scouting report in detail. It was a few minutes after six when he told his reserves and managers to go back to their rooms and to be ready to leave for Butler Fieldhouse at 6:45, instead of 7:00, as originally planned. Then Barnes and Doc Barnett kept their five seniors in the basement, sitting around talking not only about their game plan but also about their season, Barnes's golf handicap, his experiences flying over the Himalayan "hump" in the Army Air Corps. "When orders are written, you go, and it doesn't matter if it's dangerous, or you're scared," he told them. As they rose to go, Barnes turned serious. Looking from Garrett to Johnson to Murray, flanked by assistant coaches Barnett and Clay, he said, "This is never going to happen to us again."

Shelbyville's opponent for the Indianapolis semifinal championship was Lawrenceburg, a Seagrams distillery town on the Ohio River near Cincinnati. Lawrenceburg had lost only one game all season. They had a black player, Russell "Deke" Freeland, one of the better guards in the state, who would become a standout at DePauw University. Some favored Lawrenceburg to beat Shelbyville, and the game seemed headed that way as Lawrenceburg held leads of 13–10 at the end of the first quarter and 23–22 at the half. But in the first minutes of the second half, led by Garrett, Shelbyville reeled off seven straight points to take a 29–23 lead. They went on to win, 44–38. Garrett's eighteen points made him the leading scorer in all four semifinals.

As their cheering fans surrounded them on the floor, a final announcement came over the Fieldhouse public address system, "Ladies and gentlemen, here are the final scores from the other semifinal championship games tonight." A hush fell over the arena. "At Lafayette: East Chicago Washington 43, South Bend Central 38. At Muncie: Marion 40, Muncie Burris 32. And at Bloomington . . ." the announcer paused for an agonizing second before continuing, "Terre Haute Garfield 43, Evansville Central 38."

An instant of total silence was followed by wild cheers, hugs, and pumping of fists in the Shelbyville crowd, as the announcer continued, "Next Saturday, here at Butler Fieldhouse, in the afternoon, Marion will play Terre Haute Garfield at 1:15, and Shelbyville will play East Chicago Washington at 2:30. The two afternoon winners will play here at 8:15 next Saturday night for the 1947 Indiana State Championship."

The announcer's echo had not yet faded when a Shelbyville cheerleader shouted though a megaphone, "And we *know* who'll be waiting at the end!"

8

March 22, 1947

"A STATE OF NEAR-INSANITY" IS HOW THE *SHELBYVILLE Democrat* described the mood on the Monday before the 1947 Final Four. The IHSAA had allotted 800 tickets to each of the competing schools, and by the time Shelbyville's supply had been distributed to students, school personnel, players' families, police, and firemen, only one hundred tickets remained for the more than two thousand adult fans who wanted them. A drawing was held on Wednesday afternoon, and although they did not have to be present to win, two hundred adults filled every seat and stood four-deep in the high school assembly room. One hundred times Police Chief Walter Wintin turned a crank to rotate the big wire-mesh basket filled with self-addressed envelopes and four-dollar checks, as Principal Breck reached in. While some in the audience prayed, Breck called out the names of those who had won the right to buy one ticket to the Final Four.

Winners shouted and thanked their gods. After the hundredth envelope, the others slumped away, some bickering, many fighting tears. Their chances of finding an unwanted ticket anywhere in the state were as unlikely as their ability to afford a scalped one priced between $25 and $50—equal to about $250 to $500 today. The optimistic could hang around Butler Fieldhouse at the end of the afternoon games and hope a losing team's fan would unload a ticket for the evening game at face value. The most adventuresome could take their chances trying to sneak in, as a few fans did every year, hiding out in obscure corners of the Fieldhouse a day or two before the Final Four. (The previous year, Butler coach Tony Hinkle had called the police to pull a would-be fan from a Fieldhouse drainpipe.) For most Shelbyville fans, though, including more than fifteen hundred season ticket holders, striking out in the lottery meant they would not be present at the great moment, but instead would have to listen on one of the radio stations that would carry the games.

Shelbyville would play the East Chicago Washington Senators in the second game, at 2:30 Saturday afternoon. East Chicago had see-sawed with Terre Haute Garfield over the state's number-one and -two rankings during the last weeks of the season. Early in the final week of the tournament the professionals weighed in: "Bookies," sports pages all over the state reported, had installed East Chicago Washington as a 7.5-point favorite to beat Shelbyville in the afternoon, and a two-point favorite to beat Terre Haute Garfield for the state championship on Saturday night. In its final poll UPI had concurred, ranking East Chicago first in the state and Terre Haute second. At game time Saturday, the veteran sports reporters along press row were evenly split, half picking East Chicago and half picking Terre Haute. To win the state tournament, Shelbyville would have to beat them both on the same day.

Had they known more about the place, just the thought of East Chicago might have scared the boys from Shelbyville. Set smack against Indiana's northwest corner, where the South Side of Chicago spreads east into Indiana along the tip of Lake Michigan, East Chicago was the toughest, grimiest, most polyglot part of "Da Region"—the Calumet Region that also included Whiting, Hammond, and Gary. The Region was one of the roughest areas in all of industrial America—a stretch of orange flames burning over black refinery smokestacks, mills pouring molten steel, storage tanks stretching down to the docks, "soap works, ore docks, coal piles, cement docks, lake freighters, and endless desolate seas of swampy wasteland . . . the political machines and gangsters with rackets and sawed-off shotguns," as writer John Bartlow Martin described it in 1947.

Fifty-six different immigrant groups fed into the student body of East Chicago Washington High School, and, as the *Indianapolis News* reported, their ten-player tournament roster included "a Slovak, a

Hungarian, a Croatian, a Serb, two Lithuanians, an Irishman, a German Jew and two Negro boys," neither of whom were starters. Led by six-four Ray Ragelis, who ranked with Bill Garrett and Clyde Lovellette as one of the three best centers in the state, East Chicago had played a tough schedule and their record was 26–2.

On the Wednesday before the championship, the Kiwanis Club sponsored a banquet at the Antlers Hotel in Indianapolis, honoring the Final Four coaches and featuring a panel discussion between the sports editors of the three Indianapolis dailies and the coaches, which was broadcast statewide on WIBC radio. The questions were supposed to be softballs, but there was much between the lines. Some questioned the ages of Emerson Johnson and Marshall Murray. They were eighteen, but rumors were flying that they were twenty, the cutoff point for eligibility. The main theme that ran through the questions was "referee intimidation." On the surface, the term stood for two contradictory allegations: referees were afraid to call fouls when they should, and referees were calling fouls too quickly and intimidating teams from playing aggressive defense. The complaint of intimidation had emerged as Shelbyville had made its way through the tournament, and its subtext was clear: Referees were afraid to call fouls on Bill Garrett, Emerson Johnson, and Marshall Murray, or were calling fouls on Shelbyville's opponents too quickly, because referees were intimidated by the abuse Earl Townsend had taken and the controversy over the Townsend incident. At one point in the program, the questioning about referee intimidation became so persistent that IHSAA commissioner L. V. Phillips took over the microphone. He explained that the quality of refereeing had suffered during the war, and the current crop of referees was rusty, but Phillips insisted the problem was being addressed as fast as possible.

Frank Barnes left the banquet alongside East Chicago's coach, John Baratto. Childhood polio had left Baratto partially paralyzed, his sharp-featured face cast in a permanent scowl. Barnes turned to Baratto and said, in the singsong tone any acquaintance would have recognized as a teasing setup, "Take it easy on us Saturday, Coach." Baratto had made it to the top tier of Indiana high school coaches, but he was only 28, he did not know Barnes, and teasing banter was not his strong suit. Baratto stopped Barnes at the doorway, put his good hand on Barnes's forearm, and earnestly replied, "I've already talked to my team about that. Don't worry, Frank. We're gonna play just hard enough to win, and save our energy for Terre Haute." Barnes had what he needed from the luncheon. He chuckled to himself and patted the Buick's steering wheel all the way back to Shelbyville.

John Baratto was not alone in dismissing the Golden Bears' chances. Even in Shelbyville hope outpaced expectations. Senior class president George Glass asked his father if he could stay out all night if the Golden Bears won the state, and was told with a wink, "Sure, George." Junior varsity coach Malcolm Clay promised to usher the early service at the First Methodist Church on Sunday morning if the Golden Bears won the state Saturday night. On Thursday afternoon before the finals, the Shelbyville mayor and the police and fire chiefs met with Principal Breck to make contingency plans for the postgame celebration in case the Golden Bears won. But few really believed it would happen.

One who did believe was Frank Barnes. His team was positioned exactly where Barnes wanted them: underrated and facing an over-confident opponent. On the Saturday morning of the game, as they met a final time at the Harrison Cafeteria for a pregame brunch, Barnes sensed his players were loose and confident. They carried no expectations and had nothing to lose. Gold-and-black crepe paper was flying from almost every downtown home and business, but Garrett, Johnson, and Murray, in particular, were not burdened by the weight of civic pride; they were going to Indianapolis to play basketball and to settle a score, and their detachment and determination rubbed off on their teammates. In later years, Barnes would spin this moment into another of his pointed homilies, this one an exhortation to believe in oneself despite the odds: "There wasn't anybody in the state of Indiana thought we could beat East Chicago, except five boys and a couple of dumb coaches. They *thought* they could."

Alone among the Final Four teams, Shelbyville had not stayed in Indianapolis the night before the games. The city was in full tournament thrall by the time their three cars turned west on Forty-ninth Street toward Butler Fieldhouse shortly after one o'clock on Saturday. The first game, between Terre Haute and Marion, was just starting, and most of the lucky ticket holders were already inside the Fieldhouse, but thousands of others crowded Forty-ninth Street and milled around the parking lot, which was ablaze in the colors of the Final Four teams—gold and black for Shelbyville, maroon and white for East Chicago, purple and gold for Marion, and purple and white for Terre Haute. Everywhere people were looking to buy or sell scalped tickets, hawking parking spots in their driveways, selling special tournament editions of the Indianapolis newspapers, peddling pennants and pom-poms, or just soaking in the atmosphere.

Arriving at the team entrance, the Golden Bears made their way down the narrow ramp to their basement dressing room as the Terre Haute–Marion game was getting started. From the nearby trainers' room a radio broadcast carried into the corridor, and as the players dressed, it was clear the first game was shaping up as a blowout. Terre Haute led 28–16 at the half, and 47–23 at the third quarter. With every play WISH's Luke Walton described, they could hear the delayed, muffled roar of fifteen thousand fans in the distance above them. Up on the floor, Terre Haute's thirty-four-year-old coach Willard Kehrt, who normally looked like a tall academic in his three-piece suits and rimless glasses, was chomping a full pack of gum and turning with every basket to pound on reserve players and shout, "Whatta life! Whatta life, huh!"

When the first game ended, with Terre Haute winning 59–50, Garrett and his teammates started up the ramp to the playing floor wearing their road uniforms, the ones they had reverted to after the early season fiasco at Indianapolis Shortridge: dark-gold shorts and tank top jerseys with black numbers and "BEARS" in black letters across the front, and long-sleeved gold warm-up shirts with a big black S in front. As the Golden Bears walked up the narrow concrete ramp, they met the teams from the first game coming down, Marion boys in white uniforms, silent, heads down; purple-clad Terre Haute players running and shouting to one another, "Bring on East Chicago!"

Emerging from behind the grandstand, it was quickly clear to the Shelbyville team that this was the Final Four, not the semifinals. Sportswriters for 176 newspapers and three wire services occupied the first two rows to the players' left as they stepped onto the playing floor. Twenty-four sports broadcasters, representing radio stations as far away as Chicago, Louisville, and St. Louis, and speaking to an audience of more than two million listeners, took up the opposite front row, their big microphones forming a scrambled alphabet of white call letters. An Indianapolis Symphony concert was being broadcast nationwide that day on *Orchestra of the Nation,* but anyone in Indianapolis who wanted to hear it had to tune in to Cincinnati's WLW, for virtually every radio station in Indiana was carrying the state basketball finals.

Looking around the Fieldhouse, it was painfully apparent which teams the IHSAA expected to compete in the final game. The Shelbyville and Terre Haute cheering sections were side by side in the stands. No tournament planner would have seated the "rowdy" Shelbyville fans beside the fans from Terre Haute unless they thought one of those two teams would not be there for the championship game that night.

Shelbyville started tentatively. Garrett missed two shots, and East Chicago hit their first three, including a breakaway layup, to grab a 6–0 lead after the first minute and a half. This was worse, even, than the score indicated, for to beat a bigger, favored team it is important to stay close, eroding their confidence. Let such a team open daylight, and they are usually hard to catch.

Finally Marshall Murray hit a free throw, but East Chicago guard George Savanovich answered with another one-hander and the score was 8–1. In desperation, unable to get the ball to Garrett inside, Bill Breck threw up a long one-hander that banked in, "pure slop," as they would call it on the playground, giving Shelbyville their first field goal and making it 8–3. East Chicago began roughing up Garrett every time he got the ball, hacking him across the arms when he spun around a defender, clubbing him across the shoulders when he broke into the open. Believing Shelbyville to be a one-man team, and with strong reserves on his bench, John Baratto apparently thought his team could afford to pile up fouls and that playing rough would throw Garrett and his teammates off their game.

It worked for one quarter. At the end of the first quarter, East Chicago led 17–11. Garrett did not yet have a field goal. Johnson had not yet scored. Shelbyville had hit only two of fourteen shots. Garrett's six straight free throws were all that had kept them in the game.

The start of the second quarter was no better. East Chicago scored three quick points, bringing the score to 20–11, and Frank Barnes called for a time-out. In 1947, teams could not go to the bench to talk with their coach during time-outs; instead, the five players in the game for each team stayed on the floor and conferred among themselves. As Shelbyville's five seniors huddled, things were looking grim. They had not yet found their rhythm, and a nine-point lead would be hard to overcome against the top-ranked team in the state. They stood together silently, until Bill Breck leaned in to look Emerson Johnson square in the face and said, "Emmie, you see what they're doing. You've gotta step up."

As soon as play resumed, Johnson sliced through the East Chicago defense and hit a driving one-hander. Garrett was fouled again and hit the free throw, and Breck followed quickly with two more free throws. It was 20–16, and Shelbyville was back in the game. East Chicago scored to make it 22–16, but then Johnson launched a thirty-foot two-hand set shot that swished cleanly through the net. The score was 22–18, and now it was John Baratto who called time-out.

Returning to action, East Chicago fouled on two straight Shelbyville possessions; Hemingway and Johnson each hit free throws to draw the Bears within two points, 22–20. Two East Chicago free throws made it 24–20, but Murray hit a driving one-hander, and in the final seconds of the first half Johnson again swished a thirty-footer that tied the score 24–24. The underdogs had come all the way back.

Since their time-out early in the second quarter, when they had been trailing 20–11, the Golden Bears had found their game and had swung the momentum their way. Led by Johnson's seven quick points, they had outscored East Chicago 13–4, and they had plenty in reserve. Garrett still did not have a field goal, although he had responded to the rough fouling by hitting eight of nine free throws. Referees Walter Thurston and Dean Malaska were not hesitating to call the game closely, putting several East Chicago players in foul trouble. East Chicago was getting only one shot per possession, since Garrett was sweeping every defensive rebound.

The Shelbyville players, if not their coach, were again loose and confident. As Barnes made his way up the ramp for the second half, his face as gray as his lucky cardigan, a hand lightly touched his left shoulder. Coming up from behind, Bill Garrett smiled at his coach, "Don't worry, Mr. Barnes, I'll hit 'em this half." He bounded past Barnes and out onto the floor.

In the first thirty seconds of the second half, Emmie Johnson swept an offensive rebound and hit a backhand reverse layup just as East Chicago's Randy Balas pushed him to the floor in frustration. On the play referee Walter Thurston called Balas's fifth and final foul, sending him to the bench. With less than thirty seconds gone in the second half, East Chicago's best defensive player, assigned to guard Garrett, was out of the game, and Shelbyville had a three-point play and a 27–24 lead.

On the next possession Johnson intercepted a pass, drove the length of the court, and scored again. Emmie had now scored the last two points of the first half and the first five of the second, and since Bill Breck's challenge to him early in the second quarter, Johnson had outscored the entire East Chicago team, 12–4. Hard fouls had not rattled Garrett, and Shelbyville was proving to be more than a one-man team. With their game plan in shambles, it was East Chicago that wilted.

With three-and-a-half minutes left in the third quarter, Bill Garrett finally opened up. He hit a one-hander from twenty feet. With Balas out of the game, he spun around Andy Spencer at will, hitting reverse layups or passing off to teammates for clear shots. As the East Chicago team stood around looking dumbstruck, the Shelbyville players began having fun. It showed in the subtle dance Johnson did while dribbling at the top of the key, and it showed when East Chicago's Ray Ragelis blocked a Garrett shot, and Bill handed the ball to Hank Hemingway saying, "Take it. I'm gettin' outta here." At the end of the third quarter, it was Shelbyville 43, East Chicago 36.

Early in the fourth quarter Garrett hit two turn-around jump shots. When East Chicago made a little run, pulling within six points late in the game, in a span of one minute Garrett first drove from the right wing across the free-throw lane, switching the ball from his left hand to his right in midair and burying a one-hander, and then stole the ball and hit a pull-up jumper, causing sportscaster Luke Walton to shout into his microphone, "Bill Garrett breaks loose from East Chicago, and they don't know what to do with him!"

When the final horn sounded, the score was Shelbyville 54, East Chicago 46. Garrett got twenty-five points, including thirteen free throws. Four different East Chicago players had guarded Garrett, and three of them had fouled out. Garrett had gotten almost every defen-

sive rebound in the second half. Taking over when Garrett was double-
teamed, Emerson Johnson had scored thirteen points and Marshall
Murray eleven. Together, Garrett, Johnson, and Murray outscored the
entire East Chicago team, 49–46. They would have their rematch
with Terre Haute Garfield after all.

Back in the dressing room, the Bears were happy but determined.
They did not greet well-wishers or linger; they were hungry, and they
needed to get showered, dressed, and out to eat and rest for a few
hours. A reporter asked Barnes how he thought the championship
game would go and got typical Barnes spin, "I guess if we stay within
15 points of them, we'll be lucky."

It was after four o'clock when they left Butler Fieldhouse. The
state championship was at 8:15. To avoid the humiliation of the previous week, Doc Barnett had arranged for the team to use the chapter
house of his fraternity, Delta Tau Delta, on the Butler campus a short
distance from the Fieldhouse. Away on spring break, the Delts, which
like other white fraternities of the time accepted no black members,
had only one condition: Garrett, Johnson, and Murray would have to
furnish their own sheets and pillowcases. Early that Saturday morning, Hanne Barnett, Doc's wife, had driven to Indianapolis and had
made up ten beds in the Delt house, all with new white sheets and
pillowcases.

When they arrived at the fraternity house, the Shelbyville boys
were not ready to rest. Teenagers who had just beaten the top-ranked
team in the state in front of fifteen thousand people, they needed to
let off a little steam before they could focus on the state championship only a few hours away. They were all in a single, dorm-style
room when Emerson Johnson turned to Bill Breck and, without
expression, smashed him in the face with a pillow. In an instant ten
boys were on top of each other, swinging pillows, hooting, and
laughing. This went on for almost an hour, and when they came
down to the dining room for their takeout pregame meal, the giddi-
ness was gone, and they were ready to concentrate.

Frank Barnes sat at the head of the table and spoke for only a few
minutes. He never mentioned they were playing for the state championship, never said it was the rematch they had been wanting, never

reminded them of the controversy surrounding their loss to Terre Haute in early January. Instead, Barnes briefly laid out a simple game plan. Terre Haute's defense would sag around Garrett, under the basket, leaving others open. The rest of the team would have to accept the challenge, take the open shots, and hit them. If they did, Terre Haute would be forced to come out and guard the others more closely, and with their defense spread, Terre Haute could not match the quickness of Garrett, Johnson, and Murray. Clyde Lovellette might be six-ten, but he was slow. If Shelbyville could hit early shots, spread Terre Haute's defense, and isolate Lovellette on Garrett fifteen feet from the basket, they would force Terre Haute to play their game.

On defense, Marshall Murray would guard Ronnie Bland, Terre Haute's leading scorer. Hank Hemingway and Bill Garrett would double-team Clyde Lovellette, Hemingway playing behind Lovellette as the towering Terre Haute center posted up, Garrett playing in front of Lovellette off to one side. Hemingway's role was to block Lovellette from getting to the basket for layups; Garrett's was to lull the Terre Haute guards into making the soft lob passes they often used to get the ball inside to Lovellette, and then to use his quickness, timing, and leaping ability to intercept or deflect the lobs, stealing the ball and disrupting Terre Haute's offense.

Across the Butler campus, Willard Kehrt was giving his Terre Haute Garfield players their game plan. Kehrt was concerned because he thought his team was not taking Shelbyville seriously. He sensed from snippets of conversation and body language that they thought they were lucky not to be playing East Chicago, that their win at Shelbyville in January had been easy, and that Shelbyville was a one-man team. Since they had only watched the first quarter of the Shelbyville–East Chicago game before leaving for lunch and a rest, they had not seen Emerson Johnson explode for seven quick points at the end of the first half, nor heard the excitement in Luke Walton's voice as he described Bill Garrett taking over the game in the second half.

In the dressing room the Shelbyville student managers had laid out the players' home uniforms—white with "BEARS" across the front of the jerseys, above the numbers; white short-sleeved warm-up shirts with a big S on the front. The uniforms had arrived in midseason, together with the red road uniforms the Golden Bears had worn at Shortridge. Barnes had asked for white home uniforms with gold lettering and numbers, but the ones he received were white with red trim. Barnes had accepted the uniforms, laughing that he would give them to his players when they won the state championship anyway.

The basement dressing room was cramped, its floor and walls gray concrete, dark green metal lockers on three sides, and wood benches forming an L in front of the lockers on two sides. By conventional coaching wisdom, the team that had a harder game in the afternoon stayed longer in the dressing room and took a shorter warm-up at night. The Shelbyville players had known they would be going out second, but nothing could make this wait easy as they listened to the whoops and shouts of the Terre Haute team emerging from their dressing room and then heard the roar of the crowd in the distance above. For their final briefing, Frank Barnes had asked his friend Tom Downey, the coach of nearby Greensburg, to watch Terre Haute in the afternoon and to give his players a final scouting report. In his late thirties, with blond hair balding at the edges, Downey stood directly in front of the dressing room door, the only spot where all ten players, sitting on benches in front of their lockers, could see the chalkboard he had set up. Barnes and Doc Barnett stood in the corner opposite Downey. Downey had drawn a diagram of a basketball court and written the names of the Terre Haute starters at the places indicating their positions: Ronnie Bland and Jay Center, both six-two, on either side of the basket at the forwards; Clyde Lovellette, six-ten, just to the side of the basket in the middle; Gordon Neff, six-one, and Bob Skitt, five-ten, out in front on either side, at the guards.

Downey started to speak, describing how the right-handed Bland liked to fake left and make a quick move to his right, how the Terre Haute guards used high, lob passes to get the ball to Lovellette under the basket. He had been looking at the chalkboard, but when he turned to his audience, Downey paused. Slowly, he pointed to the top of the board, and then to the bottom. Not an eyeball moved. The Shelbyville players were staring beyond the board, at the door. Downey looked at Barnes, put down his marker, pulled the chalkboard out of the way, and said, "Send 'em on out, Coach. They're as ready as they'll ever be."

Bill Breck threw open the door so hard it bounced against the wall. In silence, staring straight ahead, the team trotted up the ramp to the top where a security guard with a whistle shooed milling fans out of their way. Single file, they crossed behind the grandstands and emerged through the door into the bright light of the arena to stand on a basketball court once again with Terre Haute Garfield.

As they appeared, a roar from the Shelbyville section echoed around the Fieldhouse, but there was no other fanfare. The IHSAA mandated that the final tournament games be simple and efficient. There were no decorated hoops to jump through, no bands, no baton twirlers, no costumed mascots—not even the national anthem before the afternoon and evening sessions.

The Terre Haute players were wearing the same purple uniforms they had worn at Shelbyville eleven weeks before. They had rolled into the final game on the momentum of an easy afternoon win, and they were now the prohibitive favorite with a won-lost record of 31–0. They did not have any sense that this was a grudge rematch. They thought Shelbyville was a one-man team. They knew they could not stop Garrett from scoring, but they believed Lovellette could match Garrett's point production, and that Bland and his teammates would easily outscore the rest of the Golden Bears. Willard Kehrt's game plan was exactly what Frank Barnes had expected. Terre Haute's defense would "pack it in," congesting the area around the basket, taking away Garrett's room to maneuver, and challenging the other Shelbyville players to shoot from outside. Their offense would depend on lofting high passes to Lovellette for hooks and other close-in shots over the shorter Shelbyville defenders, and on drives and outside shots by Bland and his teammates.

The starting lineups were introduced, the players received last-minute encouragement from their coaches and send-off cheers from their fans, and then Shelbyville's Golden Bears and Terre Haute Garfield's Purple Eagles squared off as Clyde Lovellette and Bill Garrett stepped up for the opening tip-off.

Lovellette, eight inches taller, controlled the tip and batted the ball backward toward his teammate Gordon Neff, but Bill Breck anticipated the play and stepped in front of Neff to steal the ball. Breck shot a pass to Murray, who relayed the ball to Johnson, who fired his two-hand set shot from thirty-five feet without hesitation. As Emmie's long shot arched toward the basket, Terre Haute players raced to get into position to rebound. Lovellette, Bland, and Jay Center formed an impenetrable semicircle directly in front of the basket, blocking out everyone else.

Hank Hemingway had learned over the years that when Johnson's high-arched shots missed, they came off the rim softly. Hank had slipped along the baseline, too far under the basket for a normal rebound, inside the three-man block-out, almost unnoticed by the Terre Haute players. As Johnson's shot touched the rim lightly and fell to one side, Hank jumped off his good leg and tipped the ball in with his right hand. After eight seconds, it was 2–0 Shelbyville.

Terre Haute brought the ball up the floor and quickly got the ball to Ronnie Bland, guarded by Marshall Murray. Bland stepped forward, leaned his face close to Murray's, and, looking at Marshall as if to say, "Watch this," faked to his left and started a quick move to his right. At Booker T., Walter Fort had taught Murray to follow the waistband of the man he was guarding. "He can fake with his head, or his arms, or the ball, but he can't fake with his belly," Fort had said. Freshman coach Ray Hinshaw had repeated the point in drill after drill on cold winter nights. As Bland faked left, Murray's eyes stayed fixed on Bland's midsection. And as Bland moved right, Murray batted the ball out of his hand.

There followed a flurry. Garrett missed, but when Terre Haute tried to loft a high pass inside to Lovellette, as they had done all year, Garrett intercepted it, drifting over to front Lovellette, and timing his jump perfectly. Shelbyville missed the shot again, but Garfield threw the ball away. Another Shelbyville miss and Terre Haute's Bob Skitt was fouled by Bill Breck and hit two free throws. With two and a half minutes gone, the score was only 2–2. Both teams had started nervously, Terre Haute had committed three turnovers, and they had not yet taken a shot from the field.

The instant Shelbyville got the ball up the floor Emmie Johnson again cut loose a long, two-hand set shot, and this time it was good: Shelbyville 4–2. Garrett swept a rebound from Lovellette, passed off to Breck, and, in a "give and go," got the ball back and drove around Lovellette for a reverse layup: 6–2. Lovellette hit a layup, and Johnson sliced through, too quick for the Terre Haute defense, for another give-and-go layup: 8–4.

In a scramble, Shelbyville got the ball out of bounds under its own basket. Breck in-bounded the ball to Murray, who looked toward Johnson at the top of the key and then made a blind, backward bounce pass to Breck, who had sneaked in-bounds under the basket for a wide-open layup, prompting Luke Walton to shout into his microphone, "A very neat in-bounds play by Shelbyville!" It was the play Murray had struggled all year to master, walking from one taped mark to another. The score was 12–6, Shelbyville.

The first quarter ended 14–8. Terre Haute had no one who could handle the quickness of Garrett, Johnson, and Murray, and the Golden Bears had been more aggressive and confident. Shelbyville had shot well—hitting seven of fifteen from the field—while Terre Haute had made only one field goal. But Garrett had two fouls, and Lovellette only one.

Johnson started the second quarter with a thirty-five-foot two-hander, to make it 16–8. Five straight points by Terre Haute brought the score to 16–13, but Garrett hit again; then Johnson drove through Terre Haute for another slicing layup, followed it quickly with a forty-foot set shot, and then stole the ball and hit a driving one-hander: three straight baskets by Johnson within thirty seconds, and the score was 24–13. Terre Haute called for a time-out, and in their players' circle at midcourt Gordon Neff, who was guarding Johnson, shot a worried look at his coach and spread his arms, palms up, in a gesture that said, "What are we gonna do? I can't handle him!" On WISH radio, Luke Walton was shouting, "That Johnson boy's on fire! I don't think he's missed one yet! Folks, he's hotter than a little red fire truck!"

The first half ended with Shelbyville leading 33–26. Barnes's game plan was working, Terre Haute's was not. Johnson's outside shooting had forced the Purple Eagles to spread their defense, opening the middle for Garrett's spin moves around Lovellette and creating space for Garrett and Johnson's quick drives—exactly as Barnes had hoped. Murray had held Ronnie Bland scoreless in the first half, and Garrett still had only two fouls, the same as Clyde Lovellette.

After his miss in the game's opening seconds, Emerson Johnson had hit four straight two-hand set shots, some from forty feet, with his feet inside the near edge of the center circle—shots that "if he'd taken them in practice, he would have been benched," as a teammate put it. At the half, Barnes told Johnson, "Emmie, keep taking those

shots, but move in a little! You don't have to shoot from that far out."
With a twinkle Johnson replied, "No need to go all the way down the
court when I can hit from halfway."

Just before the second half started, Bill Frosch, the WISH color
commentator sitting beside Luke Walton along broadcaster's row,
offered his quick analysis, "This boy Emerson Johnson and his two
teammates, his two Negro teammates, the three Negro boys for Shelbyville—Emerson Johnson, Marshall Murray, and Bill Garrett—have
been really putting on a show of hitting the basket tonight that fifteen thousand people will go home and talk about tomorrow, the
next day, and quite a few days, ladies and gentlemen. They've shot
from out in the middle of the floor, and they've taken that fast-
breaking give-off under the basket for lay-in shots. . . . And that's the
reason the Shelbyville Golden Bears are ahead."

At the start of the second half Garrett rebounded, hit a put-back,
and was fouled by Clyde Lovellette—Lovellette's third foul. Garrett
hit the free throw to complete the three-point play and make the
score 36–26. Lovellette scored on a rebound to make it 36–28, but
Emerson Johnson hit another driving layup as the normally cool
Luke Walton shouted, "That boy's ablaze! He's a rocket of fire!"

With five minutes to go in the third quarter some of the Terre
Haute players, in desperation, began to taunt Johnson and Murray.
Murray elbowed a Terre Haute player away from the ball as Lovellette
hit from the corner. A free throw made it 40–33, but Johnson came
back immediately with another two-hand set shot from thirty-five
feet, and now Luke Walton made no effort to hide his awe, "There's
Emerson Johnson again! Oh, my goodness sakes alive, he is *creating
history* here tonight!"

Garrett picked up his third foul, and Terre Haute hit two more free
throws, but the next time down the floor Johnson hit another two-
hand set shot from thirty-five feet. This time Luke Walton's voice was
more quietly respectful than excited, sounding almost wilted, "I've
never seen anything like it, ladies and gentlemen. It's like it's guided
by radar." The score was 45–35.

Lovellette scored again, hitting over Don Chambers, who had
replaced Hemingway. The next time down the floor Johnson paused,
looked at his Terre Haute defender, and sank another thirty-five-
footer. This time Walton could barely speak into his microphone,

"Oh . . . my . . . goodness. You could knock me over with a feather. This is the hottest team we've seen in a long, long time." When Garrett hit the next Shelbyville basket, a one-hander from the free-throw line, Walton dryly reminded his listeners that this was supposed to be a one-man team, "Hey! *He* hit one!" The score was 49–39.

Terre Haute's Jay Center hit from the corner, and Frank Barnes called for a time-out. The score was 49–41, but the Bears' lead was precarious. Four Shelbyville starters were in foul trouble: Murray and Hemingway had four fouls each, Garrett and Breck had three. As WISH's Bill Frosch told his listeners, while the Bears huddled at midcourt, "You can imagine how Coach Frank Barnes is sweating it out on the bench over these fouls that may still wreck the game for Shelbyville."

It got worse. Garrett hit a driving shot to make it 51–41, but Lovellette scored to make it 51–43. As Shelbyville was working for a last shot, Johnson, possibly responding to taunting, committed a foul away from the ball. Terre Haute missed the free throw, but Bland rebounded and hit a put-back—his first field goal—to make the score 51–45 at the end of the third quarter.

It had been one of the great quarters in Indiana state tournament history. Shelbyville had hit eight of fifteen shots, an almost unheard-of percentage at that time, but with the intense pace Terre Haute had gained a point, outscoring the Bears 19–18 on the strength of a 9–2 run in the last two and a half minutes.

In January, Shelbyville had gone into the last quarter three points ahead of Terre Haute, only to lose 52–44 after Bill Garrett was called for his fifth foul. Now, heading into the final eight-minute quarter, Garrett and Lovellette had three fouls each. If one of them fouled out, it would probably determine the state champion. Marshall Murray, who had held Ronnie Bland to one point, had four fouls. If Murray fouled out, Bland, normally Terre Haute's leading scorer, might take over. Without Garrett, and certainly without Garrett and Murray, Shelbyville could not win if Lovellette remained in the game, no matter how well they had played up to this point.

Early in the fourth quarter, Terre Haute hit a free throw, making it 51–46, and seconds later Lovellette stole a pass, and Gordon Neff hit from outside, bringing the score to 51–48. Shelbyville called time-out. From the Terre Haute huddle Lovellette looked up at the scoreboard and smiled, leading WISH's Bill Frosch to declare, "Big Clyde

Lovellette's saying, 'Why, shucks, that's just a couple of tip-ins. Get the ball to me, will you, fellas?' This looks to me like a mighty confident Garfield team right now."

Having played a much harder afternoon game, the Shelbyville players were getting tired. Since late in the third quarter, Terre Haute had scored seven straight points and had outscored Shelbyville eleven to two. They were down only three points and on a roll with plenty of time to go. As play resumed, Luke Walton told his listeners, "This is the crunch, ladies and gentlemen. We'll see how those boys perform now."

Terre Haute had two chances to cut the lead to one point, but they missed both. On Terre Haute's third possession Lovellette was called for his fourth foul, going over Garrett's back for a rebound. Nearing exhaustion, Garrett missed the free throw, but Murray took the rebound and drove for a clutch layup. It was 53–48, and the Golden Bears had gained a little breathing room. Then Garrett was called for his fourth foul, Lovellette hit a free throw, and the teams exchanged baskets to make the score 55–51 at the automatic time-out with four minutes left in the game. Their game in early January had been almost identical at this point: a small Shelbyville lead, and four fouls on both Garrett and Lovellette.

Ten seconds after play resumed, Terre Haute's Jay Center missed a shot from the corner. As Garrett spun to block out Terre Haute players, Lovellette, moving forward for the rebound, slammed into him and the two crashed to the floor at the feet of referee George Bender. A foul had to be called, and it could plausibly go either way. Garrett probably had the better case, for though he spun toward Lovellette, Garrett was in the more stationary position under the basket, and Lovellette had moved forward to make contact. Bender, from Indianapolis, had watched both players many times; he had refereed the Shelbyville sectional and the Bloomington semifinal that Terre Haute had won. If Bender called the foul on Garrett he might be accused of racism, but if he called it on Lovellette he would certainly be accused of giving in to "referee intimidation." It was, as Luke Walton had said, the crunch.

Bender blew his whistle and pointed down at Lovellette, then reached to help Lovellette up and prodded the big redhead to raise his hand to the scorer's bench. Having scored twenty-five of his team's fifty-one points, Clyde Lovellette was out of the game.

A moment later Johnson hit his last field goal, a long one from the right corner, and Luke Walton gave his final tribute, "He has stolen the show tonight, Emerson Johnson of Shelbyville. You can take off your hat and wave it to him, ladies and gentlemen. He has played basketball tonight."

With twenty-seven seconds to go and Shelbyville leading 66–58, Garrett was called for his fifth foul. Immediately the entire Shelbyville cheering section rose to its feet cheering wildly. And then it spread. High up on the third level a group of coaches and players from Indianapolis Crispus Attucks came to their feet. On the mezzanine at the south end, Hank Hemingway's former coach, Tim Campbell, stood clapping, followed quickly by his Franklin players. From a corner on the second level Marion Crawley—whose words in early December had proved prophetic—led a group of Lafayette Jefferson players and school officials to their feet. Along press row a lone reporter from the *Indianapolis Recorder* stood silently. The whole Marion quadrant, happy to see Terre Haute beaten, joined in, until finally most of the Butler Fieldhouse crowd was standing and applauding. On Indianapolis WIRE radio, sportscaster Tom Carnegie simply held up his microphone and let the sound of the standing ovation go out over the air.

Frank Barnes rasped, "Keep going! Keep going!" As Shelbyville's Don Chambers hit a one-hander, the gun sounded ending the game with the final score Shelbyville 68, Terre Haute Garfield 58.

Again there was a wild scene on the floor following a Shelbyville–Terre Haute game, this time a celebration. For an instant the Golden Bear players and coaches formed a tight group, embracing at the center of the floor, save for one small figure off to the side, hands on his hips, looking up at the scoreboard and beyond to the far reaches of Butler Fieldhouse, lost in his own thoughts. Asked by student manager Jack Worland if he was all right, Emerson Johnson just turned up the corners of his mouth in a weary hint of a smile.

They cut down the nets and posed for pictures. Bill Garrett accepted the two-foot-tall mahogany and gold championship trophy politely, unsmiling, no longer sweating, his white-and-red warm-up shirt neatly in place, turning to face the movie cameras looking as though nothing special had happened. Behind him, some of his white teammates could not stand still, clapping each other on the back and grinning broadly.

In the chaotic mingling that followed, sportscasters and sports-writers cornered coaches and players for interviews. Frank Barnes told one, in his singsong tone, "I wondered if my skinny little kids could keep up with those big boys, but they sure played big today, didn't they?" Shelbyville principal Breck said the magic words, "No school Monday!" His son Bill said, "Man, oh man, it's wonderful! I've waited seventeen years for this!" Hank Hemingway avoided the micro-phones and thought to himself, "Why are they asking *us* these things? We don't know anything." Marshall Murray said only, "Shoulda beat 'em the last time," and Emerson Johnson agreed, "I knew we could take Terre Haute." Bill Garrett, asked what he wanted to do in the future, told an interviewer, "I want to be a doctor."

Leaving through the same door, the Shelbyville and Terre Haute fans were a volatile mix. Winning fans were always noisy, and for the Shelbyville crowd this night had an undertone of revenge and poetic justice. The Terre Haute crowd had arrived that evening thinking the game would be easy and expecting to celebrate; instead, their team had lost for the first time all season. As the two groups mingled, Terre Haute fans vented loudly, "Goddamn refs afraid to call fouls on those nig-gers." "Our guys even look at those jigs and they get called. They *gave* those bastards the game with that foul on Junior." Junior was Clyde Lovellette's nickname. It continued all the way to the far side of the parking lot and on down the sidewalks, "Black Bears. Isn't that what they call them? They'll be playin' 'Ol Black Joe' in Shelbyville tonight."

More than fifty years later, to mention Shelbyville in the city of Terre Haute is to invite a tirade about referee intimidation and that last foul on Clyde Lovellette, but the score book tells a different story. The referees called twenty-three fouls on Shelbyville—a final-game record—and sixteen on Terre Haute Garfield. Garfield shot a record-setting thirty free throws and hit twenty of them, another record. Shelbyville shot sixteen free throws and hit eight. Lovellette alone shot thirteen free throws, an individual record. Three Golden Bears' starters fouled out of the game—Garrett, Murray, and Hemingway—while only Lovellette fouled out for Terre Haute.

After missing his first shot, Emerson Johnson hit eleven straight, most of them from near the center circle. His outside shooting had not only forced Terre Haute to spread its defense—allowing Bill Gar-rett to use his speed at will—it had shocked the unbeaten, overconfident Purple Eagles, destroyed their confidence, and changed the whole dynamic of the game. Very few players—among them pro stars Oscar Robertson and George McGinnis—would ever again put on a performance as dominant as that of five-foot-eight, 135-pound Emmie Johnson, in an Indiana state championship game.

Security guards had stopped trying to hold back the crowd that now filled the basement hallway and spilled into the locker room where Tom Downey's chalkboard lay folded against one wall. There were photographers and reporters, a few adventurous fans, and more than a dozen of the country's top college basketball coaches, who were always hungry for recruits.

Indiana University's Branch McCracken congratulated Frank Barnes, waved to the Shelbyville players, and headed over to the Terre Haute dressing room to talk to Clyde Lovellette, Ronnie Bland, and Willard Kehrt. So did Butler's Tony Hinkle, Indiana State's John Wooden, Stanford's Everett Dean, North Carolina State's Everett Case, Tulane's Cliff Wells, and all of the other college coaches present. Wells, a former Indiana high school coach whose teams had won two state championships, told *Shelbyville Democrat* sports editor Bill Holtel, before heading over to see Lovellette and Bland, "That shooting by Shelbyville was the most amazing exhibition I have ever seen in high school. Had I not taken a second look, I would have sworn it was Adolph Rupp's Kentucky Wonders."

It was a telling choice of words. Rupp's University of Kentucky basketball teams were all white until 1970, Rupp's fortieth year as the Kentucky coach. Rupp had vowed publicly that he would never recruit a black player and had asked Kentucky sports editors to place asterisks beside the names of black high school players who appeared in their stories, so the Kentucky coach would know not to contact them. But Rupp only stood out for being explicit. Of the dozen coaches beating a path to Lovellette and Bland in the basement of Butler Fieldhouse, only John Wooden had ever coached a black basketball player at the college level.

It was almost 11:00 P.M. when the Golden Bears finally emerged through the players' exit at the east end of Butler Fieldhouse, most in casual slacks and letter sweaters, battered felt hats, and trench coats. A light mist reflected the flashing lights of state police cruisers flanking the cars of Frank Barnes, Doc Barnett, and Malcolm Clay. A state trooper stood beside the passenger door of each car. One shouted to Barnes, "Stay between us. And keep up! We're gonna *move!*" Barnes stopped, put his hand on the trooper's shoulder, and replied, "Take it easy boys . . . I'm an old man tonight!"

Although it was Saturday night, Shelbyville had been at a standstill during the championship game. Those who couldn't be at Butler Fieldhouse had hovered near radios. Outside there was little traffic. With two minutes to go in the game, a deputy sheriff had stepped out of the Shelby County jail and walked a half-block to the front corner of the courthouse to stand watch over the logs and brush that had been piled there a few days earlier. There really would be a bonfire, after all.

The quiet lasted a few minutes after the game ended, as people listened to the awards ceremony and postgame interviews, and then it broke loose: car horns, whistles, sirens, church bells, and fireworks could be heard all over town as thousands poured into the streets surrounding the square. The plan to delay the bonfire until the team arrived was abandoned, and a crowd soon gathered around the blaze. Teenagers snake-danced through the downtown streets and into every open building, looping through the aisles of the Strand Theater until the manager stopped the movie and the moviegoers joined in. Soon thousands of people from around the state were crowding in to watch the celebration.

Approaching Shelbyville, the Golden Bears' motorcade passed through a gauntlet of cars parked on both sides of the road with fans beside them, on top of them, on their hoods, waving, cheering, and reaching out for the hands of the players who had brought them glory. Just before the bridge over Blue River that led into town, the local police had managed to clear a spot for the procession to pull over. The town fire truck, a thousand-gallon pumper stripped to its bare essentials, sat waiting to carry the team into town. In the rush to pile on, someone set off the truck's sprinklers, and the team had to scramble off to avoid getting soaked. After a moment they climbed back on, and, led by Police Chief Walter Wintin with siren and lights flashing, the fire truck crept across the bridge and headed for the bonfire a half-mile down Harrison Street.

It was two in the morning when the fire burned out and the crowd began to disperse. Like many, the Garretts held an impromptu open house on Locust Street, with family and friends dropping by throughout the night. It had been, as the *Shelbyville Democrat* put it the following Monday, a greater spontaneous celebration than the one following VJ Day—the day in August 1945 when Japan had surrendered, ending World War II.

In the days that followed, the town and state that had tried so long to sweep race relations under the rug could talk of almost nothing else. There had been black players on state champion teams since 1930; from 1940 to 1946, five of the seven state tournament winners had black players. The year before Shelbyville's victory, Anderson's 1946 champion team had two black starters, one of whom, Johnny Wilson, became the state's 1946 "Mr. Basketball." But until 1947, no team had ever had three blacks on its starting five or three in such dominant roles. The *Indianapolis Recorder* quoted IHSAA commissioner L. V. Phillips as saying that "the screwiest question of all time" had come into his office during the week following Shelbyville's win, "How many Negroes is a team allowed to have?"

Despite Hoosiers' long habit of treating the subject with euphemism, race was the unavoidable story of Shelbyville's state championship. Some people talked in code; some were eloquent, and some were awkward. All demonstrated, in their ways, that race was on their minds, and that many whites, especially, wanted badly to feel good about themselves on race relations. At a victory banquet for the team held at the Second Baptist Church, Booker T. Washington principal Walter Fort drew sustained applause for his opening statement, "I am deeply proud to be connected with the Shelbyville school system because it has proved its belief in the fundamental principles of American democracy. Not only in sports, but in every activity, each and every pupil, regardless of race, creed, or considerations of family influence or the lack of it, is given and encouraged to use every opportunity to develop his or her talents to the fullest. Democracy is practiced as well as taught in our Shelbyville schools." William Loper, the superintendent of Shelbyville schools, told the Second Baptist audience that the Golden Bears were "champions now, but they will be on their own when the tumult and shouting of the great victory dies down." He spoke of hate in the United States and in the postwar world, and said, "As long as there is a person in this life not getting a square deal, you are not free, and I am not free." Shelbyville's Postmaster, Gordon Thurston, told the audience that every Negro should be proud of the members of their group who contributed to Shelbyville's state championship. Ernest Ford, the pastor of First Christian Church, praised the Golden Bears' teamwork and said it was "incidental to the school's idealism that three members of the team were colored."

Swept up in the moment, the *Indianapolis Recorder* ran a "Salute to Shelbyville." Calling the state championship "merely a reward and triumph of the perennial practice of sound civic principles in every phase of community life," the *Recorder* went on, "Unperturbed by the conflicts of diverse racial groups that sap the vitality of many other communities, Shelbyville has consistently and successfully remained a well-knit community with an unusually high proportion of its citizens working consciously and with a purpose for the common civic good of all. . . . The town has never had serious racial conflicts . . . and doesn't exhibit many of the common forms of racial discrimination and segregation."

In its first issue following the state championship, the *Shelbyville Democrat* splashed across the front page stories of the victory and of the celebration to follow in the coming days. A front-page editorial declared that the civility of the Saturday night celebrations had "erased once and for all" the reputation for rowdiness caused by the Townsend incident (There had been only one arrest, of a drunk who parked on the railroad tracks). Just below the middle of the front page a prominent notice read, "A victory dance in celebration of the state tournament will be staged tonight at the Rec . . . according to Rev. Ernest L. Ford, director. . . . With three colored boys in main-stay roles on the championship team, colored students at the local high school will be welcome at the celebration. The whole team will be present throughout the evening."

Bill Garrett, Emerson Johnson, and Marshall Murray attended the dance at the Rec with their teammates. But their siblings and black classmates spurned the one-night pass, which for many still stung more than fifty years later.

After ten days of banquets, speeches, and dances, Shelbyville's celebrations came to a close on Wednesday, April 2, the day before spring break at Shelbyville High School. Despite a light drizzle,more than ten thousand people, one of the largest crowds ever assembled in town, jammed the streets to watch a torchlight parade of more than one hundred floats drift up Harrison Street behind a flower-bedecked replica of a basketball court carrying the players, coaches, managers, school officials, and cheerleaders. The parade ended at the public square, where the crowd spilled into adjacent buildings and onto fire escapes. From the second-floor balcony of the Shelby Hotel the speakers agreed that the Golden Bears had pulled off one of the greatest upsets in state tournament history by beating the two top-ranked teams on the same day, that they had played the best state championship game ever, and that the trio of Bill Garrett, Emerson Johnson, and Marshall Murray had performed magnificently and had led their team to the championship.

But of all the college basketball coaches in the country who had followed the Indiana high school state tournament, including those who had crowded into the basement of Butler Fieldhouse after the final game, not one attended this celebration in Shelbyville. Instead, the main speaker was Alvin "Bo" McMillan, Indiana University's head football coach, whose 1945 IU football team had won the Big Ten with several black players in prominent roles.

The evening ended with a dance for high school students at the National Guard armory, a few blocks east of the square. It was hot, crowded, and noisy in the armory, and shortly before 2:00 A.M., Roann Weaver, a pretty, blonde senior, was standing with her twin sister at the edge of the dance floor when a classmate appeared at her elbow. He was graceful and elegant in a dark gray suit, white shirt, and blue tie. A talented musician with a great collection of 78-rpm records, he was cool and by general consensus the best dancer in the senior class, though more often than not he had no one to dance with. As Max Wilson and his orchestra struck up "Mood Indigo," Emerson Johnson asked quietly, "Roann, would you like to dance?"

Roann stiffened for an instant. What would people think? But then, he had asked so nicely, and he didn't have anyone to dance with, and it was two o'clock in the morning before spring break and they were celebrating the state championship, so she said yes. They took a few steps onto the armory floor, turned slightly toward each other, and then he paused, reaching with his right hand into his left breast pocket. As he stood facing Roann Weaver, for his first and only dance of the evening, Emmie Johnson slowly took a neatly pressed white linen handkerchief from his pocket, carefully unfolded it, and wrapped it around his brown left hand so it would not be in contact with Roann's small, white, right one.

PART TWO

Monday, March 24, 1947

Hammond Times, Hammond, Indiana
An Open Letter to K. L. (Tug) Wilson, Commissioner,
Big Ten Conference

Dear Mr. Wilson:—I attended the Indiana state basketball finals Saturday in Butler Fieldhouse and saw Shelbyville's great team win the state title. The outstanding stars for Shelbyville were Bill Garrett, Emerson Johnson, and Marshall Murray, three Negro boys. . . .

Virtually every coach who was in Indianapolis Saturday was agreed on two things (1) that Bill Garrett of Shelbyville was the classiest individual player ever to appear on an Indiana high school floor (2) that the attitude and conduct of the Negro contestants were above reproach at all times.

The point is, Mr. Wilson, we keep hearing that the Big Ten conference has an "unwritten agreement" not to use Negroes in basketball. If so, WHY?

If the biggest, braggingest athletic conference in the middle of the greatest country in the world can use Negroes like Buddy Young, Ike Owen, Dallas Ward, Duke Slater, George Taliaferro and the like to draw $200,000 crowds for football . . . and Negroes like Jesse Owens and Eddie Tolan to win Olympic crowns—why can't it use them in basketball?

Sincerely,
John Whittaker
Sports Editor

9

The Sheriff

HE EMBODIED INDIANA BASKETBALL THE WAY LINCOLN embodied America. He had grown up on the "frontier" of Hoosier basketball, an archetypal Indiana boy of the 1920s, shooting baskets barefoot in the haymow after a day's work on the farm. Starting humbly, and without social graces, he had reached the top of his field. He, too, looked as though he had been designed for his role: six-four, with a big shock of salt-and-pepper hair and bushy black eyebrows, his massive shoulders built throwing hay bales under an Indiana sun, he had the strong face and alert eyes of a Scotch-Irish Hoosier farmer. But there, the Lincoln parallels stopped. No one ever called Branch McCracken melancholy, gentle, or poetic. To the fans and sportswriters who followed his teams and the young men who played on them, he was the gruff and intimidating "Sheriff," or "Bear."

Branch McCracken's voice was unforgettable, a deep bass gone gravelly from overuse, rumbling out of that big frame projecting authority and reaching his players over the din of a packed fieldhouse. His dedication was complete and his schedule was punishing. When he wasn't running practices or coaching games, McCracken was often driving the state selling Indiana University basketball: meeting for hours in the homes of high school stars and their parents, coaxing young athletes to come and play for him at IU in return for a free education; speaking tirelessly on Indiana's rubber chicken circuit of high school banquets, service club dinners, and alumni cookouts from Fort Wayne to Evansville; showing the face of Indiana University basketball and maintaining his ties to fans, coaches, young prospects, and alumni contributors. For these speaking engagements, his compensation was usually a few cents a mile gasoline expenses from the IU athletic department. In the 1940s college basketball coaches did not have television shows, shoe contracts, or seven-figure incomes. Alums might slip the coach a few perks on the side—a car, a trip, a free tab at a haberdashery—but his income came mainly from his university salary, which was about the same as that of a full professor in 1947.

He had grown up on a farm near Monrovia, a community of five hundred some twenty miles southwest of Indianapolis. At tiny Monrovia High School, his size and agility caught the eye of Indiana University basketball coach, Everett Dean, who, in 1926, persuaded McCracken to come and play for him in Bloomington. By 1930, his senior year at IU, McCracken was an All-American.*

In the fall of 1930, McCracken, twenty-two years old and fresh out of IU, became the head basketball coach at Ball State, then a small teachers college in Muncie. There he was twice named small-college Coach of the Year. In 1938, when Everett Dean left Indiana University to become the basketball coach at Stanford, Dean recommended McCracken, his former player, to be his successor. It was a big step up, from then-small Ball State to the Big Ten. It would mean fighting hard to recruit top high school players, in competition not only with the biggest nearby universities—Purdue, Illinois, Michigan, Ohio State—but also with major universities nationally. It would mean consistently producing winning teams that filled the seventy-five-hundred-seat IU fieldhouse, and doing it within a budget; so it would also mean, in those days of looser enforcement of recruiting rules, that McCracken would have to stay in touch with well-heeled boosters who were willing to help out now and then.

He would have to do all this while staying out of trouble, both for

---

*Another All-American from Monrovia that year was Johnny Wooden, then a sophomore at Purdue, who had grown up on a farm adjacent to McCracken's until his family moved a few miles south to Centerton. In the spring of 1947, UCLA would offer its head basketball coaching job to Branch McCracken, who would turn it down and recommend instead John Wooden, then the coach of Indiana State. Wooden, as even the most casual basketball fans know, became "the Wizard of Westwood," far and away the most successful college basketball coach in history. As college basketball coaches, Wooden would win ten national championships, and McCracken two.

the way he ran his basketball program and for his players' conduct. He and his players would be public figures of sorts, the best-known faces of a university that depended on the state legislature for much of its funding. If McCracken got caught violating recruiting rules, if his players failed academically or got arrested, the coach and the IU basketball program might become fodder for the press and the politicians. And if that happened often enough, McCracken's job would be in jeopardy.

He got off to a good start. In his second year at Indiana, his Hoosiers won the 1940 NCAA Tournament, beating the University of Kansas 68–40 in Kansas City. In 1943, saying he was eager to support "my boys," McCracken enlisted in the Army Air Corps, where he spent part of his three-year hitch teaching pilots to relax and, like basketball players shooting clutch free throws, not freeze under the pressure of combat. He returned to Bloomington at the end of the 1946 basketball season to find an IU basketball program that was mostly a ragtag collection of walk-ons and ex-GIs.

McCracken needed to rebuild the IU basketball program at the same time that college coaches from all over the country were increasingly poaching Indiana high school talent. For decades, college basketball coaches—many of whom got their start coaching high school teams in Indiana—had been recruiting top Indiana high school players because they considered them to be better coached, more accustomed to strong competition, and less rattled by large crowds. By the 1940s Indiana boys were playing everywhere. Michigan State had fielded a starting team composed entirely of Hoosiers. At one Vanderbilt–Ol' Miss game twelve of the twenty players suited up came from southern Indiana. And there were so many Hoosiers on California college teams that Cal-Berkeley's pep band once greeted the University of Southern California team by playing "Back Home Again In Indiana." Raids on the state's talent pool got so bad that McCracken would eventually declare a new recruiting policy: Each year he would pursue only the five best players in Indiana. The rest of the country, he announced, "could fight over the table scraps."

In March 1946, Indiana University's basketball season was overshadowed by headlines about that year's surprise Indiana high school state champion, Anderson High, and its star, a six-one black center named Johnny Wilson. Unranked Anderson had come out of nowhere to upset two of the top teams in the state on the final day of the state tournament. Wilson had carried Anderson to the championship, set a new scoring record for the last four tournament games, and tied the record for the final game by scoring thirty points. Gifted with quickness and vertical leaping ability, "Jumpin' Johnny" Wilson was the best high school player in the state and on his way to being named Indiana's 1946 "Mr. Basketball." He wanted badly to play at Indiana University.

A month after Anderson won the state, Branch McCracken was the featured speaker at a victory banquet in the Mulberry Room of the Anderson YMCA. He spoke from the head table, an inverted U with McCracken in the middle, the Anderson players and their coach along the sides, and the audience of several hundred some distance in front. McCracken described the difficulties of rebuilding a team and boasted that Tom Schwartz, the state's 1945 Mr. Basketball, was one of the cornerstones of his rebuilding effort. Then McCracken took questions. A guest near the back of the room asked the one on everyone's mind, "Coach, can Wilson play at IU?"

The audience froze. It was the hot potato question every big-time college basketball coach feared facing in public. Indiana University had never had a black player, nor had Purdue, Notre Dame, or Butler—the other universities in the state with major basketball programs in 1946. It was an open secret that the basketball coaches of the Big Ten—the conference to which IU and other large midwestern schools belonged—had a "gentleman's agreement" not to recruit or play blacks. Only one black basketball player, Dick Culberson, had ever suited up in a Big Ten basketball uniform, and he had seen only limited action for Iowa in part of one season during World War II. Because there were no integrated teams in the South, and because almost all the universities in the North followed gentleman's agreements of one type or another, very few blacks had ever played major college basketball in the United States in 1946.

In the five years he had coached Indiana University, McCracken had quietly passed over several black high school players who were the best, or near best, in the state. No one had ever put him on the spot over segregation in IU basketball quite so publicly and pointedly as his anonymous questioner at the Anderson YMCA.

It was Branch McCracken's Huck Finn moment, as he leaned forward and squinted into the audience. In that instant he had to be remembering yet again his responsibilities—to his fellow coaches in the Big Ten and around the country; to his players, the fans, the IU alumni, university administration, and the board of trustees. A wrong move and his basketball program, his base of support, his career, even, could all spin out of balance, maybe with a players strike, an opponent's boycott, a fan revolt, or the loss of alumni support. As the Anderson audience waited, McCracken had to be asking himself whether he had the right to ignore all those responsibilities, to speak for all those others, to be the one to stick his and his university's neck out, in a single, off-the-cuff reply.

Looking out over the heads of Johnny Wilson, his coach, and his teammates, Branch McCracken gave his answer, "I don't think he could make my team."

With those words the dream died for Johnny Wilson, and for those who had hoped he would break the color barrier at Indiana University. Sporadic efforts to get Wilson to IU continued into the summer, but they had lost their spark. In May, as expected, Wilson was named Indiana's "Mr. Basketball," and in June, also as expected, wearing number one on his white uniform, he led the Indiana High School All-Stars to a win over the Kentucky High School All-Stars.

His high school coach, Charles Cummings, riding the crest of Anderson's state championship, had accepted the head coaching job at Boston College. But he was too new to make waves by trying to recruit Johnny to Boston, and BC was too white, too far, too expensive, and too unfamiliar for Wilson to want to go there. Of all the major university basketball programs in the country, only UCLA and the University of Southern California expressed any interest in Wilson, but he knew nothing of California and did not want to live half a continent from home. His choices came down to a few nearby all-black colleges and a couple of Indiana's small private colleges. In the end he stayed home, enrolling at Anderson College, then a school of a few hundred students, most of whom were white southerners, members of the evangelical Church of God. The Anderson College student body embraced Wilson, and he thrived there. In his freshman year, with some major college teams on the schedule, Wilson averaged more than twenty points a game, sixth among all college players nationwide.

In 1976, thirty years after he led Anderson to the state championship, Johnny Wilson was voted into the Indiana Basketball Hall of Fame. At the induction ceremony he met his high school coach, Charles Cummings. During Wilson's years at Anderson High, coach Cummings had encouraged Johnny to take advanced math, history, and English literature, courses that would prepare him for college, overriding guidance counselors who tried to steer Wilson away from academic courses and into shop and driver training so, they said, "he can keep his eligibility." Cummings and Wilson had never had much of a chance to celebrate together Anderson's 1946 state championship, because, the night of their victory, Cummings's father had died suddenly in Missouri. Now, at the Hall of Fame ceremony, the coach had something he wanted to say. "I'm sorry, John. It could have been you."

Wilson was puzzled. "What do you mean, Coach?"

His eyes brimming, Cummings told Wilson what had been in his heart all those years. "I'm sorry *I* didn't have the money to send you to IU. They would have had to play you."

10

"Comin' Out a Man"

ON THE NIGHT OF JULY 6, 1944, SECOND LIEUTENANT JACK Roosevelt Robinson boarded an Army bus to ride from his base, Fort Hood, Texas, to the town of Temple, an hour away. Robinson took a seat in the middle of the bus, and the driver ordered him to the rear. Aware the Army had recently banned segregation on military buses, Robinson refused and engaged in an angry exchange with the driver. The confrontation was potentially violent—in North Carolina a white bus driver had recently killed a black soldier for resisting an order to move to the rear (and had been acquitted for it). But Robinson, outspoken and tough, had grown up fighting for himself on the streets of Pasadena. He stayed put. When the bus reached Temple, military police arrested him, and he was soon court-martialed on three counts of insubordination.

Jackie Robinson was acquitted after a four-hour trial and, at his request, soon honorably discharged. But the country had not heard the last of him. As he would later say of his stint in the Army, "I learned that I was in two wars, one against a foreign enemy, and the other against prejudice at home."

More than any other event in history, World War II galvanized black Americans to press for their civil rights. Wartime necessity forced the integration of jobs previously reserved for whites, offering black workers better pay, greater responsibility, and rising expectations. Black soldiers abroad got a glimpse of life without Jim Crow.

The success of protests, organized and individual, in breaking down military segregation gave encouragement that progress, however halting, was possible. And—most basically—the irony of fighting for freedom abroad while being denied it at home was too great to ignore. Membership in the NAACP surged 900 percent during the war. When the *Pittsburgh Courier* launched its "Double V" campaign—for victory at home and abroad—in 1942, millions of blacks signed on. They organized Double V clubs, sported Double V pins, dresses, and hats, displayed the Double V salute in photos, painted "Double V" on their fighter jets, and promised to keep the pressure on until change arrived. As a corporal declared in 1945, "I spent four years in the Army to free a bunch of Dutchmen and Frenchmen, and I'm hanged if I'm going to let the Alabama versions of the Germans kick me around when I get home. No sirreee-bob! I went into the Army a nigger; I'm comin' out a man."

The country did not make it easy for them. As white veterans returned from the war and factories reverted to peacetime production, black workers lost their jobs or had them downgraded. Black veterans could not take advantage of the GI Bill to the same degree as whites because many colleges had quotas or would not accept them. Redlining and racially restrictive covenants limited their home-buying options, and the housing construction boom occurring in cities throughout the country did not extend to black neighborhoods. As a result, the postwar expansion of the white middle class largely passed by blacks. Despite the high-minded slogans the war had generated, in its wake racial discrimination—in the North and South—remained largely unchanged.

But in those first postwar years, Americans, black and white, had no stomach for sharp protest and confrontation. After two decades of depression and war, they finally had disposable income and the leisure time to enjoy it, and they badly wanted to catch up with normal life. And yet for blacks to have that normal life—to "come out a man" from their wartime experiences—the status quo of segregation had to change.

Sports were their Trojan horse. With many Americans using their extra cash to buy tickets, sporting magazines, radios, and even televisions, and with their extra time to attend games or play in them, competitive athletics were at the heart of America's common culture. The ideals of athletic competition—the "level playing field"—represented what Americans wanted to believe about themselves and their country. The language of athletic competition—"may the best man win"— contrasted uncomfortably with the reality of racial discrimination and offered a race-neutral code for integration. Every successful black athlete, from peewee to Olympian, debunked racist stereotypes and posed unspoken challenges to segregation. Blaine Patton, the sports editor of the *Indianapolis Star,* understood what was happening when he wrote, "Fair and open sports competition will do more good in a just cause against race bigotry than a lot of oratory!"

Johnny Wilson did not make it to Indiana University on this wave of change, but here and there, all around the country, powerful individuals—people with deeper pockets and greater clout than Charles Cummings—were deciding to go to bat for athletes like him. The most famous example appeared on the national stage three weeks after Bill Garrett and his Shelbyville teammates won the Indiana state championship, when on April 15, 1947, the Brooklyn Dodgers broke the color line in major league baseball by starting Jackie Robinson at first base in their season opener at Ebbets Field.

Since the early 1930s, leading black weeklies such as the *Baltimore Afro-American* and the *Pittsburgh Courier,* and the American Communist Party newspaper, the *Daily Worker,* had waged a campaign to integrate major league baseball. By the early 1940s, Branch Rickey, president of the Brooklyn Dodgers, had quietly signed on to the effort. Called "the Mahatma" by some sportswriters, Rickey was a deeply religious, charismatic man who, in later years, often told the story of an incident that had occurred in 1910 when he was the baseball coach of Ohio Wesleyan University. A hotel in South Bend, Indiana, where Rickey's team was to play Notre Dame, had refused to take Ohio Wesleyan's only black player, a catcher named Charles Thomas. The hotel finally agreed to put an extra cot in Rickey's room and turn a blind eye, but when Rickey got to the room he found Thomas sitting on the bed in tears, pulling at the skin on his hands and saying, "It's my skin, Mr. Rickey. If I could pull it off, I'd be just like everybody else." Rickey said the scene haunted him for years.

Intent on breaking baseball's color line—and realizing that doing so would give him an advantage in tapping the pool of black players— Rickey sent Dodger scouts to find a young black baseball player with the talent to succeed in the major leagues and the self-control to take the abuse that would be thrown at him. In the summer of 1945 the scouts identified Jackie Robinson, then a twenty-six-year-old shortstop for the Kansas City Monarchs of the Negro Leagues. At UCLA from 1939 to 1941, Robinson had been a four-sport athlete—an All-American football halfback, the national champion long jumper, twice the leading basketball scorer in the Pacific Coast Conference, and the starting shortstop in baseball. His physical talent was not in question. But Robinson was also an emotional competitor and, as he had shown in the Army, a proud, combative man with a reputation for not tolerating discrimination.

A lot of major league baseball players were hard-case Southerners in the 1940s. A black man attempting to break into the all-white major leagues would face merciless taunting and even physical abuse. If he lost his nerve, it would confirm the prejudices; if he fought his tormentors, he would risk setting off a race riot in the ballpark and maybe the surrounding city. Branch Rickey needed to know that his chosen trailblazer had the courage and self-control not to publicly react, before he was firmly established, to the abuse he would inevitably face. At a now-famous meeting with Robinson in the Dodger offices in Brooklyn on August 28, 1945, Rickey got straight to the point. "We can't fight our way through this, Robinson. . . . We can win only if we convince the world that you're a great ballplayer *and* a fine gentleman." And then Rickey asked his central question, "Have you got the guts to play the game no matter what happens?"

Robinson's first reaction was incredulous anger, "Mr. Rickey, are you looking for a Negro who is afraid to fight back?"

Rickey roared back at him, "I'm looking for a ballplayer with guts enough not to fight back!"

Rickey, who had been both a major league baseball player and a manager, described the insults Robinson could expect and mimicked opposing players' taunts, mincing no words. "Suppose you are the shortstop," he asked Robinson at one point, "and a white player comes down from first base and slides, spikes high, and cuts you on the leg; and as you feel the blood run down your leg, the white player laughs in your face: 'How do you like that, nigger boy?' he sneers." Rickey handed Robinson a quotation, "Whosoever shall smite thee on the right cheek, turn to him the other also," and concluded with

his bottom-line demand of Jackie Robinson: "You will have to promise me that for the first three years you will take everything they hand
out, and not react. Three years. Can you do it?"

Robinson spent the 1946 baseball season with the Dodgers' top
farm team in Montreal. The next year, he joined the Brooklyn
Dodgers for the 1947 season. One of the Dodgers' early opponents
was the St. Louis Cardinals. The Cardinals were the reigning champions of baseball, winners of the World Series the previous fall. St. Louis
was a four-hour drive straight west of Indianapolis, and many people
in central Indiana rooted for the Cardinals as their "local" major
league team. At the beginning of May 1947, shortly before the Cardinals were to play the Dodgers, Cardinals' owner Sam Breadon heard
that some of his players were threatening a boycott with the hope of
stirring the whole league in revolt against Jackie Robinson. Worried
about a disruption of the baseball season, Breadon flew to New York
to meet with the president of the National League—a country boy
from Indiana.

Ford Frick had grown up in Brimfield, a crossroads about thirty
miles north of Fort Wayne. He had worked his way through DePauw
University, taught high school English, taken up journalism, become
head of publicity for the National League, and finally, in 1934, its
president. People in Indiana were proud of Frick and considered him
an example of hard-headed Hoosier common sense in the larger
world.

Frick told Breadon to tell his players, "This is America, and baseball is America's game. Tell them that if they go on strike, for racial
reasons, or refuse to play a scheduled game, they will be barred from
baseball even though it means the disruption of a club or a whole
league." A short time later, Breadon reported back to Frick that the
players had dropped their threats. The Cardinals took the field
against the Dodgers, and talk of a boycott blew over.

But a few days later, *New York Herald Tribune* sports editor Stanley
Woodward published the story of how Frick's stance had stopped the
Cardinals' threatened strike. Woodward's published account of Frick's
answer to the Cardinal players quickly became a signpost of the
changing era, a part of the national consciousness and of baseball history: "If you do this, you will be suspended from the league. You will
find that the friends you think you have in the press box will not sup-

port you, that you will be outcasts. I do not care if half the league strikes. Those who do it will encounter quick retribution. All will be suspended and I don't care if it wrecks the National League for five years. This is the United States of America, and one citizen has as much right to play as another. The National League will go down the line with Robinson whatever the consequences."

11

Gentleman's Agreement

ON MARCH 31, 1947, AS JACKIE ROBINSON WAS HEADING north to start his first season with the Brooklyn Dodgers, Branch McCracken again stood at a head table looking out over the newly crowned Indiana high school basketball state champions, as he had done at the Anderson YMCA the year before. The parallels between 1946 and 1947 would have been too striking to miss, least of all by the Indiana University basketball coach. Again an underdog had upset two of the top teams in the state on the final day of the tournament. Again the winner had three black players, this time all starters. Again the state champions were led by a black center who was the best player in the state and had set a new scoring record in the final four games of the tournament—for Bill Garrett had broken Johnny Wilson's record of the previous year. And again, as McCracken spoke, his IU team was coming off a mediocre season.

This time the event was an end-of-season banquet hosted by the Shelby County Coaches Association in the gymnasium of Addison Township School, a redbrick primary and junior high on the Michigan Road at the eastern edge of Shelbyville. McCracken had accepted the invitation to be the guest speaker before Shelbyville's upset victory in the state championship, and now he was surely regretting his decision. But the coach got lucky; this was an easier audience than the one he had faced in Anderson. McCracken used most of his allotted time to show an IU highlight film and took no questions.

Behind the scenes, though, questions were being asked. A few hours earlier McCracken had visited the Shelbyville home of an IU booster and old friend, Nate Kaufman, and Kaufman had gently pressed the coach, "You oughtta think about Bill Garrett. He's a good student, a good, serious kid. Look at what Wilson's done."

McCracken waved his hand. "Couldn't do it if I wanted to. Other coaches'd have my hide."

It had a familiar ring, for Kaufman knew all about gentleman's agreements.

Nate Kaufman's life was an American success story. His father, Sam, had arrived penniless and alone at Ellis Island in 1905, his wife and four small children waiting back in Poland. Upon clearing immigration, Sam had been met by representatives of the Jewish Agency, a private organization established to disperse newly arriving rural, Eastern European Jews to jobs around the country. In Poland Sam had been a carpenter, and Shelbyville's furniture factories were advertising for cabinetmakers. Before he left Ellis Island, Sam had a job with the Davis-Birely factory—the largest table maker, it boasted, in the world—and a one-way ticket to Shelbyville.

For Sam, the new land had kept its part of the promise, and he kept his. He worked hard, saved his money, and within two years sent for his wife, Rachael, his daughters, Belle, Esther, and baby Ann, and his three-year-old son, Nathan. When Rachael complained that fresh fruit and vegetables were rarely available in Shelbyville, Sam saw an opportunity. Rising before four and catching the first interurban train to Indianapolis's central market, Sam brought back fresh produce to sell to Shelbyville's grocery stores. Soon Sam saved enough money to quit the furniture factory and open his own fruit stand, and he multiplied his profits by investing in prime downtown real estate. Less than twenty years after arriving in Shelbyville, Sam Kaufman was one of the wealthiest men in the town.

His son, Nate, helped with the family fruit business and became an outstanding high school athlete, tall and handsome with black hair parted down the middle. In 1922, the University of Illinois offered Nate a basketball scholarship, but that summer his younger sister, Ann, a promising opera singer, was offered a chance to study voice in France. Basketball scholarships were paltry in the 1920s; the Kaufmans could not afford to send Nate to college and Ann to France, so Nate turned down the scholarship, joined his father full-time at the fruit stand, and never looked back.

By day Nate worked with Sam, and by night he played semipro basketball and coached the basketball team at St. Joseph, Shelbyville's Catholic high school. In 1926, just four years out of high school, Kaufman coached St. Joe to the Catholic national championship finals at Loyola University in Chicago. He began refereeing high school basketball games and quickly became the best high school referee in the state. In the Indiana state tournament, referees, like teams, advanced through the rounds on merit. In the late 1930s Kaufman was chosen to referee five straight state championship games, something only a few others have done in the tournament's ninety-five-year history.

Nate bought properties around Shelbyville, building on Sam's investments. When his real estate deals created a need for insurance, he got a broker's license and began selling home-owners policies and then life insurance for the Indianapolis Life Insurance Company. Within a few years, Nate had established himself as the most successful life insurance agent the company would ever have.

Nate Kaufman and Branch McCracken became friends when they were both young and on the way up, McCracken the coach at Ball State, Kaufman the high school and small-college referee from Shelbyville. When McCracken moved up to IU, it seemed natural that Kaufman would move up with him to referee in the Big Ten. At McCracken's request the IU athletic director asked his Big Ten counterparts to certify Kaufman as a referee. Their response became a story Nate would tell all his life. According to his son, Bart, McCracken told Nate that when his name had come up for certification, one athletic director had said, "There'll never be a kike in the bunch as long as I'm here." The rest went along. It was a blackball—in effect, a gentleman's agreement—and apparently because of it, Nate Kaufman never made it to the Big Ten.

In 1947 Kaufman knew the Big Ten had a gentleman's agreement barring black basketball players, but he was not one to accept such things. He had spent his life overcoming others' prejudices by keeping his head up and his antennae out, constantly talking to powers-that-be all over Indiana and the Midwest, keeping up with friends in New York, Cincinnati, St. Louis, and Chicago, reading people and sensing where things were going. In 1946 he had kept his silence when McCracken rejected Johnny Wilson. It was plain to him that McCracken and IU were the worse for it, and that the days of segregated Big Ten basketball were numbered. Too many good black players were coming out of Indiana high schools. It was just a matter of time before one of the Big Ten coaches broke ranks; the only questions were who, when, and with whom. Watching from the front row of Paul Cross Gym as Bill Garrett developed into a dominant player, an unflappable presence, and a good student, Kaufman had formed his own answer.

He had succeeded as an outsider by knowing how to persuade, when to float an idea, when to push, and when to back off. He realized McCracken would not respond well to being pressed publicly about Garrett joining his team, so instead he had raised the issue privately. McCracken brushed him off at their meeting before the County Coaches Association banquet, but Kaufman wasn't done.

On the first Sunday in May, as expected, the *Indianapolis Star* announced that Bill Garrett was Indiana's 1947 Mr. Basketball. Sportswriters had chosen him as the state's best high school basketball player, and he would wear number 1 in the upcoming All-Star game, an annual charity contest between the ten best high school players in Indiana and the ten best in Kentucky. The state of Indiana watched closely the announcements of the members of the Indiana All-Star team, which the *Star* released one by one over three weeks in May. College basketball coaches around the country also watched the Indiana All-Star selections, just as they had scouted Indiana high school talent throughout the season and the tournament. It is a safe bet that during the 1940s every major college basketball coach in the country knew the name, position, and achievements of Indiana's Mr. Basketball for the current year and knew which other colleges—if any—were recruiting him. Most would have followed all other members of the Indiana All-Star team almost as closely.

At the end of May, Emerson Johnson also made the Indiana All-Stars, announced by the *Star* as the eighth-best player in the state, to delighted shouts of "Emmie made it!" in the halls of Shelbyville High School. After a week of practices at Indianapolis's Central YMCA, which bent its whites-only policy for the integrated team, the Indiana All-Stars beat their Kentucky counterparts easily, 86–50, in front of a sellout crowd at the Indiana State Fairgrounds Coliseum. Garrett led all scorers with twenty-one points; Johnson hit two long shots in limited playing time. At game's end the "Star of Stars" award, decided by a vote of the Indiana and Kentucky sportswriters covering the game, went not to Garrett but to his white teammate Joe Keener of Evansville Central, who had scored thirteen points. Outraged at the snub, and noting that Johnny Wilson had also been denied the "Star of Stars" award the previous year, Charles Preston, sports editor of the *Indianapolis Recorder*, wrote, "There will have to be a signal advance—such as Negro players on the IU and Purdue teams, before the hearts of Hoosier basketball fans will recover from this." In response the *Recorder* solicited donations to give pen-and-pencil sets to Garrett and each of the other four starters on the Shelbyville team in honor of their integrated success. It became the most successful donation campaign the *Recorder* had ever run, with contributions pouring in from as far away as Texas. Later, in a letter that the *Recorder* published, Garrett specifically thanked the paper for including his teammates.

In early June, the *Recorder's* Preston had caught up with Garrett in the infield at the state high school track finals in Indianapolis (where Garrett placed third in the high hurdles). Throughout the year, often on the front page, the *Recorder* had been pressing the question of whether Garrett would integrate IU basketball. At the state track finals in early May, as news of Ford Frick's reply to the St. Louis Cardinals was spreading across Indiana, Preston pointedly asked Garrett where he was going to college. "I may go to UCLA or Southern California—that's what it looks like. I haven't made any definite plans yet. Coach Barnes is helping me," Garrett replied. Preston persisted, asking where Garrett would go if he had his "free choice." After hesitating, Bill answered, "Oh, IU, of course."

But he did not have his free choice. That summer, as Branch McCracken and other college coaches were scouring the state to complete their recruiting of high school basketball players, Garrett could read in the papers of their successes. McCracken's prizes were Phil Buck, a five-ten guard from Rossville, number 5 on the Indiana All-Stars, and Gene Ring, a guard from South Bend Central who had narrowly missed making the All-Star team. Of the other top five Indiana All-Stars, East Chicago's Ray Ragelis, All-Star number 2, was headed to Northwestern. Number 3, Terre Haute's Ronnie Bland, was going to Purdue on a football scholarship, and number 4, Joe Keener, had accepted a basketball scholarship to Georgia Tech.*

The plaudits of spring—Mr. Basketball, the state championship, the sportswriters waxing about "such amazing accuracy, blinding speed and sheer determination . . . never exhibited to a higher degree than . . . by Bill Garrett, Shelbyville's great Negro all-star"—were forgotten come summer, "all just moonglow," as the *Recorder* had feared. No one had understood that better all along than Bill Garrett, Emerson Johnson, and Marshall Murray. Already at the state championships, as one sportswriter had noticed, "The Garrett-Johnson-Murray combination was a sober one by the time the team had finished with the trophy presentations on the floor."

Of Garrett's white Shelbyville teammates, Hank Hemingway had accepted a basketball scholarship to New Mexico State University, where coach Ken Gunning was a former Shelbyville and IU basketball player. Bill Breck was preparing to put competitive basketball behind him and enter DePauw University. By midsummer, out of the ten Indiana All-Stars and the five Shelbyville starters, only Garrett, Johnson, and Murray remained without college plans as they played on into the summer evenings on the court behind Booker T.

Garrett was collecting trash for the city of Shelbyville, a good summer job for a teenager. He had received a letter from UCLA shortly after the state championship, but in the 1940s California seemed so far away as to be almost unreal to a boy from Shelbyville, and UCLA was not yet the basketball power it would become. He had heard from Anderson College. With Johnson and Murray, he had visited Wilber-

---

*Ragelis was injured during practice and was replaced on the All-Star team by Earl Roberts, a six-six black center from Muncie Central High School. Bland declined the invitation to join the team. Consequently, some histories omit Ragelis and Bland from the 1947 All-Stars or list the players' numbers differently from their original sequence given here.

force, Kentucky State, and Tennessee A&I State, well-known all-black colleges within a few hours' drive.

And that was it. Those college coaches who had crowded into the basement of Butler Fieldhouse after the state championship had all disappeared. Branch McCracken remained silent. Tony Hinkle, the coach of Butler University, the host of the state championship and the principal speaker at Shelbyville's basketball awards program in the spring of 1947, never wrote or called. Notre Dame showed no interest. Illinois, Northwestern, Michigan, Ohio State—all nearby Big Ten schools—ignored Indiana's Mr. Basketball. Purdue's head basketball coach, Mel Taube, had expressed interest in Garrett, but for the most cynical of reasons: Finding Frank Barnes in the basement of Butler Fieldhouse after the state championship, Taube asked Barnes to talk Garrett into going to Purdue. As Barnes later told it, "I asked Taube, 'Would you play him if he did?' And he said, 'No, but at least I'd know he wouldn't be playing against me.'" "Well," Barnes replied, "I hope he goes to IU and beats you every time you play."

Barnes had done his best, describing Garrett in interviews as "the best team player a coach could hope for," and spreading the word through Indianapolis sports reporters that "some" of the seniors from his team might not be able to go to college, pointedly noting that Bill Garrett was a baseball player and track hurdler as well as Mr. Basketball.

Nate Kaufman had continued to press Branch McCracken. But McCracken was middle management. Like the vast majority of whites in Indiana he saw race discrimination as something unfortunate that just happened, like the weather or farm prices, for which he had no responsibility and over which he had no control. If pressed, the coach might say it was not about what he thought, he had nothing against Negroes; it was about what others thought—the board of trustees, the state legislature, the alumni, his players. They would never accept it, they did not want trouble, and he did not see why he should be the one to take a chance.

All summer long, a buzz ran through Shelbyville, "What's Bill gonna do?" In the 1940s a lot of college coaches spent their summers collecting new players and driving them to school. Recruiting rules were fuzzy and rarely enforced. A coach could feel only moderately confident that he had a recruit once the boy was in the car and the two were heading out of town at a good clip.

In August, New Mexico State coach Ken Gunning loaded up Hank Hemingway and caught Highway 66 southwest toward Las Cruces. Coach Joe Fletcher picked up Emmie Johnson and Marshall Murray and drove them south to Kentucky State, in Frankfort. On a Saturday morning in mid-August, Bill Garrett showed up at the back door of the Kaufman home on West Broadway. He had come to say good-bye, and to thank Nate and his wife, Hortie, for their help. Coach Vernon McCain had arrived to drive him to Tennessee State in Nashville. They had a strong basketball program there, and Bill put the best face he could on it, but as he, Nate, and Hortie stood in the kitchen the words would not come. The best efforts of one of the best-connected men in the state, with the best high school basketball player in the state, who had all the right athletic skills and personal qualities, had not been enough. Nate, without his usual smile, could only take Bill's hand in both of his, wish him luck, and turn away. As Bill took Hortie's hand and then turned toward the door, she grabbed his arm, stopping him, holding him there, tears streaming down her face, her eyes blazing, for a silent moment until she practically screamed at him in despair, "Bill Garrett! Bill Garrett!" Bill waited as she searched for words. And then her voice softened, "The next time you come here, you come to the front door . . . or you don't come back!"

12

The Chief and the President

ON ANOTHER SATURDAY MORNING IN THE LATE SUMMER OF
1947, Faburn DeFrantz, executive director of Indianapolis's Senate
Avenue YMCA, was also driving south. DeFrantz had slipped out of
the capital early, leaving his home on Indiana Avenue as nightlife on
"the Avenue" was falling silent and the city was coming awake.
Despite the hour the humidity was already oppressive, and it sat on
DeFrantz and his four companions like a sullen, sweaty child. The
open windows of DeFrantz's sedan provided little relief, just more hot
air and the cicadas' steady buzz. The men's suit jackets were neatly
laid out in the trunk, ties folded in the pockets. Their sleeves were
rolled up and their shirt collars open a button or two, exposing their
necks to the rare bits of breeze.

When DeFrantz had called them two days earlier, the men had
known this would be their uniform for the trip, so they had set about
making sure their Sunday suits were ready by Saturday morning.
DeFrantz favored three-piece suits and insisted on a sense of decorum
for the most mundane occasions, and today was not ordinary. On the
phone Thursday night, he had told each of his companions, "I'm
going down to IU to see if we can do anything about getting Bill Garrett on the basketball team."

Life had outlined Faburn DeFrantz in bold. Sixty-one years old,
well over six feet tall and solidly built, so fair-skinned that friends jok-
ingly prodded him to take off his hat and show his curly hair, lest he

be mistaken for white, DeFrantz seemed to tower over everyone around him. It was, a friend said, as if DeFrantz was always in the foreground, and everyone else a step or two back. His wife called him "Fay," but to just about every other black person in Indianapolis he was "Chief."

He was born in Topeka, a child of "the Exodusters"—thousands of former slaves his father, Alonzo, had helped lead from the violence and poverty of the post-Reconstruction South to the relative freedom of Kansas. Alonzo, a deeply religious man, passed his faith on to his children and instilled in them a commitment to help other black Americans and a willingness to stand up for them no matter the cost.

Taking his father's lessons to heart, DeFrantz chose his fights carefully and did not back down. When the Ku Klux Klan announced their intention to parade down Indiana Avenue, the heart of Indianapolis's black community, in the early 1920s, DeFrantz told the city's mayor he would have men stationed on every street corner ready to cause "real trouble" at the first sign of a white sheet. The Klansmen marched, but without the anonymity of their sheets and under DeFrantz's withering stare. When a supervisor at the Commons Cafeteria in Indiana University's Union Building tried to steer DeFrantz to a table marked "Reserved" and set aside for blacks, he thundered, "I don't want this kind of hospitality. I haven't ordered any table reserved. This table must be for somebody else!" and instead sat at a table in the middle of the room. When a white fan of the visiting team shouted, "Get that nigger!" every time Indiana's Archie Harris had the ball during a football game between IU and Texas A&M, DeFrantz loudly compared the man to an ugly dog and encouraged a companion to toss a cigar butt at the back of the man's neck. A friend of DeFrantz's, visiting from Texas, was so certain they were about to be lynched that he collected Coke bottles to use as weapons, but in the end, it was the white man and his companions who skulked out of the stadium before game's end.

DeFrantz's combativeness was tempered by his personal warmth and political skills. He brought influential whites to speak at the Senate Avenue Y and involved them in fund-raising campaigns. Every Christmas Eve, with the Y Quartet in tow, DeFrantz sang carols at the North Meridian homes of the governor, pharmaceutical tycoon Eli Lilly, and other prominent citizens. He understood that those in power wanted to think well of themselves and feared bad publicity, and he used those attitudes to his advantage. As the Indianapolis NAACP devolved into back-biting and ineffectuality, DeFrantz and the Senate Avenue Y were at the center of every local effort against discrimination. As he liked to say, "As long as I stay in this town I shall see to it that the Negro is in the picture of what is going on."

By 1947 DeFrantz had been executive director of the Senate Avenue YMCA for thirty-one years, and the line between man and institution had long since blurred. Under his leadership the Y had grown from a handful of members leading Boy Scouts and Bible classes in 1916 into the largest black YMCA in the world and the social, political, and cultural heart of black Indianapolis. By the 1940s, the Y, a three-story brick building at the corner of Senate Avenue and Michigan Street, offered more classes and clubs than most large high schools and many colleges.* Y members provided job placement services, relief programs, support in juvenile court, and college counseling. The Y's dorm housed traveling orchestras, destitute men, and visiting black athletes and entertainers who were barred from Indianapolis's white hotels. In 1947, more than 110,000 people used the Y, an average of three hundred a day 365 days a year.

The Y's showcase was its annual Monday-night lecture series, the Monster Meetings, whose name parodied the weekly "Big Meetings" held at Indianapolis's all-white Central YMCA. DeFrantz had developed the series from a thumping pulpit for local preachers into the best-attended and longest-running black public forum in the country. The lectures ran from November through March and—reflecting DeFrantz's belief that all areas of life concerned the black community, not merely politics or the "race question"—the speakers were a who's who of black America in the twentieth century: from W.E.B. Du Bois to Langston Hughes, Jackie Robinson to E. Franklin Frazier. Thousands attended, mostly black men but also a handful of whites and,

---

*Y activities included three basketball leagues, a softball league, a track and field team, twenty-eight different intramural teams, a tennis club, swimming and life-saving classes, boxing, golf, volleyball, badminton, weight lifting, a choir, a band, piano lessons, and classes in English, German, French, Spanish, algebra, drafting, typing and shorthand, psychology, literature, public speaking, philosophy, religion, sociology, history, art, parent education, first aid, bookkeeping, auto mechanics, Bible study, checkers and chess clubs, a singing quartet, two sororities, two fraternities, a fathers' club, a ladies' auxiliary, an intercollegiate club, at least seven recreational and civic clubs for boys, and a summer camp.

on special occasions, women of both races. The Y's gym was always crammed full with an overflow crowd often standing shoulder to shoulder in the lobby and listening via loudspeakers. And when the Y couldn't hold them all, as when Eleanor Roosevelt or Ralph Bunche visited, the meetings were held in larger facilities such as Indianapolis's Murat Temple or Cadle Tabernacle.

The Monster Meetings gave black Indianapolis a forum where, in question-and-answer sessions, the audiences could voice their reactions, objections, ambitions, and hopes. Some came with prepared notes, many spoke off the cuff, and a few, lost for words, sang their responses. The vast majority, DeFrantz later wrote, "have spoken by simply being present—silent witnesses to a crusade for inclusion in every facet of American opportunity."

It was at the Monster Meetings that the idea of a campaign to integrate Indiana University basketball was first raised in earnest. Local blacks needed a sign of change and a symbol of hope, for the dispiriting postwar conditions of blacks across the country were especially acute in Indiana. In 1947, Indianapolis had pervasive segregation, one of the highest unemployment rates in the country for black men, and some of the worst housing conditions for blacks of any Northern city. In Indianapolis, almost half of all black veterans and their families were doubling up with relatives in cramped homes or were living in trailers, run-down hotel rooms, or tourist cabins, and there was no sign of housing relief in sight. A few loosely organized sit-ins had made some headway toward integrating the city's cafés and soda fountains, but at least one drugstore chain had fired all of its black employees in Indianapolis in retaliation. The Indianapolis police chief had recently declined to issue a permit for a dance at the Antlers Hotel downtown because the event would be integrated. Asked what policy he was enforcing, the chief had said, "My policy." Refusing to overrule the police chief, Mayor Robert Tyndall told the dance's sponsors, "My administration has been marked by good race relations and I don't intend to see this record marred."

Against this bleak picture, DeFrantz and others at the Senate Avenue Y saw the integration of IU basketball as a ripe target for scoring a public victory and giving some hope. Along with black leaders nationally, they were watching as Jackie Robinson made history with the Brooklyn Dodgers in the spring of 1947, and they were also watching something else: side by side with stories of Jackie Robinson in the black press nationally—and overshadowing Robinson in the *Indianapolis Recorder*—were stories of integrated Shelbyville's state championship and of Indiana's 1947 Mr. Basketball, Bill Garrett. DeFrantz and his friends saw a golden opportunity for a Hoosier Jackie Robinson in the sport that dominated the state of Indiana.

They knew it would not be easy. DeFrantz had a cordial working relationship with IU president Herman Wells and football coach Bo McMillan. Both spoke regularly at the Senate Avenue Y, always promoting "fair play" and "sportsmanship," generally understood code words for integration. But at IU, as in Indiana generally, football was a minor sport compared to basketball, and IU basketball was the domain of Branch McCracken.

DeFrantz had tried to break the Big Ten's color line before, most recently in March 1946, after Johnny Wilson led his integrated Anderson team to the state championship. On a Sunday morning, as the state was waking up to headlines of Anderson's victory barely twelve hours before, DeFrantz had driven to Bloomington to meet with IU president Wells.

It had seemed to go well. DeFrantz had brought along his brother-in-law, Frank Ward, an attorney and IU alum, and had ticked off Wilson's accomplishments and asked for Wells's help. Wells had called Coach McCracken, who arrived at the president's office bleary-eyed from watching Wilson score thirty points at Butler Fieldhouse the previous evening. According to DeFrantz, Wells had told the coach, "Any boy who can make the grade is a candidate for our team and must be given the opportunity to play." A few weeks later McCracken, picking up the letter of Wells's statement if not the spirit, had told an Anderson audience he did not think Johnny Wilson could make his team.

DeFrantz had learned from the Wilson experience. In 1947, he waited until the state championship dust had settled and the speech-making had finished. He gave Nate Kaufman a chance to succeed with Branch McCracken and the coach time to play his cards. And when it was clear that soft persuasion had failed, and this opportunity too was slipping away, DeFrantz again went to the top, smarter and stronger than he had been the year before.

At the last moment, DeFrantz had drafted Rufus Kuykendall, Al

Spurlock, Everett Hall, and Hobson Ziegler to join him. Spurlock, a teacher at Indianapolis Crispus Attucks High School, provided historical perspective. In 1936, as a sprinter, he had been the first black to win a varsity letter at the University of Illinois, where his coach had sometimes passed him off as "Indian" in order to get him into hotels and restaurants on the road. Kuykendall and Hall were IU graduates, both now well-connected attorneys in Indianapolis. Ziegler was DeFrantz's assistant at the Y. DeFrantz brought this larger group to serve as witnesses and an unspoken threat—of potential lawsuits and controversial publicity should IU again refuse to integrate basketball. Together the five headed south toward Bloomington determined to confront Herman Wells and get their answer.

They didn't say much on the two-hour drive. The heat precluded idle talk, and DeFrantz had already planned his strategy. He told the others, "I'm not going there to talk in generalities. Wells needs to know that we, and just about every other citizen of this state, want Bill Garrett at IU. He's the best player around, a good student, a good kid, from an integrated school; he's had white teammates, white friends." DeFrantz paused, staring ahead. "If Indiana University can't handle Bill Garrett on their basketball team, I don't think they're ever going to take anybody."

Herman Wells was a perfect match for Faburn DeFrantz but a curious fit for his hidebound state. Five-seven, 310 pounds, gregarious and suave, he looked like Santa Claus's urbane younger brother with a trim mustache instead of a beard. His appetites were gargantuan and his tastes eclectic, running from thick chicken gravy and fresh catfish to antiques, opera, and the best French wines. Wearing custom-made suits and the occasional coonskin cap, Wells tooled around Bloomington at racing speeds in his sky-blue Buick convertible.

A lifelong bachelor who called IU his "mistress" and the students "my children," the president scheduled meetings at times that enabled him to cross the campus just as classes let out, so he would see as many students as possible, many of whom called him by his first name. He held open office hours every week, when students could drop in to discuss everything from course work to their love lives. He liked to tell of a student who breezed into his office early in his presidency and announced, "You're too fat, Hermie. Give me two evenings a week and I'll train 70 pounds off you." Wells would spend a lifetime fighting a losing battle against his ever-expanding waistline—what he called "my mis-shapenness"—often joking, "Diets are easy; I've lost over six hundred pounds on them."

He had been dismissed as a lightweight, a temporary placeholder, when he agreed to be IU's acting president in June 1937. He was thirty-four years old, lacked a doctorate, and had been dean of the IU Business School for only two years. But Wells never considered himself "acting" anything. He seized the reins of IU with such authority that within a year the board removed the qualifier from his title, making Wells, at thirty-five, the youngest university president in the country.

Wells quickly set about waking IU from years of sleepy complacency and transforming it into a nationally recognized institution, recruiting top-notch professors, overseeing the rise of IU's world-famous music school, expanding foreign-language and international programs, tripling the size of the campus while protecting its trees, and vigorously defending academic freedom—most famously that of IU zoologist and sex researcher Alfred Kinsey. He did these things even though Indiana, in the 1940s, was stone-cold isolationist, suspicious of foreigners, and resistant to change. Wells regularly took flak for being too permissive and too radical.

But the IU president knew his state. An Indiana native and IU graduate, he had been field secretary for the Indiana Bankers Association at the height of the Depression, when banks were failing and farms were being foreclosed in large numbers. Wells traveled often to all of Indiana's ninety-two counties, talking survival with community leaders and farmers—and keeping card files on all of them, noting spouses, children, secretaries, sometimes even menus and flower arrangements, a practice he maintained all his life. As IU's president, Wells set out to extend the benefits of the university to everyone in the state. He started a traveling art collection that went not to museums ("the privilege of the few") but to schoolrooms in run-down neighborhoods, country churches, and labor union halls. He sent out IU graduate students to conduct community forums on economic and social issues, and he brought local leaders and opinion-makers to Bloomington for seminars to brush up on new developments in their fields. Practical as well as visionary, Wells knew that spreading support for the university dulled challenges to academic freedom and helped get IU's budgets passed by the legislature.

Like DeFrantz, Wells understood Hoosiers' dislike of confrontation and controversy, and he used it to his advantage, often making progress when no one was looking. He integrated the IU Union Building's Commons Cafeteria by telling the manager to quietly remove the "Reserved" signs designating tables for black patrons. By the time anyone noticed the change, it was a done deal. He ended segregation at the university swimming pool by sending a popular black football lineman, J. C. Chestine "Rooster" Coffee, to swim there at the busiest hour. "I doubt anyone realized a policy had been changed," Wells wrote later. He squelched red-baiting at IU by telling the American Legion he would be happy to accommodate their demand for an investigation of communists among the IU faculty—if only the Legion would first show him evidence they existed. To those who urged him to be more confrontational, Wells had a reply, "I want to win every battle, and not lose one."

In the summer of 1947, Wells was worried about two impending controversies: one over Alfred Kinsey, the other over segregation at IU. Both had the potential to do serious harm to Wells's plans for the university. Kinsey was preparing to publish *The Kinsey Report on Sexual Behavior in the Human Male*. Everyone involved expected the book to train a national spotlight on Kinsey's sex research at Indiana University, and on the controversy surrounding it. (As the *Indianapolis Star* would summarize in a headline, " 'Science' Says Kinsey: 'Dirty Stuff' Says U.S.") Wells, who once described Kinsey as the only person capable of making sex boring, was anticipating the firestorm.

Wells's second worry in the summer of 1947 involved segregation on the Bloomington campus. At the time, IU had only a couple of hundred black students among a student population of more than twelve thousand. They were barred from the dorms and most campus dining halls, honorary societies, and university social events, from the barbershop in the Union Building, white fraternities and sororities, and most Bloomington restaurants. Black student teachers could not do their practice teaching in the segregated Bloomington schools, and instead had to travel fifty miles north to Indianapolis. Black men were barred from IU's otherwise compulsory ROTC program by a local doctor's blanket diagnosis that they all had flat feet, and every year the university admitted no more than eighty-four black women—the number of off-campus rooms available for them.

Integration of the IU campus had long been one of Wells's top priorities. His first student assistant, a black zoology major named John Stewart, had helped Wells understand the extent and effects of campus segregation. Only six years younger than Wells, Stewart would become one of the president's closest friends, and regularly reported to him on IU's "blind spots." Wells had once told a carefully selected audience, "We must prepare to renounce prejudice of color, class and race. Where? In England? In China? In Palestine? No! We must renounce prejudice of color, class and race in Bloomington, Monroe County, Indiana."

Wells worked to integrate the IU campus the same way he approached other innovations: with subtlety and finesse. If critics tried to speak in racist code, Wells stole their veneer of respectability by feigning incomprehension, forcing them to make a crude statement or keep quiet. Once his changes were made, few ever publicly challenged them. "In taking the steps required to remove those reprehensible, discriminatory rules," Wells later wrote in his autobiography, "we tried to make a move, if possible, when the issue was not being violently discussed pro and con on the campus. I felt that making moves in this manner would, and in fact it did, prevent any backlash that might set the whole program back."

But stealth and charm had not been enough to budge IU's biggest racial barriers—the women's dorms, practice teaching, ROTC, and basketball. For years Wells had been worried about *Missouri ex. Rel. Gaines v. Canada,* a 1938 U.S. Supreme Court decision requiring the University of Missouri Law School to admit a qualified black applicant. *Gaines,* a forerunner of *Brown v. Board of Education,* increased the risk that state universities would be sued over segregation. Soon after the decision came out, Wells asked IU's legal counsel, George Henley, to review the university's vulnerability to lawsuits in light of *Gaines.* After receiving Henley's report, Wells followed up by asking specifically about blacks' participation in intercollegiate athletics. In June 1940, Henley sent Wells a memo: "No written rule in the Big Ten regarding participation in athletics. The unwritten rule subscribed to by all schools precludes colored boys from participating in basketball, swimming, and wrestling."

Basketball, swimming, and wrestling. All that skin, sweat and contact, so close to the fans. It would take only a small extension of the
Gaines case to open up Indiana University to lawsuits and embarrass-
ment.

By the summer of 1947 the pressure to speed up campus integration was bearing down on Wells. Faburn DeFrantz liked Wells, and
the NAACP's national office considered him "a decent fellow" on a
reactionary campus, but DeFrantz and the NAACP were doing everything they could to keep up the pressure, including threats of more
public confrontations. Future Supreme Court Justice Thurgood Marshall, then the top litigator of the NAACP Legal Defense Fund, had
met with black IU students in Indianapolis a year before; and Walter
White, national NAACP president, was preparing to visit Bloomington and discuss legal action if there was no visible progress in the
coming year.

These threats had to be depressingly frustrating to Herman Wells.
He hated the thought of expensive lawsuits and controversial publicity, and yet IU was at risk of both, over racial discrimination Wells
would have preferred to end long before.

But he had so little room for maneuver. A public university, IU
depended every year on a very conservative state legislature for its
funding. The president of the IU board of trustees, Ora Wildermuth—
effectively Wells's boss—adamantly opposed integration. In refusing
either to fund a dorm for black women or to integrate the existing
dorms, Wildermuth had written to the board's treasurer at the end of
1945, "I am and shall always remain absolutely and utterly opposed
to social intermingling of the colored race with the white . . . the fur-
ther we go in encouraging social relationships between the races the
nearer we approach intermarriage and just as soon as colored blood is
introduced the product becomes black, and if the white race is silly
enough to permit itself to intermarry with the black and thereby be
swallowed up, it really, of course, doesn't deserve perpetuity. If a person has as much as 1/16th colored blood in him, even though the
other 15/16ths may be pure white, yet he is colored."

A founding citizen of Gary, and graduate of IU's law school, Wildermuth had been elected to the IU board in 1925 and remained a
member until 1952, serving as board president for thirteen of those
twenty-seven years. For the university as he envisioned it, Wilder-

muth was a tireless supporter. He was an original incorporator of the IU Foundation, one of the most powerful engines for alumni support and fund-raising among all state universities, and he was instrumental in raising funds for expansion of the IU libraries and construction of a fieldhouse (which today is the Ora Wildermuth Center for Health, Physical Education and Recreation). But he was dead-set against integration of the IU campus. "The average of the race as to intelligence, economic status and industry is so far below the white average that it seems to me futile to build up hope for a great future," Wildermuth would write to Wells in 1948. "Their presence in the body politics [sic] definitely presents a problem."

It wasn't only Wildermuth. On the issue of integrating IU, the board, most state legislators, and many in Wells's own administration were at best unenthusiastic and often hostile. In the early 1940s, Ward Biddle, board treasurer and IU comptroller, warned Wells of a white backlash against campus integration and regularly sent Wildermuth NAACP and labor union flyers on which Biddle had scrawled notes such as, "Why can't meddlers and agitators leave us alone?" In the spring of 1947, H. Ross Bartley, known around campus as "Lord God Bartley," director of the IU News Bureau, had gone to extraordinary lengths to prevent the staff of the *Arbutus,* the IU yearbook, from publishing a picture of an integrated social event. Writing to Wells in May 1947, after a university-sponsored race relations institute held on campus, Bartley described the organizers (who had protested segregation in Bloomington restaurants) as "irresponsible" youths with "Communistic leanings," concluding, "Nothing in some time has done so much damage in Bloomington to the university's public relations." One of Wells's assistants would say, "Ross Bartley, God rest his soul, was reaction personified."

Wells was also going through a rough time personally in the summer of 1947. He had recently spent three months in Greece as an election observer, and he was being pressed to accept a one-year position as director of cultural affairs in American-occupied Berlin, activities that were not popular in Indiana, where many seethed at efforts to rebuild Europe "so they can fight us again." The IU board had opposed Wells's going to Greece, and they were threatening to deny him a leave of absence to serve in Germany. The lack of support was deeply troubling to a man who had given so much to the university.

Wells, who admitted he suffered loneliness and occasional deep depression, was trying to chart a path for himself as well as for the university.

Struggling with his own priorities and emotions, caught between the pressure to integrate IU and the resistance around him, fearing lawsuits and bad publicity, Herman Wells had to step carefully. If he moved too slowly, he risked NAACP-backed lawsuits; but moving too fast—making just one impolitic step—risked setting off the tinderbox of reactionary administrators, cautious legislators, and nervous alums, and maybe even provoking pro-integration lawsuits by publicizing the university's Achilles' heel. Like Branch Rickey in baseball, if Wells tried to integrate IU basketball with the wrong person and that person failed—at his studies or in basketball or just buckling under the pressure—it would confirm the reactionaries' every prejudice, make Wells look foolish, and set the effort back for years.

And now, with the 1947–48 school year only days away, Faburn DeFrantz was at Wells's door and the president knew the Chief expected answers.

DeFrantz and Wells saw each other as equals and knew each other well. Wells had spoken several times at the Senate Avenue Y's Monster Meetings and had brought his mother (who lived with him in Bloomington and served as his official hostess) to dinner at DeFrantz's home afterward. The two men had similar abilities and aims, and they admired each other deeply. DeFrantz would write of Wells, "In him democracy found an ally."

Wells's office faced the thickest part of the campus woods, the shade of tall oaks and thick limestone walls protecting it from the worst of the summer heat and making it a cool haven for DeFrantz and his companions. Wells greeted them with a warm smile and paused with each, asking how Spurlock came to Indiana from Illinois, when Kuykendall and Hall had graduated from IU, how long Ziegler had worked at the Senate Avenue Y. "How's Robert? Ready to start his sophomore year?" Wells asked DeFrantz, referring to DeFrantz's youngest son.

"He's fine, Herman," DeFrantz replied. "He'll be even better if he can cheer for Bill Garrett on the basketball team."

"Ahhhh . . . the basketball team," Wells said, taking a seat in his overstuffed chair.

"Herman, we appreciate all that's happened at IU. You know we do. It's made the school better and the state better," DeFrantz began, to the nods of the other men. "But in this state, basketball's what everybody looks to. Passing up Johnny Wilson didn't do anybody any good. And he's proved it with what he's done. It's embarrassing—to *everybody*. It'll be the same thing, only worse, if Bill Garrett gets away. And he's about to. I don't know if you know this, but Garrett's already gone to Tennessee State, and I'm not sure he'd come back even if he thought he could play here."

No one moved, as DeFrantz continued, "He's more than a great player. He can handle it. He's grown up around white people in Shelbyville, integrated high school, integrated team, good student, no chip on his shoulder. Hell, he's already taken all the abuse a crowd can hand out, and he's handled it."

DeFrantz leaned forward, his eyes holding Wells's, one politician's way of telling another that this mattered, that Wells's response would be long remembered by DeFrantz, his companions, and everyone they would meet in the coming years. "Herman, you know as well as I do that stupid *gentleman's*"—DeFrantz spat the word—"agreement can't last. Any year now somebody's gonna break it. And when they do, it's going to be really embarrassing—to *all* of us, Herman, and hard for all of us to explain—that the state that plays the best basketball had outstanding Negro players two years in a row, and that we asked you twice, Herman, and that somehow, some way, it just couldn't get done."

It was neither a negotiation nor a lament. Faburn DeFrantz had laid his best cards on the table and the message was clear, reinforced by the presence of the witnesses and lawyers he had brought along: Take Bill Garrett or we will do everything we can to embarrass Herman Wells and Indiana University over segregation in basketball.

The president needed to buy time. He fell back on his often-used tactic of feigning ignorance and surprise, "Chief, I don't know of any formal barrier to a Negro's playing basketball here. I'm surprised to hear you say that. I can tell you without any hesitation that Bill Garrett can come here as a student if he has the grades. But I can't order Branch McCracken to play somebody. Only the coach can decide who's good enough."

DeFrantz saw his opening. "So . . . Herman . . . if Bill Garrett comes to IU, and he's good enough to play basketball on McCracken's team, he can play here. Is that what you're telling me?"

Wells's chuckle lifted a bit of the tension. They all knew DeFrantz had won the first move, but they also knew many more moves had to play out. "I will speak to Branch McCracken about Bill Garrett," Wells said. "That's as much as I can promise you. I'd suggest you talk to McCracken, too."

DeFrantz sat back, stretched his arms, and loosened his tie. Dorothy Collins, Wells's assistant, poured coffee all around. Wells asked about the Monster Meetings of the previous spring and plans for next year. He asked Al Spurlock if Crispus Attucks was still having trouble scheduling basketball games. On a cooler day Wells might have shown them around campus and pointed out plans for new dorms, new classroom buildings, expansion of the health center, maybe stopped by his home so those who had not already done so could meet his mother. But the outdoors was not inviting, and their harder meeting was ahead of them. They finished their coffee and said their good-byes.

The minute his office door was closed Wells asked Dorothy Collins to call McCracken at his office. The fieldhouse was not five minutes' walk away, so he wasted no time. "Mac, DeFrantz brought with him two prominent lawyers from Indianapolis, a teacher from Crispus Attucks, and his assistant at the Y. They're courteous, of course, but he laid it straight out: either Bill Garrett gets a chance to play basketball here, or they will go public and do everything they can to embarrass IU, along with you and me."

McCracken started to reply, but Wells cut him off. "I told them of course Garrett could enroll at IU. I told them your job was to coach the basketball team and to make decisions about which IU students are good enough basketball players to play on your team."

There was a pause. McCracken had never been comfortable calling the president by his first name. "Mr. Wells, Nate Kaufman's talked to me about Bill Garrett, and it doesn't make any difference to me he's colored, but there's an understanding in the Big Ten. The other teams might cancel games. The conference might suspend us. Some of my own players might quit. I think we ought to step back and think about this."

Time was getting short. DeFrantz's group would be at McCracken's door any minute. Whatever Wells wanted to tell McCracken about how to balance the risks and pressures weighing on both of them, about which direction he and McCracken would take Indiana University in the days and years ahead, he had to say now. Wells paused for just an instant, his mind perhaps going back to May and the widely publicized story of how Ford Frick had backed Jackie Robinson. "Mac, I will take care of the Big Ten. I'm the head of the Big Ten Presidents Group this coming year. I will deal with the other presidents and make sure there's no suspension or canceling of games. I don't think your players will quit, but I'll back you no matter what the reaction is. All I ask is that if Garrett comes here you give him a chance, and if he's good enough to play, you play him. I'll take care of the rest."

Wells heard in the background a loud knock at McCracken's door, and the coach said, "I've got to go, Mr. Wells. They're here."

DeFrantz's group had left the president's office feeling encouraged but cautious. Wells had told them he would speak with McCracken and had strongly implied that he would tell the coach the only standard was whether an IU student was good enough to play. They believed Wells was a man of his word and that he was on their side. But as it had been with Johnny Wilson the year before, it remained to be seen whether McCracken would apply Wells's standard in good faith.

Seventeen months earlier Wells had also told McCracken the only standard was whether a student was a good enough player, and the coach had then told an Anderson audience that Indiana's 1946 Mr. Basketball did not meet that standard. It had bought McCracken only a little over a year. If he dodged again, how many more times would he have to do so? How foolish would he look holding IU back as more and more talented black Indiana high school players went to schools that were more willing to take risks, more attuned to the changing times? For the second time in seventeen months, McCracken faced a defining moment, one in which he was hit with a question that forced him to choose whether he would continue to tell black high school stars they could not make his team, or whether he would give one student as much right to play as any other.

McCracken had only met DeFrantz once, at the tense meeting in

Wells's office the previous year. He tried to be courteous, but he was uncomfortable with this group and with the meeting's subject. They stood around in the little office in the old fieldhouse while the coach rustled up enough wooden folding chairs for them all to sit, as shouts and whistles from the nearby football practice field carried through the open window.

DeFrantz tried to put McCracken at ease, calling him "Coach" and drawing him into a conversation about the last season. "I was down here for the Illinois game." IU had beaten rival Illinois in the next-to-last game of the season. "That was sweet. Played like that all season you'd a won the Big Ten."

In fact McCracken's team had floundered, finishing with a 12–8 overall record and in the middle of the Big Ten pack. "They had the talent," the coach exaggerated, "but I just couldn't get those boys to play consistently."

They were tiptoeing around the subject, feeling each other out. If either had wanted a confrontation, there was plenty of tinder. DeFrantz could have pointed out sarcastically that since their meeting last year, Johnny Wilson had become a small-college All-American. He could have asked about Tom Schwartz, Indiana's 1945 Mr. Basketball—so far the only Mr. Basketball to play at IU under McCracken—and then reminded the coach that Bill Garrett had won the award this year. But that would only have embarrassed McCracken, put him on the defensive, and brought out his combative instincts. DeFrantz understood that McCracken was limited by pressures and circumstances, and maybe outlook, and that he needed their help to find a way to do the right thing.

DeFrantz crossed his arms and leaned his elbows on McCracken's metal desk, smiled warmly, and said, "Coach, we all know why we're here. You know we've been over to see President Wells. We think Bill Garrett can help your team. You've seen him play. We think he'll be a good kid, good student, won't cause any trouble, won't react if people get on him. We know you've gotta worry about the other schools, fans, your players, alums, everything. We understand that, believe me, we do. But look at what we've got—you and me. We've got the best player in the state. He's a great kid. We've got President Wells behind us, telling everybody the only question is whether a boy is good enough to make the team."

It was an exaggeration, for Wells was not telling everybody, but the message was clear enough: *"We'll tell everybody."* DeFrantz concluded his pitch, "Somebody's got to step up. This gentleman's agreement business won't last forever."

DeFrantz leaned down until his chin was almost resting on his hands, looked McCracken straight in the eye, and dropped his voice until it was almost a whisper, "Coach, we'll take care of getting Garrett to Indiana. If we do that, and if he goes out for basketball, and if he's good enough, will you play him on your team? That's all we're asking."

McCracken's face reddened. Despite Wells's heads-up, he had expected blunt confrontation, which was more his turf than a subtle plea on a sensitive issue. He was caught off guard. Seconds before this meeting his university president had emphasized that the only standard should be whether a student was a good enough basketball player, and had given the back of his hand to McCracken's long-held fear of negative reactions. The president had said he would back McCracken completely if the coach decided Garrett could make his team. Wells had, in a stroke, taken away McCracken's defenses and given him support.

In the silence DeFrantz and his colleagues waited, avoiding any hint of impatience.

McCracken started slowly. He wasn't sure how to address DeFrantz, so he avoided using his name. "I never promised any boy he could play."

No answer.

"We've used up our basketball scholarships for this year. And it's awfully late."

Still silence. Sympathetic nods.

"But if he's here on campus . . .

"And making his grades . . .

"And he shows he can take the training and the discipline . . .

"And get along with the other players . . .

"And not react if the fans give him hell, which they might do . . ."

Long pause. DeFrantz kept his eyes on McCracken's, his expression encouraging, nodding slightly at each statement.

"And if he shows he can play well enough. . . ."

DeFrantz bolted out of his seat, grabbed McCracken's hand in both of his hands and pumped it vigorously. He knew victory when he heard it. "God bless you, Branch McCracken! You are doing the right thing! That's wonderful! They're gonna remember you for this, Coach!"

McCracken managed a weak smile. "That's what I'm afraid of."

DeFrantz had one last deal-closer. "I can't wait to tell Herman Wells. Man, he'll be proud of you!"

DeFrantz and his companions took turns shaking McCracken's hand. They would have hugged him, but they thought the better of it. Before the coach could say anything more, they said quick good-byes and hurried out the door, down the steps of the fieldhouse, and back to Indianapolis.

13

Down t'IU

ON THE RIDE NORTH TO INDIANAPOLIS, FABURN DEFRANTZ brought his group back to reality. "We've still got to get Garrett to Indiana. Find a way to pay for it. We don't even know if he still wants to go. We can't sit back and expect Wells or McCracken to do it for us."

For fifty miles the men discussed their next move. With Garrett already at Tennessee State and the fall semester starting soon, they knew they had to act quickly. DeFrantz had talked to Laura Garrett over the summer and was aware of Nate Kaufman's efforts with Branch McCracken. They decided it was time to close the loop with Nate. That evening DeFrantz reached Kaufman by telephone at his home in Shelbyville. Describing their meetings in Bloomington, DeFrantz concluded, "Mr. Kaufman, we have Wells and McCracken lined up to let Bill Garrett play if we can get him to IU. We need your help."

As soon as he hung up, Nate drove five minutes to the Garrett home on the southeast edge of town. He spoke briefly with Laura Garrett, who told him she had no objection to Bill's transferring to IU, but that in the end it had to be Bill's decision. Privately, she was relieved at the thought of his leaving the South.

Returning, Kaufman called Branch McCracken at the coach's home in Bloomington. Nate related his conversation with DeFrantz and added his own concern, "Mac, I don't want him to go down there and just sit on the bench."

McCracken pushed back, surprised at how fast word was spreading. "I never promised any boy he could play, and I'm not doing that now."

"But if he's there . . . C'mon, Mac. You know he'll be good enough to play," Nate persisted.

McCracken ran through his concerns, "He'll have to go to class and make his grades. And be on time and practice hard. Just like everybody else. I'm not gonna carry him. He'll have to get along with his teammates. Some of the fans might ride him hard. Even some of our fans. He's gotta take that and not react. I don't want to bring him here and have to kick him off."

"He'll do all those things. I'm sure of it."

Kaufman's next call was to Vernon McCain, Tennessee State's head basketball coach. "Coach, I need to speak to Bill Garrett. Could you please get word to him to call me, collect?"

McCain was wary. He knew how hard Kaufman had tried to get Bill Garrett to Indiana. "Is there something I can tell him?"

"Just ask him to call me, please."

"You know, sir, he's already enrolled here. I drove him down here myself. This is the best place for him, Mr. Kaufman, in a lot of ways."

"Coach, please just ask him to call me. I talk to a lot of basketball people all over the country, as you probably know. I think the world of you and your basketball program, and I expect I'll continue to. Just ask Bill to call me, please."

Coach McCain had good reason to say Tennessee A&I State College was a good place for Bill Garrett. Though most of its students came from modest backgrounds, the school was a few short blocks from Fisk University and Meharry Medical College, both of which educated the black elite from around the country. If he had stayed and lived four years amid Nashville's vibrant black intellectual, social, and cultural life, Garrett would have experienced the full range of black American life in the late 1940s in a setting where, for the first time, he often would have been in a majority. Black life in Nashville contrasted so completely with Garrett's previous experience in Shelbyville that even a couple of weeks at Tennessee State had to have been eye-opening for him.

In Nashville, Bill saw for the first time both Southern segregation and the beginnings of a movement that would eventually coalesce to defeat it. When he arrived in Nashville, the Solid Block, a local civil rights organization, had just succeeded in getting the poll tax abolished and would soon elect two blacks to the city council. Tennessee State was the only college in the country whose entire student body had been organized into a Double V club—fighting for victory abroad and at home—during World War II.

Tennessee State president Walter Davis was an enthusiastic supporter of intercollegiate athletics—especially basketball, football, and track—believing that athletic success promoted civil rights, enhanced the university's reputation, and increased its enrollment. The college's football program would produce scores of National Football League pros. Its track alumni would eventually include Olympic sprinter Wilma Rudolph and long jumper Ralph Boston. And the 1947–48 basketball team included Joshua Grider and Clarence Wilson, both of whom would become strong members of the Harlem Globetrotters in the early 1950s, when the Trotters were among the best basketball teams in the world.

The decision to stay at Tennessee State or transfer to Indiana was not simple for Garrett. At IU he would be returning to a small, segregated, mostly white town and campus and shouldering the burden of being a trailblazer. He had not wanted the attention or the responsibility, and he was not sure he was up to the role. At the state track finals in early May, Garrett had expressed his doubts to Charles Preston, the *Indianapolis Recorder*'s sports editor. "I don't know whether I would want to be the only Negro player at IU. I'd be too much in the spotlight—suppose I didn't make good?" A companion of Preston's had countered with a comparison to Jackie Robinson's integration of major league baseball just three weeks earlier. It had given Garrett pause, and finally he had replied with a shy smile, "That's right, Jackie is preparing the way for others, and I guess I could try that too."

It was to this sense of responsibility that Nate Kaufman appealed when he told Bill Garrett a place at IU was his for the taking. Kaufman also reminded Garrett that Bloomington was just over an hour's drive from Shelbyville, that he would be able to get home more often, and that his family could attend home games. In the end, despite Garrett's doubts, Jackie Robinson's example took hold. He knew he was good enough to play at IU, he understood what it could mean for others, and he wanted to be closer to home. Kaufman told Garrett he would send bus fare and assured him that someone from the IU basketball program would be there to meet him when he arrived.

In the postwar years a common phrase bound together Indiana's leaders and upwardly mobile citizens: a son or daughter was "down t'IU." Pronounced as one word—"downtiu"—the expression conveyed parental pride more than geography. To a generation of parents scarred by the Depression, most of whom had not gone beyond high school, Indiana was the state's flagship university, a sure path to steady jobs and better lives for their children. Purdue was the state's A&M school, its farm extension programs reaching into every rural community, its engineering department drawing techies to uphold the Boilermaker tradition. Notre Dame was only incidentally in the state, its students and football fans drawn from all over the country. Ball State and Indiana State were still small teachers' colleges. DePauw was Methodist, and Wabash was only for men, both good private schools with a connotation of small-town elites. IU was the biggest, the oldest, the prettiest, and the best known. Those who resented the university's prominence called it "the country club," and indeed its wooded campus looked a bit like one, its fraternities had a partying reputation, and joining the IU community was the conventional thing to do for those who could afford it. For even with in-state tuition, college remained a luxury, the exception rather than the rule for most high school graduates. That was changing with the GI Bill and postwar prosperity, as veterans and high school graduates streamed to college in record numbers, but the mind-set had not caught up with the new reality, and "down t'IU" still captured the pride of parents realizing a dream for their children.

As the 1947 summer heat mellowed and green leaves began to hint at the colors to follow, a variant of the phrase spread through Shelbyville. What had started as speculation—"What's Bill gonna do?"—by late August had become a factual question: "Where's Bill Garrett?" In mid-September, all over Shelbyville fathers came home from work and announced proudly to their families, "Why, Bill's down t'IU! He's gonna be the first colored boy to play there."

Bloomington's little Trailways station was crowded and chaotic when the bus pulled in. Garrett retrieved his cardboard suitcase and stood waiting for someone from the basketball program—an assistant coach or maybe a student manager—to come forward as Nate Kaufman had said they would. But as the station emptied, it became clear that no one was there to meet him. He was on his own.

Seen from a shared taxi in the evening's fading light, the university's stately limestone buildings stood out, pale and glowing against a heavy screen of trees. On a closer look, cranes, dump trucks, and acres of newly turned soil were everywhere. Herman Wells insisted that IU accept all qualified returning veterans who sought admission, and the result was akin to several years of high school graduating classes descending on the Bloomington campus at once. The year before—when 60 percent of the incoming class had been returning veterans—Wells had been forced to postpone the start of classes for three weeks as administrators scrambled to cope with the flood of students, and when classes finally began, students were sleeping in the fieldhouse and the board of trustees' meeting room. Over the course of the 1946–47 school year, IU had built six new dormitories and eighty-one thousand square feet of new classrooms and labs. During the summer of 1947, Quonset huts, trailers, and barracks had been trucked to Bloomington from Bunker Hill Air Force Base, one hundred miles north. Still, IU had turned away some two thousand prospective students for lack of housing.

If Bill Garrett was expecting his dorm to be one of the elegant limestone buildings, he was surely disappointed. A bed had been found for him in Hoosier Hall, a grandly named set of wood barracks lining a former intramural field just beyond the open end of the football stadium. Garrett's "room" was an upper bunk and a metal locker in Hoosier Hall Number Six, a jock dorm consisting of a long open space lined with rows of bunks separated from one another by low partitions. Hungry and tired, Garrett set down his suitcase, climbed into his bunk, and fell asleep.

Nate Kaufman had told Bill to go to the fieldhouse on his first morning at IU, and to look for the red door. Inside, Kaufman assured Garrett, he would find head trainer Dwayne "Spike" Dixon, and maybe freshman basketball coach Jay McCreary and some of the players. Coaches told athletes to stay out of the training room unless they had an injury requiring attention, but the room was a hangout, the athletes' clubhouse, and someone in the basketball program could almost always be found there.

The fieldhouse sat on a little rise with its back only steps from Hoosier Hall. Built in 1928, it was, literally, a field house: four walls of weathered gray Indiana limestone with a high vaulted roof enclosing a vast dirt floor that, depending on the season, was used for class registration, a fall carnival, indoor track, baseball practice, and, from November through March, big-time college basketball. Every year, as Halloween approached, the fieldhouse became a 10,500-seat arena with a basketball court assembled in sections at its center, two feet above new sawdust spread over the dirt floor. The best seats were in the single row encircling the court, where the freshman team, nearby high school players, and visiting recruits sat with their elbows on the playing floor, eye level with Branch McCracken and his bench. A corridor separated that row from the rest of the temporary, backless wooden bleachers.

Back in one corner of the building, far beyond the end of the playing floor, a small square cement-block room with a red door jutted out from the wall, interrupting the building's interior lines. Behind the red door was Branch McCracken's inner sanctum: the training room and beyond that, IU's basketball dressing room. Veteran fans learned to watch the red door at about seven o'clock on game nights to see how it opened: tentatively—bad game for IU coming up; viciously flung open—get ready for a barn burner.

Garrett opened the door slowly and peered inside. Student trainers were taping football players' ankles, and burly linemen were soaking their legs in whirlpools. The smells and sounds—old sweat, analgesic ointment, and the crisp crack of tape being smartly applied— reminded him of Frank's Office. Amid the unfamiliar faces Garrett recognized Phil Buck, with whom he had roomed and become fast friends during the week leading up to the Indiana-Kentucky All-Star game.

"Phil?" Garrett asked. "Phil?"

Buck stopped sweeping the floor and burst into a broad smile. "Bill! We heard you might be coming! Great to see you. Come and meet Gene Ring, from South Bend Central. Gene, this is Bill Garrett, Mr. Basketball."

Ring, a six-one blond guard, was a gym rat who played with an intensity coaches loved. "Think I don't know who he is?" Ring chided Buck while shaking Garrett's hand, trying to reconcile his loose handshake and mild demeanor with the determined competitor he had watched in the state finals. "Been hearing maybe you'd come here. What took you so long?"

Garrett hesitated, then smiled and answered, "Traffic."

The training room's buzz had quieted when Garrett walked in, and football players exchanged glances. Everyone knew who he was, but most of them, black and white, were upperclassmen, varsity football players, and Garrett was a rookie. Whatever their individual attitudes, the most recognition Bill was going to get was a nod. The room fell into an awkward silence until, finally, a gruff voice broke the tension, "Garrett! Grab a broom!" It was Spike Dixon, the trainer. "And when you're done, be back here at 2:30."

As they swept, Buck explained that as part of their basketball scholarships he and Ring assisted in the training room and at football practices, and then every afternoon they played pickup games in the practice gym upstairs. Buck walked Garrett over to the equipment room, where a student manager sorted clothing inside a wire enclosure. "Hey, John," Buck said, "this is Bill Garrett."

"Think I don't know?"

"He'll need stuff." The manager didn't look up. He was used to big-time jocks. "What size shoes?" With a few flicks of his hands he tossed Garrett gray gym shorts and a graying-white T-shirt with "IU basketball" in fading red letters on the front, a new jock, and socks. "Freshmen use these till they're ready to stand up in the corner, then you hand 'em in and get more." With a second toss the manager added a clean towel, a pair of black and white gym shoes, and a padlock for Garrett's locker in the freshman area.

When they finished sweeping, Garrett, Ring, and Buck had forty minutes before lunch started at the athletes' training table in the Union Building. They changed shoes, grabbed a ball, and hurried up a long, metal stairway to the second-floor practice gym. Bill dribbled toward one of the baskets, enjoying the familiar feel and sound of the ball bouncing off the floor. Players clustered around the other baskets glanced over, but no one said anything. Bill squeezed off a one-hander, sending the ball on a long, slow arc to the basket. It was good.

Through September and October, Garrett worked with Ring and Buck as student managers of the football team, and every afternoon, after their football duties were done, they played two-on-two, or three-on-three with other freshmen. Building on the friendship Garrett and Buck had formed on the All-Star team in May, the three became friends. They were all from modest backgrounds, the first in their families to go to college, new to the pace, size, and seeming sophistication of the big university, trying to find their way with almost no money in their pockets. On Sunday afternoons, when other students were riding around in cars or out on dates, Buck, Garrett, and Ring "would slip into the fieldhouse and shoot baskets. We didn't have any money to do anything else," Buck remembered.

Bill Tosheff, a twenty-two-year-old freshman from Gary who had been a pilot in the Army Air Corps, soon joined their pickup games. Six feet tall, thin and wiry, slightly stooped, with wavy black hair and a pointed face, Tosheff was a tough, funny wiseguy from "Da Region," who had worked in Gary steel mills from the age of thirteen. A gifted athlete, Tosheff had been scouted as a pitcher by the Chicago Cubs and as a quarterback by Notre Dame; he had set a high school broad jump record and had been all-city in basketball at Gary Froebel High.

They tagged one another with nicknames. Ring called Garrett "Bones" for his skinny physique—a nickname that would stick throughout his IU years. Tosheff called Ring "Polskie." Tosheff talked trash in pickup games and quickly discovered that needling brought out Garrett's own sly sense of humor. Early in the first semester, when Garrett said he wanted to be an opthamologist, Tosheff told him, "Bones, you know what you gotta do to be an eye doctor? Take chemistry and all those science courses. It's hard stuff, especially if you're gonna play basketball." Bill was quiet a minute and then replied, "I guess you're right, Tosh. Maybe I'll be a foot doctor instead."

Like Garrett, Tosheff would be going out for freshman basketball as a walk-on, but in life he was streaks ahead of Garrett, Buck, and Ring. In the fall of 1947 he already had completed one semester at IU, having enrolled on the GI Bill the previous spring. As a football walk-on, he was the first-string quarterback on the freshman team. Older, more wordly, confident, and sharper-tongued than the other three, Tosheff gravitated to Garrett, Buck, and Ring because the four of them were the best freshman basketball players. The three accepted Garrett without giving his race a thought, and Garrett saw nothing unusual in their friendship. "We seemed to group together and to go through things just naturally," he recalled years later.

But on campus their interracial friendship was unusual. Both the campus and the town were sharply segregated. Blacks and whites lived more separate lives at IU than they did in Shelbyville. Black men had been admitted to the IU dormitories only one semester before Garrett arrived, and few had accepted the invitation. It would be another year before black women could live on campus and two more years before the women's dorms would be integrated. Official university forms asked one's race. Black students were unwelcome at most university dances or other social functions. When Fletcher Henderson, the "father of swing," had played a dance on campus a few years before, black students had to ask permission to sit in the balcony and listen. Fraternities and sororities were strictly segregated, and at functions like the spring carnival they often put on skits in blackface, men with rolling eyes and "bones" through their noses, women in "Aunt Jemima" dress with red bandanas in their hair. Black students protested these activities to no avail.

Off campus, the town was even more segregated. Bloomington restaurants did not serve blacks, and when integrated groups of students tried to get sit-down service, as they did occasionally throughout the 1930s and 1940s, local restaurant owners shut down en masse. Bloomington movie theaters had "colored" and "white" entrances, admitted blacks only on weekends, and required them to sit in the balconies, referred to by some local whites as "nigger heaven." Barbers in town refused to cut blacks' hair—even the two black shop owners, who feared the loss of white customers. Blacks cut each other's hair or traveled fifty miles to Indianapolis.

Bloomington was a southern Indiana town of twenty-five thousand in a region of rolling limestone hills that more resembled Kentucky and Tennessee than the rest of the state to the north. In the hills not far from Bloomington, log cabins were common, and villages had evocative names like Gnawbone and Beanblossom. The rustic beauty of the hills drew some artists and professors to make their

homes there, but most residents of Monroe and nearby Brown counties were hill people—stonecutters who worked the limestone quar-
ries, laborers who worked the hillside apple orchards. They were not
the type who took easily to outsiders, especially black outsiders, better educated than they, who came from the affluent university they
resented. Even the storied Gables, an off-campus hangout across the
street from the president's office, where Hoagy Carmichael had composed "Stardust" as an IU law student in 1925, refused black customers. There were no exceptions for athletes. When Garrett arrived
at IU in the fall of 1947, the Gables had on its wall a large action picture of George Taliaferro, IU's star halfback; but Taliaferro couldn't eat
there.* Blacks on visiting football and track teams had to stay with
families in town or at the Senate Avenue Y in Indianapolis.

Bloomington's black population, concentrated on the west side of
town, embraced black IU students and served as an alternative community for them, offering the kind of town-and-gown cooperation
white students rarely experienced. IU's black students lived, ate,
prayed, and socialized with the laborers, washerwomen, domestics,
and practical nurses who made up the bulk of Bloomington's black
community. Most black students rented rooms in this community.
Few had cars or even bicycles. Instead, they walked the ten blocks
from campus to their west-side neighborhood, and they got to know
each other along the way. On the weekends they organized their own
supervised social gatherings and dances, often at the private homes
where black women students lived. "We'd just roll up the rug in the
front room," one woman remembered, "turn on the radio or record
player and have our dance right there." "We were there for our own
support," said George Taliaferro. "We were, in fact, out of necessity
our own best friends."

Their unofficial student union was Mays House, a private men's
residence on West Eighth Street. It had space for only sixteen men,
and the shared rooms were cramped, but at one time or another most

---

*In 1948 Taliaferro would complain to Herman Wells, who then struck a deal with the
Gables' owner: Taliaferro and a date would visit the Gables each evening for a week, and
if their presence did not drive away white customers, the Gables would integrate. The
Gables quickly became known as the place to rub elbows with the football star; white
students flocked there, and the Gables integrated. In 1949 George Taliaferro would be
the first black to be drafted in the National Football League.

black IU students, male and female, passed through Mays. They came to eat, socialize, and enjoy the warm, welcoming atmosphere. With her husband, Johnny, Ruth Mays had opened the house to boarders in the early 1920s. Ruth had long hair, a slight stoop, and, one boarder recalled, "the fortitude of a bull." She charged $22 a month for room and board, $22.50 with a radio. Her cooking was uneven; she served pork chops so often some boarders couldn't eat them for years after graduation. But to young men and women far from home in an unwelcoming environment, she was a counselor and surrogate mother. Boarders called her "Mom Mays," and she called them "my boys." Much to the consternation of her husband, who regularly threatened to throw out one or all of the boarders, she watched over them like a mother hen, so much so that some climbed in windows to avoid her wrath when they came in late.

From the beginning, Bill Garrett was welcomed into this tightly knit off-campus community, and it became the hub of his social world. When he wasn't shooting hoops with Ring, Buck, and Tosheff, Garrett often spent weekend evenings at one of the private houses for black women. On Sundays he went to the Second Baptist Church. He pledged Kappa Alpha Psi and spent hours hanging out with other black students, especially older athletes, at Mays House. Shortly after arriving at IU, Garrett joined the campus NAACP, possibly influenced by his brief stay at Tennessee State. His couple of weeks in Nashville had given him a glimpse of black attitudes very different from those he had known growing up in Shelbyville, and at IU he was curious to learn more.

Most of Garrett's fellow black students were from cities like Gary, Indianapolis, Cincinnati, and Chicago, where self-contained worlds of black schools, businesses, and culture existed apart from the white majority. Many of the black athletes had greater adjustments to make than Garrett, for until they arrived in Bloomington they had never gone to school with whites, never had to tiptoe around segregation in a small, white town. Bill and these other black students were worlds opening to each other. They wanted to know about his experiences in Shelbyville. Some thought he had a funny accent. He was curious about them as well. Many older black athletes were military veterans. They had worldly experience, goals, and perspectives Garrett lacked. If Gene Ring and Phil Buck were contemporaries with whom he went through freshman experiences, these older men were the big brothers he never had. They knew what it was like to have something to prove, and to carry the burden and responsibility of representing their race. Garrett had questions for them: where he could and couldn't go on campus; what to expect from white teammates; how much discrimination to expect on road trips; the practical jokes he had heard about. The questions all pointed toward what George Taliaferro identified as Garrett's central concern, "Am I being treated the same as everyone else?"

Official basketball practice started November 1. By then the main playing floor had been assembled in the fieldhouse, where Branch McCracken and assistant coach Ernie Andres put the varsity through its early-season drills. The freshmen practiced upstairs with coach McCreary, working on fundamentals and mastering Indiana's run-and-gun style of play. As the two hundred boys who tried out for the freshman team were whittled to twenty-two, the best remained Bill Garrett, Bill Tosheff, Gene Ring, and Phil Buck.

Garrett had arrived at IU without publicity or fanfare, but the quiet didn't last long. In October, the *Indianapolis Recorder* had carried its first story about Garrett's breakthrough, comparing him to Jackie Robinson and heralding the end of the Big Ten's gentleman's agreement. From then on, the paper never let up on the story. On New Year's Day 1948, the *Recorder* announced its annual "Race Relations Honor Roll," listing Faburn DeFrantz as number one for his "unremitting campaign over several years" to break the gentleman's agreement in Big Ten basketball, and listing Garrett as number three for being the person to do it. A month later the Indianapolis chapter of the NAACP gave Herman Wells a watch in recognition of his efforts to integrate IU, and the Senate Avenue Y presented Wells with its Emblem Club Racial Amity award. (Faburn DeFrantz would later write, "It was never more fittingly given.") By January 1948, black newspapers around the country were running stories about Garrett's breaking the gentleman's agreement, and people from as far away as Texas were writing to congratulate Herman Wells for breaking with other Big Ten schools to integrate college basketball.

By unfortunate coincidence Wells was not there to add his support. In November 1947, Wells left the campus for a now six-month stint as education and cultural affairs adviser in American-occupied Berlin. Grumbling about "internationalists," members of the board of trustees and the state legislature had done everything short of calling for his ouster to prevent him from going. Wells tried hard to cover both bases, shuttling between Berlin and Bloomington on noisy twenty-hour flights. During this period, his father, with whom Wells had been close, committed suicide. Wells would always wonder if he should have stayed home. He did not renew the Berlin job after six months and declined other foreign assignments.

Although Wells was not there to watch Garrett, a lot of others were. The freshman practice floor had no bleachers and little space for spectators, but freshman basketball practices were soon drawing crowds. Some came to show support for Garrett, others to see Mr. Basketball and because word was spreading that this small, quick bunch was exciting to watch.

In 1947, the only games the freshman basketball team played outside of practice were intrasquad curtain-raisers before the varsity's home games. In a typical year, the 10,500-seat fieldhouse was empty when these freshman scrimmages started at 6:00 P.M., with fans drifting in over the next hour. In the 1947–48 basketball season, while McCracken's varsity struggled to last place in the Big Ten, thousands of fans began turning out early to see the freshman intrasquad curtain-raisers.

Like most freshmen, Garrett had to get used to the academic demands of college. IU accepted any Indiana resident who had graduated in the upper half of his or her high school class—and then ruthlessly flunked out those who did not measure up. There was no grade inflation; A grade of A was rare, Cs, Ds, and Fs were common, and one-third of the freshman class did not return for a sophomore year. Athletes could get modest tutoring, but few professors gave them breaks, and the prospect of academic ineligibility was real. In this setting, Bill maintained a B-minus average—more than respectable for a freshman who was also playing basketball, but not strong enough for an aspiring eye *or* foot doctor at a time when competition was keen for the few places the IU Medical School allotted to black applicants. Realizing this, and perhaps seeing a future in basketball after all, Garrett switched his major to physical education and set his sights on coaching.

He dealt with the pressure on and off the court by remembering his mother's advice—"You can only put pressure on yourself"—and by shutting out all distractions. Early in the fall, he had begun dating Betty Guess, a sophomore physical education major from Madison, whom he had met at a dance at Elms House, where she lived. With her high cheekbones, wide, brown eyes, and quick mind, Betty was a catch. It was Betty who had accompanied George Taliaferro to integrate the Gables. Raised by her college-educated mother, who took in sewing and taught music in Madison's segregated schools, Betty was not only pretty, but also smart, strong-willed, and confident.

But once basketball season started, Bill told Betty he wouldn't be able to see her until spring. "I just don't have the time to court you," he told her, in the more formal language of the time. "I have to focus on school and basketball right now." Betty wasn't accustomed to being put on hold, but in Bill she saw something special, so she watched freshman scrimmages and waited. She would explain much later, "Bill was not going to fail—on the court, in the classroom, or in life."

14

The Hurryin' Hoosiers

BRANCH McCRACKEN HAD BARELY SPOKEN TO BILL GARRETT during the 1947–48 school year. "If you weren't on the varsity, you were less than zero to him," Bill Tosheff would later say. The coach rarely spoke to freshmen, but he had been watching. Having taken Garrett, McCracken wanted him to succeed. Moving up to the varsity was a big adjustment for any player; practices were harder, the travel was tiring, and the public attention unfamiliar. The IU varsity players and mainstream media also had mostly ignored Garrett as a freshman, but McCracken knew this year would be different. He wanted to make sure Bill was ready.

McCracken wanted to get Garrett out of the dorm and under the wing of an older black student-athlete. In late summer he spoke with Jim Roberson, a Kappa Alpha Psi fraternity brother of Bill's, a football lineman, and the track team's star shot-putter. In his mid-twenties and physically imposing, Roberson had been a Tuskegee Airman—a member of the famed and highly decorated unit of black pilots who trained at Tuskegee Institute during World War II. He was a junior at IU, a straight-A premed student who carried his Bible on track and football trips and was quick to help teammates, black and white, with academic or personal problems. Roby, as friends called him, was mature and focused—exactly what McCracken wanted for nineteen-year-old Bill Garrett. In August, when Roberson returned to campus for football practice, McCracken told him, "I'd like Bill Garrett to room with you this year." It was the closest the coach could bring himself to asking for a favor.

Sharing a small room and family atmosphere in a private home on West Eighth Street, on Bloomington's northwest side, Roby became Bill's best friend. Despite the difference in their ages and experience, their personalities and goals were similar. They were both easygoing yet competitive, lived quietly, and focused on sports and studies.

But Jim Roberson knew all about challenging segregation. Three years before Garrett moved in with him, Roberson and one hundred other black Army Air Corps officers had refused a direct order of their commanding officer in time of war—a violation of military law punishable by death—to protest segregation at Freeman Field, an Army Air Corps training facility outside Seymour, Indiana, thirty-five miles southeast of Bloomington. The "Freeman Mutiny" started with the local base commander's order—in apparent violation of a War Department policy—barring officer flight trainees, who were all black, from the base's officers' club, swimming pool, and tennis courts. Over a two-day period after the order was issued, 162 black officers, in small groups, entered the club only to find a military policeman waiting in the doorway to arrest them. Most of the arrested black officers were later called one by one before their commanding officer, handed a new directive barring them from the officers' club, and ordered to sign an attached statement saying they had read the directive and understood it. Roberson and one hundred other officers refused to sign. The "101 Club," as the black press called them, were court-martialed. After much negative media attention from mainstream as well as black newspapers across the country, the Army prosecuted only three of the hundred and one and convicted only one, Second Lieutenant Roger Terry, of jostling a military policeman (for which Terry was fined $150). But Roberson and the others had formal letters of reprimand placed in their Army files, ending any hope they might have had of military careers. Their protest inspired a Pulitzer Prize–winning book, James Gould Cozzens's *Guard of Honor,* and was a significant step toward President Harry Truman's 1948 Executive Order ending official segregation in most of the U.S. armed forces. Fifty years later, at the 1995 annual dinner of the Tuskegee Airmen, the Air Force formally apologized and announced it was removing the letters of reprimand from the men's files and restoring all rights, privileges, and property to Lieutenant Terry.

By the time Roberson got to IU, he was done protesting. He wanted to be a doctor, knew the IU Medical School admitted only two or three blacks per year, and was determined to be one of them. Success, not protest, he had come to believe, was the ultimate weapon against discrimination. It worked, but it wasn't conscience-free. "I wanted to get into med school, and I didn't want anything to interfere with that," Roberson explained five decades later. "So I got excellent grades, excelled at sports, made sure there was no way they couldn't take me. I was just single-minded, which bothers me today."

Branch McCracken had always been obsessed with preventing cliques from developing among his players. Partly to prevent his teams from "cliquing up," over the course of a season the coach personally made the room assignments when his team traveled, and he switched the players' roommates often. For the upcoming season, though, McCracken knew he could not randomly assign team members to room with Bill Garrett without risking serious dissension. Some of his varsity players were not happy to be sharing the basketball court with Garrett, let alone a hotel room. So he pulled Phil Buck, Gene Ring, and Bill Tosheff aside, asking each in turn if he would mind rooming with Garrett. Buck said he would be delighted; he considered Bill his best friend. Ring had no problem. Tosheff only looked at McCracken incredulously and asked, "S'matter, Coach? He snore?"

The coach who had appeared to ignore Garrett now seemed to be taking over his life. At the start of the 1948–49 season, McCracken insisted that every varsity player get a flu shot, drink at least two glasses of orange juice a day, and take two multivitamins. Like the other players, Garrett had to wear a hat whenever he was outside and was scolded if he left the fieldhouse without one. He was expected to get a minimum of eight hours of sleep every night, eat well but not too much, and tolerate McCracken's monthly checking of his grades and class attendance. This was on top of McCracken's physical training program, which was, as Roby had warned, "a whole different world from high school." Running was a key component of McCracken's basketball strategy. "My boys take a lot of pride in being able to run the other team into the floor," he once told an interviewer. "I've had my boys say to me between halves, 'Don't worry, Coach. We'll run 'em off the floor in the last ten minutes.' And they did. Our theory is never to let up."

Every afternoon during the preseason, varsity basketball players ran the three-mile cross-country course and football stadium steps. Every year, a day or two before the start of official basketball practice, McCracken held a race of the varsity players over the cross-country course. The top two finishers went to dinner with the coach and his wife; the bottom two ran the course again. McCracken watched the end of the race closely and formed conclusions about players' competitiveness and drive that could help or haunt a player all season. Veterans learned to hide in the middle of the pack, loafing for the first couple of miles and sprinting at the end when the coach was watching.

Running was just a prelude to the regular season. At practices, McCracken was always the first man on the floor, always in practice clothes—gray sweatshirt, dark slacks, and white sneakers, a stainless steel whistle around his neck. After two weeks of fundamentals and conditioning, McCracken put his team through long daily scrimmages, which he described as "fast, bruising, and punishing sessions, often lasting nearly an hour without rest periods." At any second a scrimmage might be stopped by the screech of McCracken's whistle, and the coach's deep voice would echo through the empty fieldhouse, pointing out a mistake ("That's an awful long way to run and still not score!") or handing out encouragement ("You're operatin,' you're operatin.' Now you're operatin', boys!") or instructions ("Talk to each other! Help each other out! Talk! Talk! Talk!"). McCracken rarely berated or humiliated his players on the practice floor, but he demanded total dedication, was quick to bench anyone who didn't give it, and could be physically intimidating in his private rages at players who violated his rules.

At the start of the 1948–49 season, McCracken's team had a morale problem. They were coming off a dismal previous season. There was tension between veteran players and rookies, between players from upstate cities and downstate towns, between teenagers away from home for the first time and grown men who had fought overseas. Five of the six returning lettermen were also military veterans approaching their mid-twenties. The previous year's leading scorers, Don Ritter and Lou Watson, were both back in 1948–49. Ritter, the only senior and team captain, was twenty-five years old and had flown combat missions in the Pacific as an Army Air Corps navigator. His hometown, Aurora, was a reputed sundown town. Watson, twenty-three, from Jeffersonville, where Frank Barnes had coached at the segregated white high school, had been a gunner's mate in the Navy and taken part in the invasion of Normandy. Their experiences, expectations, and attitudes were worlds apart from Bill Garrett's, adding to an already difficult mix.

The Big Ten was not high school. Everyone on the IU team had been a high school star, and no one wanted to be second fiddle now. Practices were battles to win a starting position, or at least more playing time, if necessary by roughing up a teammate and making him look bad. Up to a point, McCracken encouraged this, demanding constant intensity and praising all-out effort. Intensely competitive practices were part of the adjustment any new player had to make, and for Bill Garrett they had special complications.

In the fall of 1948, even in preseason pickup games, a few varsity players were throwing hard elbows, yelling at Garrett if the man he was guarding scored, and denying him the ball. The hostility continued after official practices began. Some of it was subtle: ignoring Garrett in the locker room. Some may have been unthinking: using insensitive language and making racial jokes in Garrett's presence. Some was unmistakable: unwillingness to room with Bill on the road. Again, the question nagged: "Am I being treated the same as everyone else?" The line between the normal struggle for playing time and the routine hazing of sophomores, on one hand, and racial discrimination, on the other, was sometimes unclear and confusing to him.

In time, Bill Garrett, some of his teammates, and practically all the black IU students who watched practices almost daily during the first weeks of the 1948–49 season, came to believe that much of the treatment Garrett was getting from a couple of the older players was racially motivated. "They couldn't come to grips with themselves to use team play," Garrett said years later, "play that would probably advance the whole team."

McCracken chose not to get involved. "I thought at the time that he should have probably come to my defense and straightened out a player or two at times," Garrett said in an interview with IU researchers years later, "but he didn't choose to do it." The coach greatly valued team morale. "There can be no jealousy or envy in a successful team," he wrote in his 1955 book, *Indiana Basketball.* "It's the coach's job to spot signs of these feelings and iron out personal antagonisms before they develop fully." But the mixture of race, competition, and hazing was too diffuse for the coach to iron out. McCracken thought the players needed to work through it themselves, if possible. Garrett had not yet proved himself on the varsity, and McCracken, who tried to avoid playing favorites, did not want to risk making a delicate situation worse by stepping in to defend the sophomore. Occasionally, in scrimmages, the coach blew his whistle and pointed out that Garrett had been open and should have gotten the ball, but he never confronted the problem directly, as Garrett thought he should have.

Friends and family told him, "Forget about it. They're just trying to intimidate you so you don't beat 'em out. If they think it'll work, they'll do it more. Just play your game." And that is what he did. Betty, who watched practices and home games, remembered, "Whatever he did at the beginning, he did by himself. He just had to make his own plays."

Garrett won a starting forward position in IU's 1948–49 season opener, his first college varsity game, an easy 61–48 win over DePauw on the night of December 4, 1948. Bill scored eight points and led the team in rebounding. They had played their usual running game, but their lineup remained an unsettled, uneasy mix. Besides Ritter and Watson, starting center Tom Schwartz was also an upperclassman and Army veteran. Garrett and Gene Ring, who started at guard, were upstart sophomores. Tosheff—a sophomore but a military veteran—had come off the bench to hit five quick shots against DePauw. It earned Tosheff a starting spot beside Garrett at forward—bumping senior captain Ritter from his starting position and raising the tension level on the team—for the next four games, in which IU beat Michigan State, Xavier, Drake, and Kansas State. Their record was 5–0 as they caught a train to St. Louis for their first road game, against Washington University on December 21, 1948.

Shelbyville, Indiana, the county seat where Bill Garrett grew up, shown here in 1950. COURTESY OF *THE SHELBYVILLE NEWS.*

Booker T. Washington Elementary School, the segregated elementary school that Bill Garrett, Emerson Johnson, and Marshall Murray attended. COURTESY OF THE SHELBY COUNTY LIBRARY.

First game of the 1947 Indiana high school state tournament: Bill Garrett controls the opening tip against Mt. Auburn at Shelbyville's Paul Cross Gym. Bill Breck is at right. COURTESY OF TOM KUHN AND *THE SHELBYVILLE NEWS.*

Crowd at the 1947 Indianapolis semifinal, won by Shelbyville after a racial incident at the team's hotel. COURTESY OF THE INDIANA HIGH SCHOOL ATHLETIC ASSOCIATION.

Arthur Trester, czar of Indiana high school basketball for thirty one years and the house that Trester built: Butler Fieldhouse, mecca of the state tournament and for decades the largest arena in the country built specifically for basketball. Now called Hinkle Fieldhouse, it is one of the oldest college arenas still in use.

Shelbyville's Emerson Johnson hits a 40-footer against East Chicago Washington in the afternoon game of the 1947 Final Four. Johnson hit six of these in a row in the championship game that night. INDIANA BASKETBALL HALL OF FAME VIDEO ARCHIVES, COURTESY OF THE INDIANA BASKETBALL HALL OF FAME.

EXHIBIT A?—Is this something of the intimidation of guards in basketball by officials? Emerson Johnson, of State Champion Shelbyville, drives in for a lay-up, but his guard, Garfield's Bobby Skitt (4), apparently fearing the whistle, lets him go and even takes pains to keep his arms back. The Giant Clyde Lovellette stays away, too. Others are Ronnie Bland (13) and Marshall Murphy (6).

Emerson Johnson drives past Terre Haute Garfield's Ronnie Bland (13) and Clyde Lovellette (16) in the 1947 state championship game. Note the picture's caption. Referee "intimidation" refers to the widespread belief among whites that referees gave special breaks to Shelbyville's black players to avoid being accused of racism by Shelbyville's "rowdy" fans. COURTESY OF THE INDIANAPOLIS STAR.

Six-ten Clyde Lovellette put back a rebound early in the 1947 state championship game. All five Shelbyville players are visible (left to right): Bill Garrett, Marshall Murray, Emerson Johnson, Bill Breck, and Hank Hemingway.

Courtesy of the Indiana Basketball Hall of Fame Museum.

Believed to be the first integrated basketball team in the country at any level— high school, college, or pro—to have three black starters, the Shelbyville Golden Bears celebrate the 1947 Indiana high school state championship. (Kneeling, from left): Louis Bower, Everett Burwell, Bill Breck, Emerson Johnson, Don Robinson; (standing, from left): Marshall Murray, Don Chambers, Bill Breedlove, Arthur "Doc" Barnett, Frank Barnes, Bill Garrett, Loren "Hank" Hemingway. *The Indianapolis News,* photo courtesy of *The Indianapolis Star.*

Shelbyville welcomes its state champions home. Marshall Murray leaves the fire truck with a pat on the back from fire chief Russ Klare, as Bill Garrett (top) waits his turn. COURTESY OF PAULA KARMIRE AND CHARLES JONES.

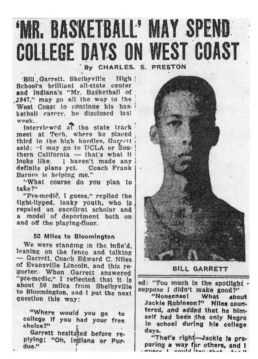

'MR. BASKETBALL' MAY SPEND COLLEGE DAYS ON WEST COAST

By CHARLES. S. PRESTON

Bill Garrett, Shelbyville High School's brilliant all-state center and Indiana's "Mr. Basketball of 1947," may go all the way to the West Coast to continue his basketball career, he disclosed last week.

Interviewed at the state track meet at Tech, where he placed third in the high hurdles, Garrett said: "I may go to UCLA or Southern California — that's what it looks like. I haven't made any definite plans yet. Coach Frank Barnes is helping me."

"What course do you plan to take?"

"Pre-medic, I guess," replied the tight-lipped, lanky youth, who is reputed an excellent scholar and a model of deportment both on and off the playing-floor.

50 Miles to Bloomington

We were standing in the infield, leaning on the fence and talking — Garrett, Coach Edward C. Niles of Evansville Lincoln, and this reporter. When Garrett answered "pre-medic," I reflected that it is about 50 miles from Shelbyville to Bloomington, and I put the next question this way:

"Where would you go to college if you had your free choice?"

Garrett hesitated before replying: "Oh, Indiana or Purdue."

BILL GARRETT

ed: "Too much in the spotlight - suppose I didn't make good?"

"Nonsense! What about Jackie Robinson?" Niles countered, and added that he himself had been the only Negro in school during his college days.

"That's right—Jackie is preparing a way for others, and I

A few weeks after Garrett was named Indiana's 1947 "Mr. Basketball," an *Indianapolis Recorder* article laments that he may play college basketball in California, if at all. Garrett told *The Recorder* that he would play at Indiana or Purdue if he had his "free choice." COURTESY OF THE INDIANAPOLIS RECORDER.

Faburn DeFrantz, Executive Director of Indianapolis's Senate Avenue YMCA, the largest black Y in the world, was determined to break the color line in the Big Ten with Bill Garrett. DeFrantz persuaded Indiana University president Herman Wells to press basketball coach Branch McCracken to give Garrett a chance to make the IU team if he was enrolled and on the campus. COURTESY OF THE INDIANA HISTORICAL SOCIETY.

Chairman of the IU Board of Trustees Ora Wildermuth strongly opposed integrating the Bloomington campus and was an obstacle to President Wells's efforts. Wildermuth wrote in 1945, "I am and shall always remain absolutely and utterly opposed to social intermingling of the colored race with the white. . . . [I]f the white race is silly enough to permit itself to intermarry with the black and thereby be swallowed up, it really, of course, doesn't deserve perpetuity. If a person has as much as 1/16th colored blood in him, even though the other 15/16ths may be pure white, yet he is colored." COURTESY OF THE INDIANA UNIVERSITY ARCHIVES.

Indiana University president Herman B Wells, shown greeting World War II veterans arriving on campus in the fall of 1947, used stealth and finesse to integrate IU. Pressed by DeFrantz, Wells told Coach McCracken that the only standard must be whether Bill Garrett was a good enough basketball player and that he would back McCracken no matter what the reaction was if McCracken would give Garrett a chance to make the team. COURTESY OF THE INDIANA UNIVERSITY ARCHIVES.

Jim Roberson, Tuskegee Airman, premed student, football and track athlete, and Garrett's friend and mentor. COURTESY OF THE INDIANA UNIVERSITY ARBUTUS YEARBOOK.

Tentatively accepted into the IU basketball program as a walk-on, Bill Garrett excelled. Here he hits a fast break lay-up against Illinois during his junior year. COURTESY OF THE INDIANA UNIVERSITY ARCHIVES.

Playing center at 6'2", Garrett set IU scoring and rebounding records. Here he rebounds against Ohio State, February 6, 1950. Photo by Frank Fisse, *The Indianapolis News,* courtesy of *The Indianapolis Star* and Frank Fisse.

Finally one of the guys. By his junior year, Garrett was widely accepted by his teammates, seen here celebrating Garrett's having hit the winning shot against Wisconsin, January 7, 1950. Others are (from left) Phil Buck, Bob Masters, Charley Meyer, Marvin Christie, Lou Watson, and Jerry Stuteville.
Photo by James Mahler, courtesy of Hoosier Times, Inc.

The Hurryin' Hoosiers of 1951, Garrett's senior year. To Garrett's left are three other starters: Gene Ring, Bill Tosheff, and Bob Masters. The fifth starter is Jack Brown, number 22. Phil Buck is number 12. The coaches are (left to right) Lou Watson, Branch McCracken, and Ernie Andres.

PHOTO COURTESY OF INDIANA UNIVERSITY ARBUTUS YEARBOOK.

Bill Garrett receives the Balfour Award for outstanding performance and conduct on the Indiana University basketball team, in the spring of 1951, his senior year.

PHOTO COURTESY OF THE INDIANA UNIVERSITY ARCHIVES.

Garrett and his mentors at Shelbyville's "Bill Garrett Night," March 19, 1951. (From left): Branch McCracken, Nate Kaufman, Frank Barnes, and Walter Fort.
Courtesy of Tom Kuhn and *The Shelbyville News*.

Bill and Betty on their wedding day, August 2, 1951.
Courtesy of Betty Garrett Inskeep.

Betty, Bill, and Leon Garrett, Bill's father, at the Garrett home in Shelbyville, August 3, 1951. Courtesy of Betty Garrett Inskeep.

Laura Garrett, Bill's mother, shown here with Bill and Betty's children. (Clockwise from left): Tina, Judy, Laurie (on floor), and Billy (on Laura's lap).
Courtesy of Betty Garrett Inskeep.

Garrett with "Goose" Tatum, left, and Walter Dukes, center, during his days with the Harlem Globetrotters. COURTESY OF THE HARLEM GLOBETROTTERS.

Coach Bill Garrett and his Crispus Attucks High School team celebrate the 1959 Indiana state championship. Garrett remains the only Indiana "Mr. Basketball" to have played on and coached a state championship team.
COURTESY OF THE INDIANA HIGH SCHOOL ATHLETIC ASSOCIATION.

Eight Who Came Before

Johnny Wilson

Bobby Milton

Chuck Harmon
COURTESY OF THE INDIANA BASKETBALL
HALL OF FAME MUSEUM.

Davage Minor
COURTESY OF CALUMET REGIONAL
ARCHIVES, INDIANA UNIVERSITY
NORTHWEST.

George Crowe
COURTESY OF THE UNIVERSITY OF
INDIANAPOLIS FREDERICK D. HILL
ARCHIVES.

Frank Clemons
COURTESY OF WARD M. CANADAY
CENTER FOR SPECIAL COLLECTIONS,
CARLSON LIBRARY, UNIVERSITY OF
TOLEDO.

Dave DeJernett
COURTESY OF THE UNIVERSITY OF
INDIANAPOLIS FREDERICK D. HILL ARCHIVES.

Jack Mann
COURTESY OF W. A. SWIFT
COLLECTION, ARCHIVES AND
SPECIAL COLLECTIONS RESEARCH
CENTER, BALL STATE UNIVERSITY
LIBRARIES.

For his first five games, Garrett's entry into college basketball had been quiet; IU fans had supported him, the mainstream press had paid no special attention, and opponents had not canceled games. But McCracken had worried about problems on the road for over a year, since he had first known Garrett would be joining the team. Before the start of the season, he had asked his senior student manager to call the hotels where the IU team would be staying, tell them about Garrett, and report back if any of the hotels balked. Usually these were the best hotels in town, for McCracken's teams traveled in comfort. In St. Louis, the Chase Hotel had bent its usual whites-only policy and said Garrett could stay there, provided he was accompanied by white players in the hotel's public areas, and he did not eat in the dining room. McCracken, still feeling his way, had reluctantly accepted the Chase's terms.

But the IU players did not get the word. The team arrived in St. Louis the day before the game and held a light workout. Returning to the Chase, a hungry group of players went directly to the main dining room where most were seated before they realized Garrett had been stopped at the door. They stared for a few seconds, trying to comprehend what was going on, until Tosheff stood up and said loudly, "If Bill can't eat here, nobody does."

He turned and walked out, and the others followed. Whatever reservations some might have had, they were not going to let an outsider tell them who could and could not be part of their group, especially after Tosheff had thrown down a gauntlet. As a team, the Hoosiers walked a few blocks until they found a Greek diner whose owner welcomed them. The following night, they beat Washington University, 51–44, for their sixth straight win. Garrett led IU's scoring with thirteen points, and Tosheff was second with eleven.

Hotels and restaurants were a constant problem that first varsity season. One hotel manager challenged McCracken to put team members' names in a hat, including his own, and to assign rooms randomly by a drawing. "If you're willing to share a room with him," the manager told McCracken, "then he can stay." With roommates chosen randomly, they stayed. Often the team could not eat in hotel dining rooms and, as in St. Louis, went looking for a restaurant that would take all of them. In Chicago to play DePaul, their hotel insisted Garrett room alone, use the back entrance and back stairs, and avoid the dining room, which he and the rest of the team members did.

Opposing players, fans, and coaches gave Garrett a hard time during that first varsity season. Often it was unusually loud booing or harder than normal elbows. Occasionally it was more direct. McCracken would later tell the story of one opposing coach shouting repeatedly at his players, when Garrett had the ball, "Get the nigger! Who's guarding the nigger?"

These incidents had to hurt and anger Garrett, but he didn't show it, and he never admitted it. He alluded to them with his family and closest friends, but, as in high school, to everyone else he appeared to shrug off the taunts and slights and play harder. All his life, he held it inside. Years later he would tell an interviewer, almost casually, "Of course, having a Negro player presented problems for the coach as far as dining room facilities."

Indiana's 6–0 start ended after St. Louis. They lost to Butler in the first game of the holiday Hoosier Classic, and then beat Notre Dame in the second game. After beating Marquette in Bloomington on January 3, the Hoosiers started the Big Ten season with a record of 8–1, ranked eighth in the country. Then it quickly went downhill. They won two of their first four Big Ten games, and then lost four straight—on the road to Minnesota, DePaul (not a Big Ten game), and Ohio State, and at home to Michigan. By mid-February their record was 2–5 in the Big Ten and 10–6 overall, and they were no longer ranked nationally.

No big-time college basketball coach tolerates a losing streak lightly. McCracken took a hard look at his team. Despite the show of unity against outsiders, the team was still split along veteran-versus-rookie lines, and some of the veterans did not fully accept Garrett. All season, Garrett had solidly held one of the starting forward positions while Ritter and Tosheff battled for the second starting forward spot. It was obvious that Garrett could be moved to center—the position he had played most of his life—so as to open up a second starting forward position, ending the Ritter-Tosheff standoff. But to start at center, Garrett would have to displace Tom Schwartz—another upperclassman and Army veteran and, like Garrett, a former Mr. Basketball.

McCracken had to make decisive changes. The veterans and soph-omores did not mesh well. Most of the veterans were slow; they played an older style of basketball, and they carried a mind-set formed by previous mediocre seasons, a mind-set that pervaded even the IU administration. In early February 1949, the chairman of the IU Faculty Athletics Committee had put his low expectations in writing, telling Herman Wells in a memorandum, "For the next two years we can expect only average seasons in basketball because we do not have the material to compete with the 'giants' we are encountering."

The sophomores played a different game. They were quicker, hun-grier, more willing to press all over the court on defense and dive for loose balls. Untroubled by Garrett's presence, they were also not accustomed to losing in an IU uniform and were willing to play all out to avoid it.

Following IU's fourth straight loss—54–47 to Michigan in Bloom-ington—McCracken went with the hungry ones. He benched Ritter and replaced him with Tosheff at one forward. He benched Schwartz and moved Garrett to center. He moved Jerry Stuteville, a junior who in personality and playing style belonged with the rookies, into the second forward position. For the rest of the season, IU's starting lineup would be Tosheff and Stuteville at the forwards, Garrett at cen-ter, and Gene Ring and Lou Watson, the only veteran to keep his starting position, at the guards.

It was an extraordinarily small lineup, even by the standards of 1949. Only Watson reached six-five. Garrett, at center, was six-two, Tosheff was six feet tall, Ring was six-one, and Stuteville was six-three. "We're a small team," McCracken acknowledged at the time, "and what we lack in height we have to make up for in speed, accuracy, and deceptiveness." And they did, playing a swarming defense all over the floor and running fast breaks every time they got their hands on the ball. McCracken had been developing the fast break for years, and in this new group he had the right players for it: Garrett in a sin-gle motion rebounding and swinging the ball to Tosheff on the left side, Tosheff passing to Ring sprinting up the middle, and Ring blind-passing to Garrett racing the length of the floor up the right side for a layup—all before an opponent could make the transition from offense to defense, often without the ball touching the floor. "When Bill went for the basket, you just saw a streak," Tosheff recalled. The fans loved it, and the sportswriters revived an old nickname that had been coined for McCracken's 1940 NCAA champions, "the Hurryin' Hoosiers."

This new lineup reeled off four straight Big Ten victories and won five of their last six games. Weighed down by their midseason losses, the 1948–49 IU team finished fourth in the Big Ten, with a record of 7–7 in the conference, 14–8 overall. Garrett, the team's leading scorer and rebounder for the season, had won his coach's respect. "A lot of the pressure was on him," Branch McCracken said years later. "But he was an exceptional guy. He handled discrimination on the floor and off the floor without changing expression."

The same starting lineup returned for Garrett's junior year. Unlike the previous season, this was a team of Garrett supporters. New sophomores had joined the varsity excited to play with Bill. Veterans who had given him a hard time had graduated, quit, or changed their views. Lou Watson, the senior captain of the 1949–50 team, who many believed had been slow to warm up to Garrett the year before, and Jerry Stuteville, the other senior starter, who had welcomed Bill from the beginning, joined Tosheff, Ring, and Buck as Garrett's defenders. In an early home game against the University of Arkansas—a rare inter-regional matchup at the time—some of the Razorbacks taunted Garrett. Midway through the first half, when Garrett drove for a layup an Arkansas player undercut him as he sailed through the air. When play resumed, Watson and Stuteville pinned the offender between them, and Stuteville looked at him nose to nose. "You fucking hill-ape, you try that again and I'm gonna knock your teeth down your throat." A few minutes later the same Arkansas player caught a sharp Garrett elbow to the mouth. IU won 86–50, led by Garrett's twenty points, and word spread, "Bill Garrett can take care of himself."

On the road it was also different this second season. Big Ten players and fans were more accustomed to seeing Garrett. Some had come to respect him; all had learned he could not be rattled by taunting. The IU basketball staff had more experience in picking hotels, and the players had a better sense of when to stick together. Garrett was included—often a target—in the easy teasing among teammates that marked acceptance. During pregame meals, when McCracken forbade even smiles, Tosheff crossed his eyes and made faces at Garrett, forcing Bill to look at his lap, until, after a few games, Garrett learned to sit beside Tosheff instead of opposite him. When they roomed together on the road, Tosheff told Garrett ghost stories and took delight when Garrett jumped at Spike Dixon's knock on their door during bed checks. On a long flight to Oregon, Tosheff, a former military aviator, persuaded the pilots of their Roscoe Turner Airlines DC-3 to let him sit in the co-pilot's seat and shout back to Garrett, whose fear of flying was well known, "Look, Bones, I'm flying the plane!" He had become one of the guys. When McCracken growled at his team in practice, "You're gonna stay here and work till you're black in the face!" Garrett could ask, "Does that mean I can go home now?"

But this team was so small that to win they had to be nearly perfect every game, something no team could sustain over a whole season. After winning their first ten games and ranking second nationally, they lost five of their last twelve. All the losing games were close—the total difference between the Hoosiers and their five opponents was fourteen points. Four of the five losses were on the road. They had reached the top of college basketball but could not quite stay there. All the heart and conditioning in the world, it seemed, could take them only so far with a front line that averaged less than six-two. They finished the 1950 season with a record of 17–5, ranked twentieth in the country. Again, as in 1949, Garrett was the team's leading scorer and rebounder.

The *Indiana Daily Student* suggested that Garrett should be an All-American, but Bill was realistic. "Our team's record really isn't good enough for members to be All-American," he told the *Daily Student*. He was starting to look ahead to life after college. During a Christmas break conversation with Bill Breck, Garrett had talked about his chances of getting a coaching job, and though there were no blacks in the newly formed National Basketball Association, the black press was reporting that some might be selected in the 1950 NBA draft. He knew All-American status and the publicity that went with it would boost his chances to play professionally, and he was looking forward to his senior season. "Our team has played together for three years," he told the IU paper, "and most of us will be back the next year. We have great teamwork, something many college teams never achieve."

After basketball season, every year the state of Indiana looked forward to the Indianapolis 500. Practice and qualifications went on the entire month of May as excitement built for the race on Memorial Day. In 1950 almost two hundred thousand were expected to turn out under threatening skies. A lucky few would watch the race from the newly built upper-deck stands, and more would fill the old bleachers scattered around the outside of the 2.5-mile track. But the real fun was on Sixteenth Street, where thousands of fans lined up their cars and then, as soon as the gates opened, raced across the vast infield in search of a spot from which to watch the race or sleep off the all-nighter.

Around three o'clock on the morning of May 30, 1950, George Taliaferro, the black IU halfback whose visits to the Gables had integrated the popular IU hangout, was awakened by a loud knock on the door of his house on Bloomington's west side, accompanied by muffled shouts of "Open up! Taliaferro, come on, damn it, let's go." It was Garrett's basketball teammate Jerry Stuteville. He, Taliaferro, and Slug Witicki, another football player, were planning to attend the 500 together, leaving Bloomington at 4:00 A.M. in order to find a spot in the infield. But Stuteville had been celebrating the end of his last final exam at a fraternity party and wanted to leave earlier. Taliaferro, trying to buy time and to keep Stuteville from driving, told him to go get Witicki and come back. "I was thinking that one of us would drive and the other would hold Jerry down," Taliaferro remembered. But neither Taliaferro nor Witicki had a phone, so they couldn't confer, and Witicki didn't want to ride with Stuteville any more than Taliaferro did. "Slug's not going because I won't let him drive," Stuteville told Taliaferro on his return. "Well, I'm not going either," Taliaferro replied, "because I know you won't let me drive." "To hell with you guys, I'm going anyway," Stuteville said, pushing Taliaferro away and ignoring his concern. He got back in his car and headed north on State Road 37.

A few miles south of Indianapolis there was a bridge wide enough for only one car at a time. As Stuteville barreled along, approaching the bridge, a truck approached from the other side. In a split second Stuteville had to decide whether to hit the brakes hard or floor it and try to squeeze through. On the basketball court he had been what they called "a slicer"—a player who could spot and slip through small holes in the defense—and this was the kind of decision he had made a thousand times before. Confident of his instinct and heading for the Indianapolis 500, Stuteville was not one to back down.

He almost made it. But as he left the bridge the truck entered it, and they collided head-on. Ten days short of his college graduation, Jerry Stuteville died of a broken neck. He had been among the first to welcome Bill Garrett, and his combative, single-minded play had typified the Hurryin' Hoosiers. In shocked silence his friends and teammates attended his funeral in Attica. "You know," George Taliaferro said fifty years later, "I'm seventy-three and I've had a tremendously fulfilling life, but that last image of Jerry shucking me off is indelible to me. I don't go to the Indy 500 because of it. When Jerry died, it just ruined my spirits for the race forever."

In the fall of 1950, senior starters Garrett, Tosheff, and Ring were joined by Jack Brown, a six-four forward who had seen limited playing time on the 1947 and 1948 IU teams before taking off for two years of military service. Brown was a rebounder more than a scorer, an all-out player as Stuteville had been. The 1950–51 starters would be Brown and Tosheff at the forwards, Garrett at center, Gene Ring and Bob Masters—a six-three junior who had been the state's 1948 Mr. Basketball—at the guards, with Phil Buck and Sam Miranda, another junior, coming off the bench. They were still small; they would again have to swarm and claw; but in the previous season they had shown they could win, up to a point. By mid-December, in the Associated Press's first rankings for the 1950–51 season, Indiana was fourth in the country, behind only Kentucky, Bradley, and North Carolina State.

The 1950–51 Hoosiers won their first six games, and by Christmas they ranked second to Kentucky in the AP poll. A few days later they lost at Bradley by two points, but they won their next seven straight games and by the end of January they were 13–1 overall, 6–0 in the Big Ten, and third in the AP national rankings, behind Kentucky and Oklahoma A&M. They had beaten their closest conference rival, Illinois, in Bloomington, but they still had to play them in Champaign. Winning the conference was the key to their season, since in 1951 only the Big Ten champion could go to the sixteen-team NCAA Tournament. As in Shelbyville in 1947, the publicity from doing well in the postseason tournament could greatly help Garrett's future prospects.

Some sportswriters questioned whether Indiana could win against opponents playing a slow, deliberate game. Michigan State tried it, but the Hoosiers beat them in East Lansing, 47–37. Then Minnesota, third in the Big Ten behind IU and Illinois, tried it in Bloomington, but the Hoosiers—perhaps to discourage that style of play—turned the tables and held the ball for eleven minutes of the second half, winning 32–26. It ended opponents' slow-down tactics but set Minnesota on a course of revenge; two weeks later they beat IU by seven points in a fast-paced game in Minneapolis. The loss put IU in a tie with Illinois for the Big Ten lead and dropped them to sixth in the AP's national rankings. They beat Iowa and Northwestern in quick succession and prepared for their showdown with Illinois on February 19, 1951, in the game that likely would decide which team would be the Big Ten champion and go on to the national tournament.

Configured like a theater in the round, Illinois's Huff Gymnasium was a hard place for visiting teams to play. The first-row fans sat so close to the playing floor they could pull the leg hairs—and in at least one case drop a lighted cigarette down the trunks—of visiting players standing in front of them to in-bound the ball. All seven thousand who filled Huff Gym for the IU-Illinois game knew it was for the Big Ten championship, for the right to go on to the postseason national tournament, possibly for the number-one national ranking, and for year-long bragging rights between the neighboring states.

The game was intense. Gene Ring and Illinois's Irv Bemoras traded punches as both dove for a loose ball. IU led 36–35 at halftime. Garrett scored fourteen points in the first half, but already he had four fouls. Trying to avoid a fifth, Garrett scored only two more points in the second half. With seven minutes to go and IU leading by two, Garrett was called for his fifth and final foul. Tosheff and Sam Miranda (who was hitting set shots "from somewhere just outside Bloomington," the *Daily Student* reported) kept the Hoosiers in the game, but with Garrett out Illinois took over and won, 71–65.

The win put Illinois one game ahead of Indiana in the Big Ten, but the Hoosiers still had a slim chance of going to the tournament. Each team had four Big Ten games remaining; if IU won all four of its games, and Illinois lost one of its four, then Indiana and Illinois would end the season tied for first in the Big Ten, and Indiana would go to the NCAA Tournament because Illinois had gone the previous year.

Both teams won their next three games in quick succession. On March 5, 1951, Indiana played Wisconsin in Bloomington, their last game of the season and the IU seniors' last home game. They still had a chance to tie for the Big Ten title if Illinois lost at Michigan State that same evening. Throughout the IU-Wisconsin game the public-address announcer periodically reported Illinois–Michigan State scores: Michigan State was leading at the half and was still ahead midway through the second half. Each announcement brought loud cheers from the IU crowd. With five minutes to go in the Indiana-Wisconsin game and IU leading by eighteen points, the PA system crackled during a time-out, "Ladies and gentlemen, here is the final score from East Lansing." The fieldhouse fell silent, and the announcer continued, "Illinois 49, Michigan State 43."

In an instant, the mood in the fieldhouse turned from hopeful to stunned. The Wisconsin game was meaningless. No matter what, Indiana would finish second in the Big Ten and would not play in a postseason tournament. Win or lose, this was the seniors' last game.

Branch McCracken had a tradition. Every year, near the end of the last home game, if the score was not close the coach would take his seniors out of the game, one by one, for their final curtain calls. This year the gesture had special meaning. This undersized, overachieving group had won the hearts of their coach and fans as no other IU team had done before, and as few, if any, would again. They had won 19 of 22 games, 12 of 14 in the Big Ten, 7 of 8 against nonconference opponents, 10 straight at home, and 9 of 12 on the road. They had beaten three major conference champions. In the final AP Coaches' Poll, Indiana ranked seventh in the country.* "No one has played every minute of every game with more intensity than did the boys of

---

*The first six teams were Kentucky, Oklahoma A&M, Columbia, Kansas State, Illinois, and Bradley. IU had beaten Kansas State and Illinois in the first of their two games, and had lost at Bradley by two points.

'50–'51," *Indianapolis Times* sportswriter Vic Rensberger wrote the next day. "They played their hearts out and worked their tails off," McCracken later said of his team.

It was a sad, proud, emotionally drained crowd of ten thousand that cheered loudly when Jack Brown and Phil Buck left the game. Then came Gene Ring, to intense applause. Tension built until, with two minutes to go, the clock stopped for a free throw and McCracken waved in Don Luft, a reserve center. The instant Luft peeled off his red satin warm-ups and hopped onto the raised floor the crowd knew what was coming, and by the time Luft reached midcourt and touched hands with Bill Garrett, all ten thousand were on their feet. The outpouring, impulsive and cathartic, went on for almost two minutes, momentarily freezing referees and players as Garrett stepped down from the court to the bench, then back up again onto the edge of the floor, looking at his coach, his feet, and his teammates until they surrounded him protectively and the referees stepped in to break the spell out on the court. It was a moment those who were there would remember the rest of their lives.

As the players left the floor, the band struck up the song they played after every home game. Set to the tune of Cornell's more famous "Far Above Cayuga's Waters," it could sound joyous or sad, depending on the game's outcome. This was a win, but the song was poignant. Fans stood silently, some in tears, as Garrett and his teammates swept past them to the red door of the training room. As one sportswriter put it, "From Hammond to Hanover, from Fort Wayne to Farmersville, strong men, little children and old women wept without shame. The more optimistic may say, 'there's always next year.' But for the majority of Hoosierdom, the fighting spirit of this season's fighting IU five will live in sports history. Never before have so few men done so much with so little height."

Two days later, Garrett, Ring, and Buck drove to Indianapolis in Buck's '39 Chevy. They dropped Bill off to see Betty while Buck and Ring went on to Butler Fieldhouse to watch an NBA game. Afterward, they picked up Garrett and headed back to Bloomington. Just south of Indianapolis, on State Road 37, they pulled into a diner with a small marquee announcing, "Hurryin' Hoosiers' Fans Welcome."

The three had just settled into a booth in the corner when the lone waiter came out from behind the counter and stood in front of them. Before they could say they just wanted burgers, the waiter said, cocking his head toward Garrett, "I can feed the two of you, but not him." Blindsided, the three friends just looked at each other, got up, and walked out. Buck and Ring tried to tell Garrett the guy was a jerk and they weren't all that hungry anyway. But perhaps because of that week's emotional roller coaster, this incident bothered him more than most. Garrett apologized to his friends because they couldn't eat, and sat in the backseat rubbing his head while tears rolled down his cheeks.

15

Coming Home

THE DAY AFTER THE INCIDENT AT THE INDIANAPOLIS DINER
the *Washington Post* announced the UPI's selection of Bill Garrett as
an All-American. A few weeks earlier, he had been named an All-
American by the *Sporting News*.* These were the first fruits of seeds
Branch McCracken and Indiana newspapers had been planting all
season. The *Indiana Daily Student* had run editorials lamenting
Garrett's lack of national recognition, one saying, "Perhaps the finest
ball player in the country is going unnoticed." Near the end of the
season the *Daily Student* had launched a campaign to get IU students
and fans to write the basketball powers that be, asking them to name
Garrett an All-American. "Perhaps in this way," the editors wrote, "we

---

*The same issue of the *Sporting News* named Sherman White, of Long Island University,
the 1951 Player of the Year. A few days later, White, along with several other college
players from the New York area, was arrested for having shaved points in college games.
In a short time, as part of the same national college basketball scandal, Bill Spivey, of
Kentucky, and Gene Melchiorre, of Bradley, both, like Sherman White, 1951 consensus
first-team All-Americans, were indicted for point-shaving during their college careers.
White, Spivey, and Melchiorre were barred from the NBA for life. But of the three, only
Sherman White, who was black, served time in prison. Spivey was tried and acquitted.
Melchiorre and two other Bradley players were given suspended sentences by a judge
who called them "repentant" and referred to their "excellent backgrounds." The same
judge, in sentencing White (who pleaded guilty immediately and expressed great
remorse) to a year at Rikers Island, called him a "hardened criminal and a semi-moron
who didn't belong in college." White's name was, and remains, removed from most
lists of 1951 All-Americans.

can reward a boy who unselfishly contributed the sum total of his splendid ability and energy toward making IU a national basketball power—and making those games in the Fieldhouse among the more exciting and memorable occasions of our lives." McCracken drove home the point, telling sportswriters all season, "He's an All-American if I've ever seen one."

In truth, there was no hard and fast definition of what an All-American was, or who was one. Any newspaper, magazine, or institution could issue a press release announcing its All-American team. In the eyes of most of the country, though, it was the better-known, mainstream institutions that anointed legitimate All-Americans, and among them there was a loose pecking order. In the top tier were AP, UPI, the National Association of Basketball Coaches, the Helms Foundation, *Sporting News,* and Converse, the maker of gym shoes. Then came national magazines and individual newspapers. Most named both a "first team" and a "second team"—their picks of the best and second-best five-man lineups in the country. Players tapped by the largest number of prestigious organizations were called "consensus All-Americans"—consensus first team or consensus second team. To be named a consensus All-American made a player famous, at least briefly, enhanced his value as a future pro, and created a calling card for a lifetime.

Garrett had good credentials for this chase. For three years he had been the leading scorer and rebounder on IU teams that improved steadily until they were among the best in the country, and he had done it while battling opposing centers nearly a foot taller. By mid-March, when all the returns were in, Garrett was a consensus second-team All-American—recognized among the top ten college players in the country and among the country's three best college centers, in a close race with Kansas' six-ten Clyde Lovellette and Kentucky's seven-foot Bill Spivey.*

For two months in the spring of 1951, awards and recognition came to Garrett in rapid succession and everything seemed to be breaking his way. His teammates voted him IU's most valuable

---

*Some of the All-American lists placed Garrett at forward, even though he had only played a few games at that position, making it possible for there to be three consensus All-American centers on the two teams.

player. Big Ten coaches and sportswriters voted him onto the All Big Ten first team. He received Indiana University's basketball Balfour Award, given annually to one player in each sport for outstanding performance and conduct. At the Hoosiers' end-of-season banquet, Branch McCracken called him "as great a player as Indiana has ever had." At Faburn DeFrantz's invitation, he spoke at the Senate Avenue Y's final Monster Meeting of 1951. Shelbyville threw an "All-American Bill Garrett Night," with hundreds crowding the Elks Club and thousands more listening on local FM radio. The featured speaker was to have been Ezzard Charles, from Cincinnati, fresh from defending his heavyweight title against Joe Louis's attempted comeback, but a blizzard closed the roads all over south central Indiana. As the crowd waited, Charles cabled a belated apology: The Michigan Road was impassable. McCracken was more accustomed to driving the state in bad weather, or maybe more motivated. He had driven the sixty miles up from Bloomington in the snow just to sit at the head table with Garrett. When word came that the heavyweight champ had begged off, McCracken agreed to speak extemporaneously.

It was almost five years to the day since the IU coach had looked out over a crowd of about the same size in Anderson and told them Johnny Wilson could not make his team. The world had changed since then, and so had McCracken. He quoted Nate Kaufman's admonition, "I'm not sending him down there to sit on the bench," and his own response, "I never promised any boy he could play, but if he's good enough, he'll play." He acknowledged having been concerned about how his players would react, and he told of their growing acceptance when they saw "Bill could play, that's the first requirement." But "more than just playing," McCracken, echoing the standard Branch Rickey had laid down for Jackie Robinson, told the crowd Garrett was "a perfect example of a sportsman and gentleman." McCracken never spelled out the real subject, but the audience understood.

Despite his having been left off the ballot, college coaches elected Garrett to the College All-Star team as a write-in, and that spring he starred with the All-Stars in games around the country against the Harlem Globetrotters. The play was rough. According to the *Indiana Daily Student,* in one game Garrett was mauled by his Trotter defender "like a professional wrestler making love to his best girl." But Garrett loved extending his playing season, and when the tour came to Indianapolis in mid-April he scored fourteen points, missed only one shot, and again received a long, impassioned standing ovation from a record crowd of fourteen thousand at the Indiana State Fairgrounds Coliseum.

In those heady weeks from February to April, it seemed that finally Garrett had grown into his trailblazer role and overcome his unease in the spotlight. He could enjoy the recognition he was receiving and hope that in the future his path might be a little smoother. As he told a *Daily Student* reporter, "It's great. Man, it's really great. I think it will be easier getting a job now than it might have been."

And then the cheering stopped.

A week after he had received a standing ovation from a record crowd in Indianapolis, the Indianapolis Olympians snubbed Garrett in the 1951 NBA draft, using their first three picks to take players who were unknown in Indiana and would never see a minute of action in an NBA game,* and their fourth pick to take Bill Tosheff, Garrett's IU teammate. The Olympians had finished next to last in their division in 1950–51, while averaging about thirty-five hundred fans a game at butler Fieldhouse. Yet they were blind even to the business advantages of drafting Bill Garrett from Shelbyville, twenty-five miles down the road, the All-American star of IU's Hurryin' Hoosiers whose crowd appeal had been demonstrated at the Coliseum in Indianapolis a few days before the draft.

The Olympians were player-owned; their principal owners, who were also their star players, had been members of the gold-medal U.S. Olympic basketball team in 1948. These same players—Ralph Beard, Alex Groza, Wallace Jones, and Cliff Barker—had also been starters on Adolph Rupp's 1948 and 1949 NCAA champions at the University of Kentucky. Before the start of their 1950–51 season they had refused to

---

*The Olympians' first three draft picks were Marcus Freiberger, of the University of Oklahoma; Scotty Steagall, of Millikin University; and Glenn Kammeyer, of Central Missouri State University.

let Johnny Wilson—Indiana's 1946 Mr. Basketball, a former small-college All-American, and a member of the Harlem Globetrotters—even try out for the team.* Indiana's other NBA team also snubbed Garrett. The Fort Wayne Zollner-Pistons—the forerunners of today's Detroit Pistons—used their first- and second-round picks in the 1951 draft to take two white players who would average less than three points a game as reserves over two NBA seasons.

Overlooked in Indiana, Garrett was drafted by the Boston Celtics in the second round of selections, making him the third black ever to be drafted for the NBA. The Celtics had integrated the NBA a year earlier when their owner, Walter Brown, had shocked his peers by announcing Boston's choice of Chuck Cooper, a six-five center from Duquesne University. After a moment of stunned silence, one of the other owners had found his voice, "Walter, don't you know he's a colored boy?" Brown's reply became part of NBA lore, "I don't give a damn if he's striped, plaid or polka-dot! Boston takes Charles Cooper of Duquesne!"†

The NBA had long maintained its own gentleman's agreement against black players. The pro league was in its infancy, with franchises struggling along from one year to the next. Many owners feared black players would drive away white fans, and they did not want to upset the unspoken détente between the NBA and the far more popular and successful Harlem Globetrotters.

In the 1920s, Abe Saperstein, a five-three white parks employee from Chicago, had started the Trotters on a shoestring. Wearing red, white, and blue uniforms sewn in his father's tailor's shop, Saperstein and his players crammed into his unheated Model T for wintertime barnstorming tours around the Midwest, where they challenged local

---

*In October 1951, Groza and Beard were arrested for shaving points during their college basketball careers at Kentucky. The NBA president announced they were barred from the NBA for life and had thirty days to dispose of their stock in the Olympians and "get out of town." The franchise folded after the 1952–53 season.

†The Washington Capitols then drafted Earl Lloyd of West Virginia State, in the ninth round. Five weeks after that, the New York Knicks bought the contract of Nat "Sweetwater" Clifton from the Harlem Globetrotters. Cooper, Lloyd, and Clifton all became NBA trailblazers in 1950: Cooper as the first black to be drafted; Clifton as the first to sign an NBA contract; and Lloyd as the first to play in an NBA game, when he took the floor for the Capitols in Rochester, New York, on October 31, 1950, one day before the rest of the NBA season began.

talent in small-town gyms and church basements, slept in the car, and barely got by from one game to the next. The clowning routines that would become their trademark developed as a survival technique, to mask their basketball superiority and to win over white crowds, after they discovered it was risky for five blacks to blow into small midwestern towns and demolish the local white stars.

By the early 1950s, the Globetrotters' combination of skill and flair had made Saperstein a rich man and the Trotters by far the most popular sports act in the world. The State Department used them to promote the image of the United States abroad and designated them "Ambassadors of Good Will"; three Globetrotter "units" were playing seven days a week almost year-round, and they still couldn't reach all the fans who wanted to see them. While the NBA averaged thirty-five hundred a game—about the same attendance as Shelbyville High School—the Globetrotters could fill the biggest stadiums in the world just by showing up.

Saperstein, who wanted to own a white NBA team, built goodwill with the league by scheduling Trotter exhibitions together with regular-season NBA games—doubleheaders that filled arenas essentially as a favor to the NBA teams. As the NBA slowly began to integrate, Saperstein was not happy about having his best players poached by a fledgling NBA he was helping to survive. Saperstein is reported to have threatened to boycott the arenas of NBA teams that signed black players he was interested in, including a threat to Walter Brown to boycott the Boston Garden if the Celtics signed Chuck Cooper in 1950.*

The Trotters had scouted Garrett throughout the 1951 season. In March 1951 Saperstein told the *Pittsburgh Courier*, "My reps . . . tell me he is the best pivot man they have seen since Charley Cooper." He could not have been happy when Garrett, like Cooper, went with the Celtics instead.

---

*Such threats appear to have been only momentary outbursts. There is no evidence Saperstein followed through on them, and the Globetrotters continued to play in the Boston Garden. Indeed, although Cooper was under contract to the Globetrotters at the time the Celtics drafted him, a week after the 1950 NBA draft Saperstein sent Cooper a telegram saying, "Considered carefully circumstances surrounding draft considering opportunity initial colored performer NBA. Agreed if satisfactory to you to relinquish my claims your services to Boston Celtics. . . . To me you were you are and you always will be a Harlem Globetrotter."

•   •   •

Done with college basketball, in the spring of 1951 Garrett turned his attention to his growing relationship with Betty Guess. Betty had graduated from IU a year ahead of Bill and had taken a job teaching swimming and modern dance at the Phyllis Wheatley YWCA in Indianapolis. For Betty, it was the fulfillment of a longtime ambition to teach black children to swim. Growing up, she and the rest of Madison's black children had been barred from the Crystal Beach public swimming pool. They swam instead in Crooked Creek, near the local glue factory. Betty was a strong swimmer, but others were not. Every year, all over the Midwest, black children barred from public swimming pools drowned in unguarded rivers and canals. Betty viewed swimming as a powerful symbol of the safety as well as the opportunities that came with integration.

On Mother's Day 1951, Bill was visiting Betty and her mother in Madison. Unlike other local black families, the Guesses lived on Main Street, near the town's business district, a couple of blocks from a jewelry store owned by a white family with a son at IU. Before leaving Bloomington for the weekend, Bill had asked the young man if his family would open their jewelry store for him that Sunday morning. The family was happy to do a favor for the IU basketball star. On Sunday morning Bill slipped out of the Guess home and walked up Main Street to the jewelry store, where he bought a small diamond ring with his earnings from the Globetrotters–All-Stars "World Series of Basketball." He and Betty had talked of marriage, but the ring was still a surprise. That summer, after he had graduated from IU with a degree in physical education and a minor in business, Bill and Betty were married in Madison.

He was graduated, newly married, and drafted by the Boston Celtics. Much later, Garrett would say, "I thought then I had it made; I know now I don't." In late June he received a draft notice from the Army. The Korean War was in full swing, and his prospect of a future with the Celtics did not impress the draft board. Garrett spent the summer with Betty in Indianapolis, looking halfheartedly into possible Army deferments and trying to figure out whether he would be going to

Boston or the Army. The Celtics did not offer help, and Bill did not ask for it. There was little anyone in the Celtics organization could or would have done anyway; after all, another Boston athlete, Ted Williams, was already flying fighter jets in Korea.

In August, Garrett teamed up with his high school teammate Emerson Johnson on the Senate Avenue Y's entry in a two-week basketball tournament held at Lockfield Gardens. The twenty-two-acre Lockfield project was at the center of Indianapolis's black community in 1951. Its basketball court, "the Dust Bowl," was the place where rising black basketball players honed their skills, punctuating good shots by shouting "Bill Garrett!" Battling Indiana's best street players, Garrett's Senate Avenue Y team advanced to the semifinal round, where they lost 56–55, as Garrett fouled out and Johnson led all scorers with twenty-four points. As the *Recorder*'s headline put it, "All-Americans Are Just Players in Lockfield Dust Bowl."

In October, Garrett began Army basic training at Fort Leonard Wood, Missouri. Betty soon took a job teaching physical education at a segregated school in Pine Bluff, Arkansas, thinking it might put her closer to Bill. But shortly afterward he shipped out for Japan, and in the spring Betty returned to IU to work on a master's degree.

Garrett worried about possible combat in Korea, but instead he spent most of his hitch playing basketball and running recreation leagues for the Army's Special Services at Camp Drake, outside Tokyo. It was good duty, but he was homesick and missed Betty terribly, as he poured out in a letter to Gene Ring, "Every guy over here, married or single, would give their right arm to be back there in the States. The thing that hurt me most was having to leave my wife. I was married three months when I got those papers, so you know about how I felt." Adding a point his IU teammate would understand, he told Ring, "We won a game last night 89–33, so that gives you an idea of the competition."

Honorably discharged from the Army in August 1953, Garrett returned home eager to join the Boston Celtics. Both the Celtics and the NBA were on the rise. At the end of the 1952–53 season, the Celtics had almost won their division and had done well in the NBA playoffs. Coach Red Auerbach had built an exciting team around guards Bob Cousy and Bill Sharman and center "Easy Ed" Macauley, with Chuck Cooper starting at one of the forwards. Practice would begin in September for the 1953–54 season. It would be a whole new life for Bill and Betty in Boston, where Bill would be playing basketball at the highest competitive level on the parquet floor of the Boston Garden.

But when Garrett got home, a shock was waiting. The Celtics had released him, and the Globetrotters were offering a contract. NBA teams still limited the number of blacks on their rosters, and the Celtics already had two, Chuck Cooper and Don Barksdale. Possibly the Celtics questioned whether Garrett could easily make the switch to forward or guard—as he would have had to do in the NBA—or maybe they wanted to accommodate Abe Saperstein.

Garrett had rebuffed the Trotters' overtures in 1951, and his mind hadn't changed in the two years since. He had played one game with the Globetrotters in September 1951, before reporting to the Army, so he knew how different life with the Trotters would be. The Celtics played seventy-two games of hard-nosed basketball, half of them at home in Boston, from November through March. The Globetrotters, by contrast, had no home base except for a few weeks of practice in Chicago. They were on the road constantly, playing three hundred games year-round, most of them exhibitions against all-white "opponents" in which the Trotters' clowning routines often played to prevailing racial stereotypes.

For a couple of years at the end of the 1940s, the Globetrotters had been the best basketball team in the world. In 1948, they had twice beaten the Minneapolis Lakers, the best white pro team of the time. By 1953 they were still among the best, but increasingly their games were mere exhibitions, and their goodwill was fading among American blacks, many of whom considered the Trotters' jokes and image demeaning. In the South, the Trotters often played the same city two straight nights, the first for a white audience, the second for a black one. Though they played to packed stadiums everywhere—and played three times as many games per year as NBA teams—Saperstein paid most of his players less than half what NBA players were making. He paid the college All-Stars more than he paid most Trotter players during the Trotters–All-Stars annual series—and defended the differential by saying blacks did not need as much money as whites. Globetrotter players had to pay for their own meals on the road and wash their uniforms every day in the sinks of hotels and rooming houses, because Saperstein made no provision for cleaning them. Saperstein had expanded the audience for basketball, employed black players when others would not, and been first to see the international appeal of the game, but he was a promoter, not a manager. Black newspaper editors increasingly lambasted the Globetrotters and the black fans who paid to see them. Marion Jackson, influential columnist of the *Atlanta Daily World,* wrote in March 1953, "To me the 'clown princes of basketball' are becoming as much a symbol of bigotry, intolerance and prejudice as the Mason-Dixon line itself."

Bill and Betty settled briefly in Indianapolis while they decided what to do. The rosters of other NBA teams were set, and the few coaching jobs available to black men in the Midwest were already taken. Bill could accept the Globetrotters' offer, or give up on playing pro basketball and look for another job at lower pay.

He joined the Globetrotters as the team returned from playing exhibition games across Europe. He and Betty spent a short time in Chicago while the team practiced there during their three-week "off-season." In late September, less than two months after he had returned home from the Army, Bill went on the road with the Globetrotters, and Betty returned to Bloomington to finish her master's degree. For the next twelve months there would be games almost every night, sometimes twice a day.

For a while he avoided the team bus, driving between cities with Johnny Wilson, by then a Globetrotter veteran. After Wilson transferred to a second Globetrotters' team touring the West, Bill rode the bus and hung out more with the other players. The veterans hazed him mildly, as they did all rookies, calling him "rook" and making him sit in the back of the bus, over the wheels where the ride was bumpier. They joked that he was in the Trotters' "rhythm section," since he was not a showman and was expected to stay in the background. As a Globetrotter employee recalled, "even in vaudeville Garrett was serious."

His hope had been to stay with the Globetrotters only a short time, and then move to the NBA, perhaps with the Celtics. But, after less than two months with the Globetrotters, Garrett badly broke his right wrist. It was set incorrectly, causing him a lot of pain, and ultimately the wrist had to be rebroken and reset. His arm was in a cast for most of his first year with the Globetrotters, as the prospect of the NBA faded. Classmates, teammates, and friends turned out to see him that year in cities all around the country. He was always glad to see them and always courteous, introducing them to his teammates, calling friends down from the stands to meet them. But most remembered that his forearm was in a cast, that he did not play, and that the man they remembered as easygoing seemed lonely and unhappy. "He would never talk about his time with the Trotters," said Al Spurlock, who would become Bill's colleague and friend, noting that Garrett was very open about other subjects. In the summer of 1954, shortly after returning from a tour of South America with the Globetrotters, Garrett told Don Robinson, a former high school teammate, that the Trotters were "show business" and that he hated it and wanted to quit.

In late 1954, Garrett bumped into Bill Tosheff in Philadelphia. Tosheff had been an immediate starter for the Indianapolis Olympians and had been the NBA's co–Rookie of the Year for the 1951–52 season. When they met in December 1954, Tosheff was in Philadelphia with the NBA's Milwaukee Hawks, getting ready to play the Philadelphia Warriors. Garrett was there for another one-night show with the Globetrotters. The two had stayed in touch over the years, and Tosheff knew how much Garrett missed real competition. "It was a sad time for him," Tosheff would say. Rubbing his head, which Tosheff recognized as sign of stress, Garrett told his old IU teammate he was unhappy with the Trotters and would be leaving them soon.

A few months later, in March 1955, the Globetrotters were in Richmond, Indiana, a town of forty thousand on the state's eastern boundary. Betty was then living in Toledo, teaching swimming and modern dance at the local black Y. Ohio was just across the state line, a stone's throw from Richmond. Shelbyville was forty-five miles to the southwest, Indianapolis a seventy-mile straight shot west. The pull of home was too great. Bill called Betty from a pay phone in Richmond and told her, "I'm coming home."

16

A Gym Needs a Name

TOLEDO WAS INTEGRATING ITS PUBLIC SCHOOLS IN MARCH 1955, and there was a lot of movement in the job market for teachers. Both Bill and Betty applied to teach and coach there for the 1955–56 school year. Betty was hired to teach physical education, but coaching jobs were scarce for black men without experience or seniority, and the Toledo school system had no place for Bill Garrett. He took a job in a steel foundry, doing piecework, getting bonuses for meeting his daily quota. He went after his quota as he had once gone for rebounds, coming home exhausted, his arms covered with cuts.

Bill and Betty wanted to be closer to home. For the following school year they both found jobs at Harry Wood, Indianapolis's vocational high school, Betty teaching physical education and Bill teaching business courses and coaching track and freshman basketball. Bill was just completing his first year at Wood when, in the spring of 1957, the most visible, pressure-filled basketball coaching position a black man could hope to occupy in Indiana opened up on the west side of Indianapolis.

Crispus Attucks High School had opened its doors in the fall of 1927, following a series of decisions by the city's school board to segregate Indianapolis's public schools. Founded on whites' low expectations, Attucks quickly became a magnet for many of the best black teachers in the country. Along with other black and Catholic high schools, Attucks had been denied membership in the Indiana High

School Athletic Association until August 1942, and for years after they joined the IHSAA the Attucks basketball team had limped along, wearing hand-me-down uniforms, riding old buses long distances, unknown by most Indiana basketball fans, until 1951. That was the year Ray Crowe moved up from Public School 17—the junior high across the street—to the head coaching job at Attucks just as several extraordinarily talented basketball players were reaching maturity there. By coincidence, 1951 was also the first year WFBM-TV televised the Indianapolis sectional, regional, and semifinal games in addition to the Final Four. That year, from late February to late March, people all over central Indiana watched on television as the Crispus Attucks Tigers, playing the best basketball ever to come out of Indianapolis, marched through the tournament to the Final Four.

Between 1951 and 1957 Attucks dominated Indiana high school basketball as no team had ever done before. Five times they went at least as far as the final eight teams in the state tournament. Led by Oscar Robertson, who would become one of the greatest players in NBA history, Attucks won forty-five straight games over the 1955 and 1956 seasons, becoming the first Indianapolis team to win the state championship in 1955 and the first undefeated team to win the championship in 1956. By the mid-1950s, Attucks, in new green and gold uniforms, was playing its regular-season home games before crowds of nine thousand to twelve thousand at Butler Fieldhouse. Athletic directors from all over the state, hoping to gain a financial boost for their athletic programs, were calling to ask politely if Attucks could find a place for them on its schedule. Alonzo Watford, the athletic director who had nurtured Attucks basketball when it was struggling, remembered those calls thirty years later, on his deathbed, in a conversation with writer Phillip Hoose, "Until he thought of those courteous phone calls, his face had been contorted with the labor of speech, of struggling to build words syllable by syllable. Then he began to chuckle, and soon laughter shook his frame. . . . 'One game with us could make the whole year for them. It got so I could play *Podunk* and make money.' Tears of laughter rolled down Alonzo Watford's face. 'Man, what a great feeling,' he said."

In April 1957, at the height of Attucks's six-year run, coach Ray Crowe announced that he wanted to leave in order to make more money, both for the benefit of his family and because, he told the *Recorder*, "salary is one of the best ways to measure advancement." As long as he stayed at Attucks, he would never make more than his teaching salary plus the uniform stipend the central school adminis-tration paid all Indianapolis high school basketball coaches—five hundred dollars in 1957, one of the lowest in the state. Crowe let it be known that he had applied for the coaching job at Lebanon, a town of ten thousand some twenty miles northwest of Indianapolis, and that he would be interested in other high school or college coaching jobs. But Lebanon turned him down, and no one else contacted him.* For a few months the *Recorder* staff let themselves hope Crowe would stay on as Attucks's coach, but in mid-July the school board issued a two-part announcement: Ray Crowe was resigning from coaching to become athletic director at Crispus Attucks, and Bill Gar-rett had accepted the job as Attucks's head coach. Under a front-page headline, the *Recorder* mourned Crowe's departure, saying, "It appears that despite all the hoopla about basketball sportsmanship, prejudice still rules Hoosierland and the man who should be coach of Indiana University is compelled to leave the profession," quoting an observer as saying, "I guess the school board wanted to end Attucks' reign," and adding, "All one can do for Crowe's successor, the talented and popular Bill Garrett, is to pray."

In retrospect, Garrett was the obvious choice. There were few black basketball coaches around, and no one else had his combina-tion of coaching experience (though only one year), strong basketball credentials, and proven ability to handle himself in a public role where race and sports mixed. At twenty-eight, amid controversy, Gar-rett succeeded one of the most successful high school coaches in the history of Indiana basketball and became a symbol of the black com-munity in Indianapolis. He started slowly, but in Garrett's second sea-son his unheralded Attucks team improved steadily and won the 1959 state championship. Bill Garrett became the only Indiana Mr. Basketball to play on a state championship team and coach one, a record that still stands.

Garrett was the only black varsity basketball player in the Big Ten during his four years at Indiana University, but that fact is deceptive.

---

*The *Recorder* mentioned repeatedly that the head coaching job was open at Muncie Central—one of the state's strongest basketball powers—but Muncie showed no inter-est and Crowe did not apply.

In his senior year, the 1950–51 season, two players, John Codwell at Michigan and Rickey Ayala at Michigan State, were playing freshman basketball and getting ready to join their varsity teams as sophomores. The next year, under a one-year, Korean War exception allowing freshmen on varsity teams, not only sophomores Codwell and Ayala but also four freshmen—Don Eaddy at Michigan, McKinley "Deacon" Davis at Iowa, Ernie Hall at Purdue, and Walt Moore at Illinois—joined Big Ten varsity basketball teams. Thus, the year after Garrett graduated from Indiana, six black players were on five Big Ten teams. As Ernie McCoy, the Michigan coach, said, summing up the feelings of coaches all over the northern United States, "I'd love to have a player as good as Bill Garrett."

It captured the irony. Garrett had wedged the door open but the opening was narrow. Coaches wanted Bill Garretts, and there weren't many. "Bill Garrett left such a strong legacy that it could never be reversed," said Wally Choice, Indiana University's second black basketball player. Basketball integrated by ones and twos throughout the 1950s, as most coaches accepted only strong students of starting-five quality—like John Codwell—or superstars like Wilt Chamberlain, who integrated basketball at Kansas (and in the Big Eight Conference) in 1956. The pool of black basketball prospects most college coaches would consider recruiting was limited. There were not many blacks of marginal ability warming college benches in the 1950s. "Bill Garrett set the bar so high that in a way it was almost more difficult for those who came after," said Stanley Warren, a coworker of Garrett's at Attucks and later the director of Black Studies at DePauw.

Along with the steady march of a few black players into more and more college basketball programs, there were spurs that accelerated the process. Bill Russell and K. C. Jones led the University of San Francisco to back-to-back NCAA championships in 1955 and 1956. Wilt Chamberlain dominated college basketball from the fall of 1956 through the spring of 1958. Along with Chamberlain, Oscar Robertson, at the University of Cincinnati, and Elgin Baylor, at Seattle University, were college basketball's best players in the late 1950s. Loyola University of Chicago won the 1963 national championship with four black starters. Then Texas Western (now the University of Texas at El Paso), with five black starters, beat Adolph Rupp's all-white Kentucky team for the 1966 national championship, "and the walls came tumbling down," as Frank Fitzpatrick has described in a book of that title.

More than any other college basketball coach, Branch McCracken started this movement, and yet, among many blacks, especially in Indianapolis, McCracken is unpopular. The rough-edged "Bear" who came of age in 1920s all-white Morgan County never sought the role of integrationist; he just wanted to win basketball games. Bill Garrett had indeed been his "perfect person," for Garrett was small town and was low-maintenance. The coach never quite got the hang of dealing with urban blacks in a changing time.

Wally Choice, his second black player, like Garrett, was from an integrated high school in a predominantly white city, Montclair, New Jersey. Choice, who enrolled in the fall of 1952, was the team's leading scorer and an All Big Ten selection in his senior year. IU's third black player, Hallie Bryant, arrived in the fall of 1953 carrying high expectations—McCracken's and his own. Bryant, from inner-city Indianapolis and Crispus Attucks High, had been Indiana's 1953 Mr. Basketball. The cultural gap between Bryant and McCracken was large, and it grew as Bryant did not live up to expectations, was not a starter in his sophomore year, and had "only" a solid IU career, averaging fourteen points a game as a junior and eleven as a senior. Many in the Crispus Attucks community thought McCracken did not give Bryant a chance, or use him well, and they drew the conclusion the coach was prejudiced.* It was a conclusion that the coach, in his awkwardness, did little to dispel. In the summer of 1953, shortly after McCracken recruited Hallie Bryant to IU, a high school basketball coach in Omaha wrote to McCracken on behalf of one of his players, and received the following reply, "Your request for an athletic scholarship for Robert Gibson has been denied because we already have filled our quota of Negroes." Bob Gibson went on to be a Harlem Globetrotter, and then one of the best major league baseball pitchers of his era, but forty years later he remembered Branch McCracken's slight: "I remember watching Bryant play on television over the next few years and thinking to myself, 'They got the wrong Negro.'"

---

*Bryant himself said nothing negative about McCracken or his experience at IU in his interview with the authors.

Then McCracken failed to land Wilt Chamberlain in 1955, and Oscar Robertson in 1956, two of the greatest players in basketball history, both urban blacks (Chamberlain from Philadelphia, Robertson from Indianapolis) who visited IU and appeared to be leaning toward going there. This fed the belief of some that the coach had a problem with blacks, but the truth was more complicated. McCracken may have been overconfident that he had won the recruiting battle for Chamberlain; he was blindsided when the entire community of Lawrence, Kansas, put on a full-court press emphasizing the town's history of antislavery activity and liberal politics, which contrasted with Bloomington and subtly highlighted McCracken's rough edges. In addition, rumors about prohibited payments persisted throughout Chamberlain's two-year varsity career at Kansas ("No NBA team can afford to pay him what he gets at Kansas now and [Kansas coach] Phog Allen gave it all to him," Boston Celtics' owner, Walter Brown, said publicly in 1957, in opposing Chamberlain's early entry into the NBA).* McCracken, it appeared, had been outrecruited, and maybe outbid. The next year the city of Cincinnati successfully wooed Oscar Robertson after McCracken (possibly still smarting from the Chamberlain experience) had been gruff in his one meeting with Robertson and his coach.† McCracken had been outrecruited again. The rumors about Hallie Bryant's experience at IU may also have been a factor; Bryant would remain the only Crispus Attucks graduate ever to play basketball at IU, despite Attucks's dominance of Indiana high school basketball throughout the 1950s.

Branch McCracken continued to recruit black players when he could, most notably Walt Bellamy, an athletically inexperienced six-eleven giant from the small town of New Bern, North Carolina. Under McCracken's training, Bellamy became a first-team All-American, a

---

*Whatever the amount might have been, Chamberlain appears to have thought it was not enough: "Look at the revenue athletes generate . . . it was said that I helped to build the Kansas Turnpike—they needed it, so people could come to Lawrence to watch me perform at KU. If this is true, they didn't pay me *nearly* enough money for my three years as a Jayhawk."

†In his autobiography, Robertson has said that when he and his coach visited IU, McCracken began the conversation by saying, "I hope you're not the kind of kid who wants money to go to school."

starter on the 1960 U.S. Olympic Team, and the most successful NBA player McCracken ever produced.

In the early 1960s, when the Big Ten was threatening to expel Indiana University for repeated football recruiting violations, Herman Wells brought in a new athletic director named Bill Orwig with a mandate to clean up the athletic department. Orwig set about creating a single, central account, under athletic department control, for all monetary contributions by athletic boosters—akin to the varsity clubs at most major universities today. Branch McCracken had spent his career traveling the state and building up his basketball program, and he did not want to share his life's efforts with IU's weaker football program and other nonrevenue sports. It was new school versus old school, and they were bound to clash. McCracken dug in his heels, and Orwig made the coach's life miserable in the ways an athletic director can, asking him at one point to take a lie detector test. Near the end of the 1965 season, worn down despite having a strong basketball team, McCracken offered a letter of resignation to IU president Elvis Stahr. "Word quickly leaked out," as several publications delicately put it, and with one game still to go in the season McCracken's resignation was publicly accepted and Lou Watson, McCracken's assistant, replaced him.

Old before his time, McCracken died five years later at the age of sixty-one. After he had retired, a reporter asked him to name his favorite players among all those he had coached in his twenty-three seasons at Indiana University. Branch McCracken's spontaneous reply was, "Now what would Bill Garrett say . . . or a hundred other boys if I'd leave one of 'em off the list?"

Herman Wells retired as president of Indiana University in 1962, saying publicly that twenty-five years in one job was enough, and privately that too many people were agreeing with him. He served without salary as IU's chancellor—its wise man—until his death in March 2000. Wells had transformed IU and the world of education, helping to create the National Endowment of the Arts and National Educational Television (a precursor to the Public Broadcasting Service). He received twenty-six honorary degrees, chaired the American Council on Education, served on the boards of the Carnegie Foundation and the Brookings Institution, and contributed to the rebuilding of Germany. Into his nineties, he continued to hold open hours for students. A few weeks before his death, sensing the end was near, Wells summoned IU president Myles Brand. He wanted to say good-bye, and he had one last question, "Is there anything more I can do for the university?"

When Wells died at the age of ninety-eight, the IU flag that had stood beside his desk for more than sixty years draped his coffin, as he had requested, and the board of trustees commissioned a life-size statue. It portrayed Wells not in a grand pose designed for a museum—"the privilege of the few"—but instead sitting on a favorite bench in the middle of campus, where it would be surrounded by as many students as possible and shaded by the trees he had fought to protect.

Faburn DeFrantz turned sixty-five in March 1951, a few days after Bill Garrett played his last game as a "Hurryin' Hoosier." He had fought many battles with Indianapolis's all-white Central YMCA, of which the Senate Avenue Y was a branch, and the relationship was a bitter one. DeFrantz's sixty-fifth birthday finally gave the Y adminis-tration the upper hand, and they forced him out though it was well known that he was a few months shy of qualifying for Social Security benefits. In a tribute to DeFrantz upon his retirement, the editors of *The Y's Men,* the Senate Avenue Y newsletter, compared him to Moses.

Without DeFrantz's leadership, and with integration diffusing the compact black community that had been its nucleus, the Senate Avenue Y could not survive. It closed in 1959. Faburn DeFrantz died five years later at the age of seventy-eight. The Monster Meetings he had built into the most dynamic and longest-running black forum in America continued into the 1970s, at the Fall Creek Y on Indianapo-lis's West Tenth Street.

Nate Kaufman continued his insurance business and involve-ment in civic affairs. He was a founder of the Shelby County United Fund, made sure it included the Booker T. Washington Recreation Center, and was for years its biggest fund-raiser. He helped establish the Shelbyville Boys Club, where basketball is still played in the Nate Kaufman Gymnasium. Before his death, in 1981 at the age of seventy-eight, he was instrumental in raising the money that took the Indiana Basketball Hall of Fame from an idea and a small office to a museum of the state's high school basketball tradition, the only one of its kind in the country. He never stopped delivering fruit to his insurance customers and friends, and there are still people around Indiana who say they haven't had really good strawberries since Nate Kaufman died.

In stark contrast to Ray Crowe's experience, nine high schools and two universities tried to hire Frank Barnes in the days following his Golden Bears' 1947 state championship, but Barnes quickly decided to stay on in Shelbyville with a new three-year contract and "a substantial increase in salary," as the *Shelbyville News* described it in a front-page story. Five years later Barnes announced he would retire from coaching at the end of the 1952–53 season. His 1953 team made it to the Sweet Sixteen semifinals at Butler Fieldhouse, where in the first afternoon game they upset Crispus Attucks in a contest marred by lingering claims of referee bias. All that stood between Barnes's team and the Final Four—a grand finale to Barnes's coaching career—was an unknown burg from the southeastern part of the state called Milan. Though still one year away from the 1954 state championship that would ensure Milan's place in the national consciousness—as "the Milan Miracle" in books and "Hickory" in the 1986 movie *Hoosiers*—Milan demolished Barnes's exhausted Bears, 43–21. Barnes became Shelbyville's athletic director and basketball elder statesman, president of the Indiana High School Basketball Coaches Association, and a member of the Indiana Basketball Hall of Fame. In an interview the year before his death in 1989, at the age of eighty-six, he still would not refer to Terre Haute Garfield by name, calling them "that team."

For two years after the 1947 state championship Doc Barnett stayed on as Frank Barnes's assistant, but then he and Barnes parted ways. They were very different men, and they responded differently to the glory of the championship, Barnett publicly understating his role in preparing Bill Garrett and his teammates in the years leading up to 1947, Barnes enjoying the limelight and his standing among the top Indiana high school coaches. Hurt by the thought that his contribution was unappreciated, Barnett eventually dropped basketball to concentrate on teaching science and coaching baseball, and then withdrew from coaching altogether to finish his career as a teacher. His players, however, never forgot Barnett's help; at his funeral, in 1984, Emerson Johnson made a point of thanking the Barnett family for Doc's role in minimizing racial incidents when the Golden Bears were on the road.

Hank Hemingway played one year at New Mexico State and then followed his coach to the University of Wichita (now Wichita State University). He played three years at Wichita, served in the Army, and returned to Shelbyville as the assistant varsity basketball coach and a small businessman. Hank and his wife, Jo, retired south of Shelbyville, where he is embarrassed to say he has a Columbus address.

Bill Breck left competitive basketball on the floor at Butler Fieldhouse. He graduated from DePauw University, raised a family, and became a respected high school principal and administrator. Bill and his wife, Katie, live near Indianapolis.

Marshall Murray spent one year at Kentucky State University, where he played basketball, then he enlisted in the Army and served in the Korean War. He returned to Indianapolis, where he worked for the U.S. Postal Service and where he still lives.

Emerson Johnson attended Kentucky State for two years and then came home to Shelbyville. College in Kentucky was too lonely, too expensive, too unconnected to any future possibilities he could foresee, and the basketball was, as he told Hank Hemingway, "like trying to shoot over tall trees." In 1954 General Electric moved a plant that made heating systems to Shelbyville, creating hundreds of jobs but also some inevitable tensions. Locals worried about "outsiders" and "labor trouble;" some of the transplanted GE people, from Schenectady, New York, referred to their new home as "Shabbyville." The head of the Shelbyville NAACP chapter wrote to national headquarters in Washington complaining that GE was slow to hire blacks.

The following year Emmie Johnson was one of the first blacks GE hired. He remained in his job there as a skilled welder for thirty-eight years, continuing long after GE had sold the plant to Wellman Thermal Systems Corporation. He married and had four children. He became a deacon in the Second Baptist Church. He lived near his mother and took care of her in her old age. He taught his kid brother to play basketball on the court behind Booker T., playing rough and giving him no breaks, and drilling into him, "When you go up, you better have a place to come down." Often, when there was a death in a coworker's family, Johnson showed up in the evening at their home with a homemade cake or pot of soup, always going to the back door.

On weekends he tended bar at Joe's Glass Bar, or Willie Farkle's, as the Nip'n'Sip was successively renamed. His old friend Jack Worland, the former student manager, occasionally stopped by to talk with him there. Still curious about why Johnson had seemed so downcast in his moment of triumph on the floor at Butler Fieldhouse, Worland tried to draw him out about the racial taunts Jack had heard in that 1947 state championship game. All Johnson would ever say was, "That's too old to talk about."

He was a longtime season ticket holder at Golden Bears' home games, where every year more and more fans brushed past the slightly stooped little man in a gray cardigan without connecting him to the big picture of the state champions hung high on the wall above the gym entrance, or to their own lingering feelings of pride; without having any idea that Luke Walton had once told a million listeners, "He has stolen the show, Emerson Johnson of Shelbyville. You can take your hats off and wave them to him, ladies and gentlemen; he has played basketball tonight."

Johnson developed cancer in the mid-1990s, and few realized how sick he was at Shelbyville's fiftieth-anniversary celebration of the state championship in early 1997, or at the class reunion later that spring when Johnson urged his 1947 teammates to get together again for a private dinner. They finally gathered on December 9, 1997. Emerson Johnson died two weeks later at the age of sixty-nine, having hung on, some thought, to join his teammates one last time.

Bill and Betty started a family in the summer of 1956, not long after they returned to Indianapolis. In quick succession they had three little girls, Tina Louise, Judith Ann, and Laurie Jean. Then in December 1964, they had a son, William Guess Garrett, whom they called Billy. Betty taught the children to swim almost before they could walk. Bill found a Y on the far southwest side of Indianapolis that accepted black girls on its swim team. Swimming practices started early—often at 6:00 A.M.—and the Y was a thirty-minute drive from the Garrett home on Indianapolis's north side. They followed a routine that maximized sleeping time for everyone: Bill got the girls up, made their breakfast, and drove them to practice while they slept in the backseat; then Bill would sleep on a bench in the pool lobby while the girls went through their workout. Swimming for the Krannert YMCA, Tina, Judy, and Laurie Garrett were the first blacks to compete in open swimming competition in Indianapolis, and became nationally ranked swimmers. Bill never lectured his children about handling discrimination; he taught them, instead, by quiet, steady example. After an official discriminated against the girls at the start of a race, Bill qualified to be an official starter for swim meets. Bill and Betty attended every swim meet and turned meets held out of town into family trips. Long afterward, the children remembered what their father had told them on those trips about competition and life:

"The only person who can put pressure on you is yourself."

"Compete with situations, not people."

"Talent is what you do when others are looking at you; character is what you do when no one is looking."

Every summer the family took vacations, which Bill planned in detail: to Washington, Baltimore, and Philadelphia to visit historic sites; to the 1964 New York World's Fair; to Benton Harbor, Michigan, and to lakes in northern Indiana. He taught the children to fish and play checkers, chess, badminton, Ping-Pong, and minigolf. And when he played those games with them, he always played to win.

Bill cooked the family big breakfasts. He was handy, kept their home in good repair, and even took an upholstery course so as to re-cover most of their furniture. He worked summers, promoting the sale of heating and air-conditioning units for Peerless Corporation, and selling insurance for Indianapolis Life Insurance Company. He qualified to be a high school basketball referee and, along with Johnny Wilson, was part of a highly publicized effort to get more black referees hired to work Indiana high school games (the Indiana Officials Association did not admit black members in the 1950s, which limited black referees' opportunities to be hired by high schools). The Garrett family usually ate dinner together, even if it meant waiting for Bill to get home late from Attucks's practices or games, and they sat around the table and talked long after the meal was finished.

A month after Garrett's Attucks Tigers won the 1959 Indiana state championship, Shelbyville threw another "Bill Garrett Night," this

time at the First Methodist Church. The guest speaker was Jesse
Owens. Frank Barnes announced that Bill, at age thirty, had been
named the IHSAA's 1959 Coach of the Year. It was an honor that had
been denied Ray Crowe throughout his seven glory years as Attucks's
coach—an omission so glaring that the Touchdown Club of Columbus, Ohio, as if to mock Indiana, that year named Crowe the High
School Coach of the Year, two years after Crowe stopped coaching.
Maybe the Indiana basketball establishment's snub of Crowe and
acceptance of Garrett rankled. Crowe, who was still Attucks's athletic
director, tried to return to coaching, but the Attucks job was taken
and other schools were not hiring black men. He considered college
coaching—the *Recorder* suggested he should be an IU assistant
coach—but got no offers. By the late 1960s, when Crispus Attucks no
longer had a monopoly on talented black basketball players in Indianapolis and had become just another team, the Crowe-Garrett relationship had become difficult and Bill wanted to move on.

In 1969, Crowe left Attucks to enter politics, and Garrett replaced
him as the school's athletic director, stepping down as basketball
coach. Two years later Bill left Attucks to be director of continuing
education at Indiana Vocational Technical College, or IVY Tech as it
is known around Indiana. In 1970 and again in 1971 he ran for the
Indiana University board of trustees—seeking to become the first
black to be elected to the board—but each time he was narrowly
defeated. When Lou Watson resigned abruptly as IU's basketball
coach shortly before the end of the 1971 season, Garrett applied for
the IU coaching job, but it went to Bob Knight.

In 1973, a new university that united the IU and Purdue exten-
sions in Indianapolis—Indiana-Purdue University at Indianapolis
(which goes by the acronym "IUPUI")—needed an assistant dean
who could relate to students having academic, financial, or personal
difficulties. For Bill it was an opportunity to use the master's degree
he had earned at Butler University. He became IUPUI's assistant dean
of student activities.

All his life, a competitive fire had burned beneath Garrett's calm
exterior. Outwardly, he had shrugged off most of the racial taunts and
ugly incidents, but surely he had felt them. Coaching at Attucks kept
him in the spotlight and continued the need to project outward
calm, but he was a private man in a public role, and often he couldn't

eat on game nights. He took great interest in his players' lives, many of which were difficult. By the end of his time at Attucks, his friend Clarence Wood recalled, Garrett didn't look happy.

He had smoked since his days with the Globetrotters. Twice, episodes of heart arrhythmia had caused him to faint, and on one of those occasions he had been hospitalized. At Betty's request Jim Roberson, Bill's good friend and former IU roommate, who was a physician in Rochester, New York, talked to Bill about taking his health and his medication more seriously. But if he was worried, Bill didn't show it. He was, after all, in his forties, trim, and a former basketball All-American.

Bill had built a basketball goal in the driveway of their home, and as soon as Billy was old enough, Bill taught him the basics of the game. He had a way of teaching his son that drew on his experience as father, coach, and former star: He showed Billy each move needed to shoot a layup, and then stood nearby and watched. When Billy didn't execute all the moves correctly, Bill simply blocked his shot.

One summer day when he was nine years old, Billy missed a long shot and broke a windowpane in the garage door. The following Saturday morning, Bill measured the window and set off for Zayres, in the Shadeland Mall on the east side of Indianapolis, to buy a pane of glass. Holding the wrapped glass under his arm, he was standing in a checkout line when he collapsed with severe heart arrhythmia. An emergency room physician standing nearby leaped over a counter to his aid, but the damage was done. Bill Garrett lingered for two days and died on August 7, 1974, at the age of forty-five.

His death was front-page news around Indiana, and when the wake was held two evenings later at Witherspoon Presbyterian Church, where Bill had been an elder, police were called to control the traffic. For the simple, brief funeral ceremony on Saturday, August 10, 1974, the scores of honorary pallbearers included Emerson Johnson, Marshall Murray, George Taliaferro, Ray Crowe, and Nate Kaufman. Cars were still leaving the church parking lot when the hearse bearing Bill's casket entered Crown Hill Cemetery, more than two miles down the Michigan Road.

Bill's children learned of his trailblazing role through the eulogies, articles, and obituaries. He had never spoken to family, friends, or colleagues of his accomplishments, unless they asked. People remembered, instead, that he gave his full attention to anyone who spoke with him, and that, assigned to write about a personal accomplishment in a class at IU, he had written about winning Shelbyville's marbles tournament at the age of ten.

It was easy to list what he had done but harder to capture who he was, for, to a degree that strains the jaded's credulity, he was indeed "the perfect person," as Branch McCracken had called him, for his time and his role. By example on and off the court he showed white midwesterners that they had been wrong, in a way they could accept. Maybe that's what those ten thousand were trying to acknowledge when they stood and cheered so strongly as he left the IU court for the last time. It would take most whites a while to understand Bill Garrett's legacy, but Indiana's black community grasped it immediately and defended it vigorously. Wally Choice, IU's second black basketball player, recalled, "African-Americans made me aware that I was following an icon—not just in basketball but in personality too . . . I became aware that I couldn't mess up at IU, or I would mess up the legacy. I would be letting *him* down." Choice, who never met Garrett, continued, "As I've grown older, I've realized that he paved the way—showed an example to every other Big Ten school. Bill Garrett made it a pleasant situation for me."

Today, Tina Garrett is an attorney in Chicago. Judy is a pharmacist in Houston. Laurie is an ordained Presbyterian minister in North Carolina. Billy, who played basketball at Crispus Attucks and the University of Indianapolis, is an associate head coach at Texas A&M, with a young son named William Leon Garrett II. They were still children when the family gathered one more time in Shelbyville, six months after Bill's death.

For twenty years after the 1947 state championship season, Paul Cross Gym continued to be the home of Shelbyville basketball. But it couldn't last, for in the 1950s Indiana had begun a second generation of gym-building. Huntingburg, a town of five thousand in southern Indiana, built a state-of-the-art underground gym seating sixty-two hundred. Columbus dunned all public school teachers and city employees a week's salary to build a seven thousand-seat arena, big enough to get the sectional and regional away from Shelbyville. New

Castle, a town of seventeen thousand, built a ninety-three hundred-seat underground arena that remains the world's largest high school gymnasium. Anderson, less than twenty-five miles from New Castle, built the Wigwam, seating almost nine thousand. Eventually, Indiana would have fifty-four high school gyms seating more than five thousand, and thirteen seating more than seven thousand—allowing the state to claim all but one of the twenty largest high school gyms in the world.

Number eleven on that list, for a time, was the new facility Shelbyville built in 1967 to replace Paul Cross Gym. Round, high-domed, and seating fifty-eight hundred, it was a gym for the new era, big and versatile, with an indoor track and swimming pool, but it lacked the intimacy of Paul Cross. The scale was large and the grandstands were brightly lighted, decreasing the sense of all eyes directed to the playing floor, of the whole community hanging on every play.

For its first seven years, Shelbyville's new gym had no name. Then, in August 1974, a few days after Bill Garrett's funeral, the Shelbyville Chamber of Commerce placed a petition in the local banks, the newspaper office, and the courthouse. The first to sign was Frank Barnes and the second was Nate Kaufman. The mayor, the city council, and the school board all endorsed the petition, but those were only formalities, for there was no opposition. The petition began, "Shelbyville High School's splendid gymnasium needs a name. That name should be: The William L. Garrett Gymnasium."

The dedication ceremony was held at the half of a Golden Bears basketball game on February 7, 1975. Betty and the children were there, and Emerson Johnson, Marshall Murray, Bill Breck, and Hank Hemingway, along with most other members of the 1947 state championship team. So was the IHSAA commissioner with both his assistants, and the president of the Indiana Basketball Hall of Fame, with most of his directors. Nate Kaufman presented a plaque to be placed in the Hall of Fame, and Frank Barnes presented a bronze portrait of Bill to be displayed in the trophy case of Garrett Gym.

Among the "what ifs" of Bill Garrett's life is the question of what his undersized, overachieving Hurryin' Hoosiers would have done if they had had Clyde Lovellette, and what difference that might have made in Bill's life afterward. Lovellette, who was a year behind Garrett in school, was recruited by Branch McCracken and went to IU on a basketball scholarship in the fall of 1948, moved into a fraternity house, and was about to enroll in classes. But then—in those days of anything-goes, never-say-die basketball recruiting—Lovellette went missing, only to turn up a couple of weeks later enrolled at the University of Kansas. In 1952, his senior year, Lovellette carried Kansas to the NCAA championship, led the country in scoring, was the national Player of the Year, and was the first pick in the NBA draft. He is still the only player to have done all those things in the same year. Lovellette played eleven seasons in the NBA, mostly with the Minneapolis Lakers and St. Louis Hawks, averaging more than twenty points a game in six seasons.

Had Lovellette stayed at Indiana, it is more than possible—it is likely—the Hoosiers would have won the national championship in 1951, Garrett's senior (and Lovellette's junior) year. They had everything except a big man. With Lovellette, they might also have won in 1950, when Garrett was a junior and Lovellette a sophomore. A national championship—certainly two in a row—might have made Garrett a national sports celebrity, as the Indianapolis Olympians' Alex Groza and Ralph Beard had been following Kentucky's championships of 1948 and 1949, and it would have enhanced Garrett's market value with NBA teams, both before and after his years in the Army.

Another "what if" involves the Boston Celtics. It was deeply disappointing to Garrett that his only professional basketball experience consisted of exhibitions with the Globetrotters, much of that time with his arm in a cast. "It ate at him," Jim Roberson recalled, "that he wasn't playing 'real' basketball." By the end of the 1950s, as Garrett was establishing himself in a new career as a high school teacher and coach, the Celtics were starting a string of eight straight NBA championships, with a team that included the legendary Bill Russell.

If the Celtics had not released him to the waiting Globetrotters in 1953, Garrett might have played on the legendary Celtics teams, at least in their early years. He was only twenty-seven when Bill Russell joined the Celtics in the fall of 1956. Or, perhaps, there would have been no place in the NBA for a six-two swingman who had been a center most of his career. We will never know. For two years during the Celtics' eight-year championship run, 1963 and 1964, the team's second-string center—Bill Russell's backup—was Clyde Lovellette. Lovellette later returned to Terre Haute and served for a time as sheriff of Vigo County. He divides his time between Wabash, Indiana, and the Upper Peninsula of Michigan.

Today, Bill Garrett is remembered by a shrinking circle of classmates, teammates, opponents, and aging IU basketball fans. Of the countless books, articles, and websites devoted to the histories of sports and civil rights—even those that focus on black breakthroughs in basketball—one or two mention Garrett in passing and the rest ignore him completely. He is not in the national Basketball Hall of Fame, even though it has a special category for persons who, regardless of their playing or coaching records, made major contributions to the game.

Faburn DeFrantz watched from the stands as Bill Garrett played his last game at Indiana University March 5, 1951. The long, intense standing ovation Garrett received when he left the IU floor for the last time was, DeFrantz later wrote, something "I will never forget. Things less dramatic have happened through the years. I say 'happened' and realize at once the verb is wrong. Little progress 'happens.' Usually it must be wrestled from influences that—either belligerently or indifferently—deny it."

Postscript

MY FATHER GREW UP ON A SMALL FARM SIX MILES NORTH of Shelbyville, in the same section of the same township where his family had farmed for generations. Every afternoon, after school, he had to hurry home to help with the milking and other chores, so he was not able to play basketball at Shelbyville High School. After he graduated in 1926, he gradually gave up farming for jobs in town that left him time to watch high school basketball practices and sometimes to scrimmage with the team and scout future opponents. Eventually, he and his brother became the Ford dealers of Shelbyville, but what my dad always liked best was selling tractors to farmers. There was nothing artificial, or consciously chosen, about his rapport with farmers or his love of Shelbyville High School basketball. Both came to him naturally, without complications or questions.

A corn-picker accident cost my father some fingers and kept him home from World War II. During the war, when gasoline was scarce and tractor salesmen got an extra ration, he drove Shelbyville's freshman and B teams to out-of-town basketball games. That was how he first got to know Bill Garrett, Emerson Johnson, Marshall Murray, and their teammates, when they were ninth and tenth graders, on the way up.

As a young woman, my mother wanted desperately to get out of Shelbyville for the larger world. The star of her nurses' training class at Indianapolis's Methodist Hospital, she dreamed of pursuing the new field of X-ray technology in St. Louis, and of working at New York's Bellevue Hospital. But the year she graduated the Depression hit, and instead she found herself pasting labels on bootleg whiskey in the basement of the relatives with whom she lived in Indianapolis.

My mother gave up her dreams, worked at the Shelbyville hospital, married my father, and raised my sister, brother, and me. But she never came to terms with life in complacent Shelbyville. She was a contrarian, an outspoken supporter of underdogs, and a nonstop commentator—especially to her small children—on the hypocrisies of small-town life.

All the time I was growing up, no teachers, no peers, and almost no adults ever talked about the way we treated black people. It was just the way things were. People avoided the subject the way they avoided staring at the handicapped.

My mother did not avoid the subject. She talked to us about it in terms little children could understand. She told us repeatedly that she had gladly taken care of black people at the Shelbyville hospital when others had refused to do so, and that she had given rides to the women who cleaned our church when others had passed them by. She heaped scorn on the Daughters of the American Revolution for denying Marian Anderson access to Constitution Hall, and she rooted for Jackie Robinson's Brooklyn Dodgers. If we mindlessly said something racially insensitive, she pulled us up short and told us, in the awkward language of the time, to "just be thankful *you* weren't born colored."

I was four when Shelbyville won the state championship. I was eight and part of the crowd that gave Bill Garrett a standing ovation at the Indiana State Fairgrounds Coliseum before his College All-Stars took on the Harlem Globetrotters. A child's feeling of pride was one of the strongest influences on my early life. My friends and I pretended to be Bill Garrett while learning to play basketball, without ever thinking about the limits on the Garrett family's life in town. I made it my mission to play for the Shelbyville Golden Bears, and when I finally did, I often looked up at the big picture over the entrance to Paul Cross Gym—three blacks and nine whites in their 1947 uniforms. By my day, we used those gold jerseys in practice. When a coach tossed them at us and said, "The state champions wore these," we never failed to practice harder.

And yet, after those very same practices, I dropped off teammates at Shelbyville's "colored" teen center, and went on to the one for whites, without giving it a second thought. Or so it seemed. But of course I thought about it. Don Wallis, writing about Madison, Indiana, said it this way:

> Truly it seems that I did not know it. But of course I had to know. In some deep and silent, heartfelt way, we all had to know. Whenever one of our ball games ended . . . and we white kids went off to swim at Crystal Beach and the black kids went off to swim at Crooked Creek—in those moments we had to be thinking about it. . . .
>
> And I realize now we were forbidden to talk about it—forbidden by ourselves, forbidden by our elders in the community, forbidden by the community itself—precisely because of what we knew, what all of us in the community knew in our hearts. It was so wrong we had to keep it a secret from ourselves.

I grew up and went away from Shelbyville. I played a year of freshman basketball at Indiana University, where I was allowed to hang around in the vicinity of some of Bill Garrett's former teammates and his coach. I went east to law school and then lived in South America, Europe, and Washington.

And all that time I have thought about it.

To write this story became an obsession. For years, I told anyone who would listen that I would write a book about it if only I had time to do the research. Finally a friend, tired of listening, suggested I hire a research assistant. So Rachel, who was finishing a master's degree focused on African-American history, became my coauthor. Without her, this would be mainly a basketball book. She made it possible for us to get behind the feel-good headlines and explain better the larger significance of Bill Garrett's breakthrough.

This has been a seven-year project. Everything about it—but above all, the interviews we did—has made me reconsider many things about the world I grew up in.

I learned things that made me wince at my own past attitudes. In 1950, during his junior year at Indiana University, Bill Garrett told a reporter for a black newspaper in Columbus, Ohio, that if he had it to do over again he might not have gone to IU, but instead might have attended an all-black college, because at Indiana, he said, "They all treat me okay . . . but too many of them try to treat me like they're doing me a great favor."

When my father was growing up on the farm and only went into town on Saturdays, he sometimes felt shunned by Shelbyville's in-crowd because he had a farmer's haircut, or because he didn't know how to play pool or tennis. In the early 1950s, when tractor sales were booming, my dad bought an antique pool table and built a full-length, asphalt, lighted tennis and basketball court in a field behind our house. In time, our court became a gathering place for aspiring basketball players for miles around, but for one summer, the first summer anyone outside our family played there, all the players were blacks who saw our new court as a big improvement on the one behind Booker T. Among those first players on my family's basketball court were Emerson Johnson, Marshall Murray, and Bill Garrett's brother, Jim. On hot summer days they and their friends drank water from the hydrant near our back door and bantered courteously with my dad.

We felt good about ourselves, but in my heart I thought we were doing them a favor.

For this book, I interviewed a black former high school basketball teammate, a classmate with whom I had gone to school since the fourth grade. Awkwardly, I tried to apologize for having been so unaware of how it had been. For a moment we sat silently, and then he smiled and said, "You know, your mother was the sweetest lady. When we were playing basketball on hot days, she would bring us a pitcher of ice water, and say, 'You boys must be thirsty.'"

Tom Graham
Washington, D.C.
November 2005

The time you won your town the race
We chaired you through the market-place;
Man and boy stood cheering by,
And home we brought you shoulder-high.

To-day, the road all runners come,
Shoulder-high we bring you home,
And set you at your threshold down,
Townsman of a stiller town.

—A. E. HOUSMAN,
"TO AN ATHLETE DYING YOUNG"

Eight Who Came Before

Johnny Wilson

"Jumpin' Johnny" Wilson led Anderson High School to the 1946 Indiana state championship, set scoring records, and was Indiana's Mr. Basketball. One of the top-scoring college players in the country in each of his three years at Anderson College (now Anderson University), Wilson was twice named an All-American by nonmainstream publications. He played for the Harlem Globetrotters from 1949 to 1951, when the Globetrotters were the equal of any basketball team in the world, and again from 1953 to 1955. In 1959, Wilson became the head basketball coach at Indianapolis Wood High School, the first black to coach an integrated high school basketball team in Indiana. Bluntly outspoken about discrimination, he was repeatedly turned down for head coaching jobs at predominately white high schools outside Indianapolis, including Anderson High School. Asked in one job interview whether he thought he could coach white players, Wilson replied, "When you realize that coaching one player is the same as coaching another, you won't have to ask an asinine question like that." He left Indianapolis in the late 1960s to become head coach and athletic director of Malcolm X Community College in Chicago, where his basketball teams compiled a won-lost record of 378–135 over twenty years. After serving as head coach of the Anderson High School girls' basketball team, Wilson is now an assistant basketball coach at Lock Haven University in Pennsylvania. He is a member of the Indiana Basketball Hall of Fame and the Anderson University Athletic Hall of Fame.

Bobby Milton

A six-two forward, Milton led his Fort Wayne Central team to the final game of the 1946 state championship, where they lost to Johnny Wilson's Anderson team. He was a member of the Indiana High School All-Stars, and he joined Wilson for one season at Anderson College, where Milton and Wilson were one of the top-scoring combinations in the country. Along with Wilson, he joined the Harlem Globetrotters in 1949, played in over eight thousand games, and was a Globetrotters' player-coach for ten years. He is a member of the Indiana Basketball Hall of Fame.

Chuck Harmon

Harmon, a six-two forward, led Washington, Indiana, to the state championship in 1942. As a freshman at the University of Toledo, he was a key starter on the Toledo team that lost to St. Johns in the final game of the 1943 National Invitational Tournament at Madison Square Garden. Harmon began a professional baseball career with a minor league team in the Cincinnati Reds' organization in 1947, shortly after Jackie Robinson broke the color line in major league baseball. He made it to the major leagues and became the first black to play for the Cincinnati Reds in 1954. After a four-year major league baseball career with the Reds, the St. Louis Cardinals, and the Philadelphia Phillies, Harmon returned to Cincinnati and worked for the court system. A member of the Indiana Basketball Hall of Fame, Harmon still lives in Cincinnati, where, in late March 1993, he was chosen to throw out the ceremonial first pitch for the first game to be played in the city's new baseball stadium, the Great American Ball Park.

Davage Minor

Minor is believed to be one of the inventors of the jump shot. In 1941 he led Gary's Froebel High School to the Final Four of the Indiana State Tournament. That year, an Indiana University alum from Gary wrote to President Herman Wells asking that Minor be considered for the IU basketball team. Wells suggested Coach Branch McCracken look into recruiting Minor, but Minor never heard from the coach. Minor played two years at the University of Toledo, spent three years in military service, and then finished his playing career at UCLA. At the start of the 1947 season, *Time* said of him, "UCLA's Davage Minor is being talked about as the best Negro player in basketball history." Several publications named him an All-American during his years at UCLA. He was among the first blacks to play in the NBA, joining the Baltimore Bullets in the 1951–52 season, and playing for Baltimore and Milwaukee in 1952–53. Minor, also six-two, worked in a family business in Gary, where he died in 1997.

George Crowe

Indiana's first Mr. Basketball, in 1939, Crowe led Franklin High School to the final game of the 1939 state championship. At six-two, 210 pounds, he was the center and star of Indiana Central College's nationally ranked teams in the early 1940s, then played seven years of professional basketball for the all-black New York Rens, Los Angeles Red Devils, and Harlem Yankees. In the 1950s, Crowe played eight years of major league baseball for the Boston (later Milwaukee) Braves, Cincinnati Reds, and St. Louis Cardinals. His brother Ray Crowe was the coach of Oscar Robertson at Indianapolis's Crispus Attucks High School during Attucks's early glory years, and Bill Garrett's predecessor at Attucks. Both George and Ray Crowe are members of the Indiana Basketball Hall of Fame. George Crowe lives in upstate New York.

Frank Clemons

As a starting guard, Clemons helped Anderson High School to the Indiana basketball state championship in 1937, his junior year. When his team played on the road in high school, crowds were often so hostile that police had to escort Clemons to and from the dressing room, and his coach sometimes took him out of games for his own protection. In the summer of 1938, after his senior year, Clemons's coach, Archie Chadd, spoke to Indiana University's new incoming basketball coach, Branch McCracken, about the possibility of Clemons playing basketball at IU. According to Clemons, McCracken told Chadd the Big Ten athletic directors had an agreement not to take black players because of problems they would face on the road, but McCracken was sure the agreement would be broken in a few years. At the University of Toledo, Clemons became a member of the school's Athletic Hall of Fame for three sports: basketball, football, and track. In New York with his Toledo basketball team to play in the 1942 National Invitational Tournament finals, Clemons and a black teammate were excluded from a performance by Jimmy Durante at the hotel where the NIT teams were staying. (Durante, hearing of their exclusion, invited Clemons and his teammate to sit with him onstage, introduced them to the audience, and told them they were his guests.) As an Army officer in the Pacific in World War II, Clemons was awarded the Bronze Star for bravery in the Philippines. He lives in Toledo, where in 1992 he was president of the University of Toledo Alumni Association.

Dave Dejernett and Jack Mann

Dejernett, six-five, and Mann, six-seven, were not only two of Indiana high school basketball's earliest black players, they were also the state's best early big men at a time when their heights were rare. Dejernett outscored Mann in the 1930 state championship game, in which Dejernett's Washington, Indiana, team beat Mann's Muncie Central. The next year Mann's Muncie team beat Dejernett's Washington in the round of eight, and went on to win the 1931 state championship. Dejernett graduated from Indiana Central College (now the University of Indianapolis) in 1935, where he was an outstanding basketball player. He played professional basketball with the Chicago Crusaders, Harlem Globetrotters, and New York Rens. Mann attended Wilberforce University, where he played basketball for two years. He played professional basketball for several years with the Chicago Crusaders and then was a longtime member of the Muncie police force. Both Dejernett and Mann are members of the Indiana Basketball Hall of Fame.

Acknowledgments

This book is the product of two lifetimes of thinking and seven years of research and writing. Along the way we have enjoyed the help of many individuals and institutions across the country. We are grateful to all who gave us their time and we are honored that they entrusted us with their knowledge and memories. We hope our book does right by them. If *Getting Open* ever was our project alone, it ceased being that a long time ago.

The book could not have been written without the support and involvement of the Garrett family: Bill's children, Tina Garrett, Judith Shelton, Laurie Garrett Cobbini, and Billy Garrett; Bill's siblings, Jim Garrett, Mildred Powell, and Laura Mae Wicks; and, especially, the wonderful Betty Garrett Inskeep.

In the course of our interviews we often heard, "I don't think I really have anything to tell you," and never found that to be true. Every interview revealed some facet of the story. We would particularly like to thank Bart Kaufman, Bill Breck, Phil Buck, Don Chambers, Faburn DeFrantz, Jr., Hank Hemingway, Jack Krebs, Gene Ring, James Roberson, George Taliaferro, Bill Tosheff, Johnny Wilson, and Walt Wintin. We are indebted to Al Spurlock for speaking up and saying, "I was there," thus offering us an eyewitness account of the August 1947 meeting between Herman Wells and Faburn DeFrantz, about which Mr. Spurlock had never before spoken, because, he told us, no one had ever asked.

When the book was still little more than a pipe dream, Shelbyville High School athletic director Steve Drake lent us the school's thirteen brittle 78-rpm records, on which we heard Frank Barnes call out to Bill Garrett on the floor of Butler Fieldhouse, and Luke Walton say of Emerson Johnson, "That boy's hotter than a little red fire engine!"

Larry Sandman let us spend hours in his basement listening to his collection of 78-rpm records of Tom Carnegie's broadcast of the 1947 semifinal and Final Four games. The Indiana University History Department provided a research fellowship in the summer of 2001, and IU professors Jim Madison and Bill Wiggins offered advice, information, and encouragement. The Indiana Historical Society supported this project with its extensive archival resources and, in the summer of 2001, with a generous Cleo Grant. The Indiana Basketball Hall of Fame gave us access to its archives, and the Hall's best guide, Don Chambers, who was also Bill Garrett's high school teammate, led us through them more than once. The Indiana High School Athletic Association helped us navigate its archives, and Joe Gentry, of the IHSAA, helped us find and copy many photographs. The IT Department at King & Spalding LLP talked us through many computer crises.

Reference librarians and archivists are a breed apart—their work often seems more a calling than a job—and over the course of this project we have tested the patience of many. A particular thank you goes to those at the Library of Congress's manuscript room, the Indiana Historical Society, the Indiana State Library, Multnomah County Library, the State Library of Ohio, where Connie McCleary Ostrove spent her free time tracking down the newspaper article naming Ray Crowe "Ohio High School Basketball Coach of the Year," and the Jeffersonville Township Library, where Jeanne Burke made a special effort to find and send us articles about the controversy surrounding coach Hunk Francis and the 1935 state championship. At the IU Archives Brad Cook and, especially, Dina M. Kellams helped us find the images and information that put meat on this story's bones. Barbara Floyd, University Archivist at the University of Toledo, helped us understand why Toledo accepted black basketball players long before most other Midwestern universities, and put us in touch with one of those players, Frank Clemons. Christine Guyonneau, University Archivist at the University of Indianapolis, went to great lengths to find pictures of Dave DeJernett and George Crowe, and to explain why they were able to play basketball at Indiana Central (forerunner of the University of Indianapolis) at a time when they could not play at most other schools. All of these people made the work of research a pleasure.

Any research into Indiana's African-American history must start with Wilma Moore, archivist, African-American History, at the Indiana Historical Society, and Stanley Warren, dean emeritus of education, DePauw University. Their knowledge is both broad and deep, and they share it generously. Wilma long ago transformed from a contact into a friend.

Rosemond Graham, Jan Reid, Nigel Jaquiss, John Schrag, and Bart Kaufman waded through our drafts and came out with helpful comments, encouragement, and insight. David McCormick, our agent, had confidence in our project and helped us navigate the publishing world. Our editor at Simon and Schuster, Malaika Adero, shepherded our manuscript into a final book.

What began as a father-daughter endeavor quickly morphed to encompass in one way or another much of our families. Peggy Cliadakis read early drafts and provided comments, information, and memories. Pat Lux, a terrific researcher, spent countless hours scouring microfilms, scanning articles and photographs, and finding persons with stories to tell. Norman Morris gave us a scrapbook of photos and clippings, as well as his memories. Rosemond Graham and Tom Cody have been our best cheerleaders, counselors, and mediators, offering indulgence, support, and reminders to celebrate each step in a long process. Charlotte and Eve Cody were the most perfect distractions. To all of them, and to the many friends who have listened to us talk endlessly about the book, thank you.

Notes

All of the events portrayed in this book happened as described. Almost all the statements we quote either were reported to us by persons who said them or heard them directly, or were reported as quotations in publications. Some, including many of Frank Barnes's aphorisms, were heard firsthand by Tom Graham. In the few instances in which we have reconstructed statements or dialogue, we have done so after cross-checking multiple sources, and we have confirmed with persons who were present that the reconstruction accurately represents the tone and content of what was said.

Prologue

xi *most popular sports act:* Green, 233.

Chapter 1

3 *more than six thousand a month:* Department of Veterans Affairs, "America's Wars," online.
5 *condemned by the State Board of Health:* McFadden, 203–04.
5 *"that old, ugly, dilapidated building":* Indianapolis Recorder, May 10, 1930.
6 *the first black students to play:* 1920–1940 Shelbyville High School *Squibs.*
7 *"It'll be OK, son":* Interview, Loren Hemingway, June 30, 2001.
8 *"wanna shoot with me":* Ibid.

Chapter 2

9 *"the mean that is sometimes":* Martin, 8.
9–10 *"impassable, hardly jackassable":* McFadden, 77.

11 *Bijou roller rink:* David Craig, "The Birth of Golden Bears Basketball," *Shelbyville News,* June 23, 2004.

12 *"With a heart just as full":* Shelbyville Republican, June 13, 1918.

12 *"the great sympathetic heart":* Ibid.

12 *"ranks the highest":* 1920 Shelbyville High School *Squib,* 23.

13 *"I am the law":* Martin, 184.

13 *Indiana had a long history:* Lutholtz; Lyda; Madison (2001); Martin, 184–200; Moore; Leonard Moore, "Ku Klux Klan," *Encyclopedia of Indianapolis,* 879–82; Edward Price Bell, "Creed of the Klansman," *Chicago Daily News,* 1924, Indiana Historical Society Pamphlet Collection, HS 2330, K63. For the Klan in Shelbyville, see McFadden, 292; "Local Officers of the Ku Klux Klan in Indiana," Indiana Historical Society Archives Collection #SC2419; David Craig, "Klan Had a Rally at Fairgrounds," *Shelbyville News,* July 28, 1999.

13 *membership numbers (fn):* Moore.

14 *a higher per capita black population:* Thornbrough (1993), 229 n44. Among northern cities only Philadelphia, New York, St. Louis, Chicago, Kansas City, and Pittsburgh (in order) had higher absolute numbers of black residents than Indianapolis, but, with the exception of Kansas City, blacks averaged about 2 percent of the other cities' populations, while in Indianapolis blacks were almost 10 percent (compared with almost 11 percent in Kansas City).

14 *Hancock County:* Thornbrough (1993), n 222–23.

14 *Riverboat captains:* Thornbrough (2000), 3.

14 *the governor of Georgia:* Thornbrough (1993), 276.

14 *"Sundown towns":* Loewen; Thornbrough (2000), 3, 116. Martin, 189.

14 *"foremost mass psychologist":* Martin, 193.

15 *a Klan-sympathizing country preacher: Criterion,* April 23, 1982. Cf. Moore, 25.

15 *burn down St. Vincent Catholic Church:* "St. Vincent Church Destroyed by Fire Early This Morning," *Shelbyville Democrat,* April 4, 1924; "Officers Investigate Report of Prowling," *Shelbyville Democrat,* April 5, 1924.

15 *ladies corset salesmen:* David M. Chalmers, *Hooded Americanism: The History of the Ku Klux Klan,* Durham: Duke University Press, 1987, 162.

15 *"bootlegging Catholic Democrats":* Martin, 192.

15 *"conduct unbecoming to a Klansman":* Martin, 194.

15 *Convicted of second-degree murder:* Almost all the details came from Madge Oberholtzer's "dying declaration" (a statement by a person who knows he or she is about to die that is allowed into evidence after the person's death). Stephenson and his supporters claimed he had been framed by political enemies, but Oberholtzer told a con-

sistent story to several people over a period of weeks, and parts of the story were independently verified. The Oberholtzer family attorney, Asa Smith, who took the declaration, made sure Madge Oberholtzer confirmed it line by line, and signed it, in front of several reputable witnesses. For a detailed account of the case against Stephenson, see Lutholtz, 178–96.

16 *On the night of August 7:* Madison (2001); Cameron (1994).

16 *"These people can't help":* Editorial, *Shelbyville Volunteer,* December 19, 1869. Cf. McFadden, 203.

16 *The racial violence:* See Thornbrough (1963, 1993, and 2000); Madison (2001), 13–24.

16 *The town's only lynching victim:* McFadden, 174–75; Wetnight, 110–16.

16 *speakers such as Frederick Douglass:* McFadden, 204; Thornbrough (2000), 128–29.

16 *"Ebon onslaught":* W. Jennings Day, "Yazoo, Indiana-Shelbyville" (Works Project Administration of Indiana, 1936), 4–5. Indiana State University Archives.

17 *Shelbyville was a segregated:* Coauthor's personal observation; interviews with thirty-three former or current residents of Shelbyville, both blacks and whites. For segregation in Indiana towns generally, see McFadden; Thornbrough (2000); Martin; Loewen; Lynd and Lynd (1929, reprint 1956).

17 *Walter Fort:* Ron Hamilton, "Fort Was Remarkable Elementary School Educator," *Shelbyville News,* October 6, 2000; "The State of Indiana: Shelbyville," *Indianapolis Recorder,* May 17, 1930.

18 *"Nobody said directly":* Interview, Mildred Powell, July 20, 2000.

18 *Laura Belle O'Bannon Garrett:* Interviews, Garrett family and contemporaries; Gray (2001), 18–24; "Rites Set for Laura Garrett," *Shelbyville News,* June 7, 1965.

19 *marbles champion:* Interviews, Garrett family; Gray (2001), 26.

19 *tennis champion:* Interview, Jim Garrett, June 30, 2001; interview, Mildred Powell, June 30, 2001.

20 *"silent assassin":* Interview, Bob King, July 5, 2001, quoting Bob Collins, columnist and sports editor of the *Indianapolis Star.*

22 *"That boy could be a tremendous basketball player":* Interview, Louis Bower, April 25, 2001.

Chapter 3

23 *Coach Frank Barnes:* Much of the material about Barnes comes from stories and aphorisms that Tom Graham heard from Barnes directly. Other facts and quotations are taken from published interviews and

from the authors' interviews of Barnes's former players and contemporaries. More specific citations are given where appropriate.

23 *picked to win:* Bill Fox Jr., "Shootin' Em Shouts It's Shelbyville!" *Indianapolis News,* February 24, 1942.

24 *gentle with the many:* Jim McKinney, "Remembering Frank Barnes," *Shelbyville News,* April 17, 1989.

24 *players taped rancid:* Interview, Joe Crosby, March 5, 2004.

25 *Hunk Francis:* "Janis Francis Quits Coaching Game: Crimson Tide Mentor Leaves Under a Cloud," *Jeffersonville Evening News,* March 18, 1935; "Belief Grows Francis Was Drugged: Came to Game Groggy After Taxi Cab Ride: Effort to Revive Coach Was Ineffective," *Jeffersonville Evening News,* March 19, 1935; Larry Thomas, "After 69 Years, Players' Questions Still Unanswered," *Jeffersonville Evening News,* July 26, 2004.

25 *never able to beat:* May, 175–212.

26 *Shelbyville's "Negro star":* Among the very few Indiana sportswriters who consistently did not mention black players' race in the 1940s were brothers Jimmy Angelopolous of the *Indianapolis Times,* and Angelo Angelopolous, of the *Indianapolis News.*

27 *chucked scores of hot dogs:* Interview, Wava Stephens, September 11, 2003.

27 *refereeing had been outrageous:* "Officiating . . . resembled that of a sour lemon . . . with the weight of poor officiating in the final quarter definitely harming Shelby's chances. The red-hot Columbus team pulled away . . . only after Bill Garrett had been forced from the contest with five personal fouls, the last two of which had been very questionable and drew the ire of all the Shelby fans. The complexion of the game changed like night and day." *Shelbyville Democrat,* March 2, 1946.

27 *spring awards ceremony:* "Paul Cross Medal Goes to Bill Garrett," *Shelbyville Democrat,* April 12, 1946.

Chapter 4

29 *few, if any, basketball coaches:* While it is virtually impossible to confirm this statement exhaustively, the authors made inquiries on relevant websites, asked interviewees and research librarians, and read relevant sources, and found no instance in which a predominately white college or pro team had used three or more blacks on its starting five as early as 1947.

29 *"Hell, they're the three best!":* Interview, Walt Wintin, April 4, 2001.

29 *"thought we didn't want to be there":* Interview, Jim Garrett, June 30, 2001.

29 *flouted convention together once:* Interview, Don Robinson, April 14, 2001.

29 *Sports historian (fn):* Behee, 41.

30 *"the Black Bears":* This was common knowledge in Shelbyville in 1947 and for years afterward, and was confirmed by numerous interviews.

30 *On the road:* Interview, Mildred Powell, July 20, 2000. Interview, Jim Garrett, June 30, 2001.

30 *never coached a black player:* At Jeffersonville, where Barnes had last coached, the high school was segregated and the city did not allow blacks into the five-thousand seat high school fieldhouse during games in the late 1930s. Blacks would gather outside and watch home games through the windows. Interview, Richard "Peachy" Hughes, April 3, 2004.

31 *"it's what they want you to do":* Interview, Jim Garrett, July 8, 2000.

31 *"don't mess with":* This was a common Barnes admonition.

31 *"I don't know which team it was":* Interview, Loren Hemingway, June 30, 2001.

31–32 *paid basketball coaches poorly:* "Here's Why Crowe, Other Naptown Coaches Are Hot," *Indianapolis Recorder,* April 13, 1957.

32 *went to Shortridge:* Interview, Loren Hemingway, June 30, 2001; interview, Louis Bower, April 25, 2001.

Chapter 5

33 *Paul Cross Gym had been:* Bill Holtel, "Hard-Fought Net Game Here Is Marred by Demonstration by Fans," *Shelbyville Democrat,* January 4, 1947; Dan Thomasson, "Historic Night 50 Years Ago Woke Community to Injustice of Racism," *Shelbyville News,* February 15, 1997; Dan Thomasson, "The Way It Was," *Indiana Basketball History Magazine,* summer 1999; interviews, Shelbyville players, students, fans who were at the game, Terre Haute Garfield players and fans, and both referees. The view that race was a factor in the officiating was and is not unanimous, even among those on Shelbyville's side, but it was a widely held view in Shelbyville at the time, and it remains a majority view among those who were present.

33 *Lovellette looked into:* Interview, Clyde Lovellette, August 18, 2000.

34 *"You're responsible":* Interview, Earl Townsend, May 6, 1999.

34 *winter's worst storm:* Bill Holtel, *Shelbyville Democrat,* January 3, 1947.

34 *two hundred of them:* Interview, Jim Byers, March 19, 2001.

35 *Barnes told his team:* Interview, Louis Bower, April 25, 2001.

36 *"one of the 'blackest'":* Bill Holtel, "Hard-Fought Net Game Here Is

Marred by Demonstration of Fans," *Shelbyville Democrat,* January 4, 1947.

36 *"someone pulled a giant drain":* Interview, Walt Wintin, April 4, 2001.

Chapter 6

39 *"All any of us thought about":* Interview, Jim Garrett, June 3, 2002.

39 *Townsend, indignant over:* "Indicates No Charges in Game Disturbance: Official at Net Tilt Here Says Players, Coach not to Be Blamed," *Shelbyville Democrat,* January 6, 1947.

39 *America's most popular amateur sport:* "Most Popular Game," *Time,* April 1, 1946.

40 *state tournament of the 1940s gone national:* "The NCAA Basketball Tournament is the Indiana basketball tourney gone national. It *is* what it *is* because of the Valpos, Princetons and College of Charlestons. It's the stories of the small schools beating the big guys. The story of a son playing for his father on a Cinderella team. Terms like 'Final Four' and 'Sweet Sixteen' began in Indiana." Bill Benner, former *Indianapolis Star* sports columnist, as quoted in Jeremy Dann and Julie Wolinsky, "Hoosier Hysteria: The Tradition and Business of Indiana Basketball," Case Study prepared for the Harvard Business School, May 1, 1998, 7.

40 *Chuck Taylors:* Naismith Memorial Basketball Hall of Fame, website.

40 *"sure turns out some swell forwards":* Kyle Crichton, "Indiana Madness," *Colliers,* February 6, 1937.

40 *Naismith had invented:* Naismith (1894 and 1941); Naismith Memorial Basketball Hall of Fame website.

40 *McKay brought basketball straight:* Schwomeyer, 3–37; Hoose (1986), 36–70; Beck (2003), 33–43; Gould, xiii–13.

41 *"You don't play against opponents":* Correspondence with Bob Hammel, April 12, 2005.

41 *schools too poor or too small:* David Halberstam, "The Basket-Case State," *Esquire* (June 1985).

41 *"a sport for the lonely":* Ibid.

41 *Indianapolis had fewer:* U.S. Census Bureau.

42 *He made the goals:* Kansas Sports Hall of Fame website, "Dr. James Naismith."

42 *"laboratory for moral development":* Naismith (1996), Ch. XI, "The Values of Basketball."

42 *barns, church halls, warehouses:* Schwomeyer, 8–37; Hoose (1986), 37–39; Beck (2003), 33–39.

42 *many referees packed revolvers:* Gould, xiii.

42 *Between 1913 and 1944:* Schwomeyer, 18–37; Hoose (1986), 38–52.

43 *"Two things hold this state together":* Jimmy Angelopolous, "Bob Jewell Gets Big Hand at Reception for Attucks," *Indianapolis Times,* March 19, 1951.

43 *"state's woodshed":* Hoose (1986), 42.

43 *"rules are clear":* Ibid.; "Essay by Bob Hammel," in Beck (2003), 80.

43 *"our nightclubs":* David G. Martin, "Gymnasium or Coliseum? Basketball, Education and Community Impulse in Indiana in the Early Twentieth Century," ed. William Reese, *Hoosier Schools Past and Present* (Bloomington: Indiana University Press, 1998), 134.

43 *When Arthur Trester took charge:* Schwomeyer, 62, 190; *The Indiana High School Athletic Association Annual Handbook* ("IHSAA Handbook"), 1913, 1944.

43 *radio audience of some two million:* In 1947 there were no surveys or polls to determine the size of radio audiences with precision, so of necessity this figure is an estimate. Tom Carnegie, who broadcast the 1947 Final Four for Indianapolis WIRE, told the authors that "the whole state listened," and said that when television broadcasts of the tournament finals began (in 1951), it was confirmed that 85 percent of the state's TV-watching audience watched the state championship (which he called "completely unheard of anywhere"). Indiana's population was about 3.7 million in 1947. If even 45 percent of that population listened to the 1947 state championship, then the radio audience in Indiana alone would have been almost 1.7 million—not including listeners in surrounding states, including the nearby cities of Chicago, Louisville, and Cincinnati.

43 *more than the total attendance:* Live attendance at all rounds of the 1947 Indiana state tournament was 1.241 million *(IHSAA Handbook, 1947).* This exceeded by more than 10 percent the total combined live attendance of approximately 1.113 million at the other 1947 events listed: World Series, 390,000 ("Baseball Almanac, Online"); Indianapolis 500, 168,000 (Encyclopedia Britannica, *Book of the Year, 1947*); Kentucky Derby, 120,000 (est.); Rose Bowl, 84,000 ("Rose Bowl," website); Orange Bowl, 60,000 ("Miami Hurricanes, the Miami Orange Bowl," website); Cotton Bowl, 46,000 ("The Handbook of Texas Online"); Sugar Bowl, 69,000 ("Nokia Sugar Bowl," website); NCAA Championship game, 18,000 ("Wikipedia, the free encyclopedia," online); NIT Championship game, 18,000 (approx. Madison Square Garden 1947 capacity); pro football championship, 31,000 *(Encyclopedia of the National Football League,* 183); Basketball Association of America championship game, 16,000 *(Official NBA Basketball Encyclopedia,* 43); United States Professional Tennis Singles Championship final, 16,000 (est.); Notre Dame–Army game, 59,000 (Notre Dame Stadium 1947 capacity);

Louis-Walcott fight, 18,000 (approx. Madison Square Garden 1947 capacity).

44 *"not publicly open to all"*: Beck (2003), 90–92; Hoose (1986), 105; Stanley Warren, "The Other Side of Hoosier Hysteria: Segregation, Sports and the IHSAA," *Black History News and Notes,* November 1993.

44 *difficulties the struggling schools:* Richard Pierce, "More Than A Game: The Political Meaning of High School Basketball in Indianapolis," *Journal of Urban History,* November 2000.

44 *Brokenburr finally got:* Ibid.; Stanley Warren, "The Other Side of Hoosier Hysteria;" "Senate Bill Hits IHSAA Bar," *Indianapolis Recorder,* February 15, 1941; "Will Affect Negro High Schools Entrance to Tourneys." *Indianapolis Recorder,* March 1, 1941; Bob Stranahan, "IHSAA to Admit Catholic, Negro Schools," *Indianapolis Star,* December 22, 1942, cf. *Indianapolis Recorder,* April 9, 1955.

45 *the IHSAA's Report:* IHSAA Handbook 1947, 103.

45 *"well-known basketball referee":* Interview, Earl Townsend, May 4, 1999.

Chapter 7

47 *"those uniforms aren't wet":* Jim McKinney, "Cold January Night Sent '47 Bears to Title," *Shelbyville News,* March 28, 1986; interview, Loren Hemingway, June 30, 2001; interview, Jack Worland, June 9, 2002.

47 *Thirty years later:* Jim McKinney, "Cold January Night Sent '47 Bears to Title," *Shelbyville News,* March 28, 1986.

47 *"Just tell the man we're sorry":* Interview, Loren Hemingway, June 30, 2001.

48 *ranked Shelbyville twenty-first: Indianapolis Times,* February 18, 1947.

48 *Jack Estell, picked Shelbyville:* Jack Estell, "Here's Jack's Story on Choice of Golden Bears," *Shelbyville Republican,* February 28, 1947; Eugene J. Cadou, "Jack Gets Pat on the Back from Managing Editor," *Shelbyville Republican,* March 28, 1947.

49 *almost a million people would turn out:* The actual figure was 981,000; *IHSAA Handbook 1947.*

50 *makeshift "broadcasts": Shelbyville Democrat,* March 1, 1947.

51 *"Athens of the prairie":* R. W. Apple, Jr., "A Farmland Showcase for Modern Architecture," *New York Times,* December 5, 2003.

52 *jury-rigged long-distance: Shelbyville Democrat,* March 8, 1947.

52 *worst physical and verbal abuse:* Based on numerous interviews with players and fans. See also Bill Holtel, "Bruins Coast to Title after Hard Afternoon Tilt," *Shelbyville Democrat,* March 10, 1947.

53 *"I just can't hit in the daytime":* Ibid.

53 *"it must be us"*: Interview, Loren Hemingway, June 30, 2001.

53 *"the Big, Bad Boy"*: *Indianapolis Times,* March 12, 1947.

53 *"Turn Eyes to Shelbyville"*: Charles Preston, "CAHS Tigers Out, Many Fans Turn Eyes to Shelbyville:" *Indianapolis Recorder,* March 8, 1947.

53 *"Golden Bears again"*: Interview, Louis Bower, April 25, 2001.

54 *Butler Fieldhouse:* William D. Dalton, "Hinkle Fieldhouse," *Encyclopedia of Indianapolis,* 682; "New Era Opens in Butler's History," *Indianapolis News,* December 31, 1928; William Herschel, "New Athletic Plant at Butler University, Modern in Every Detail, a Far Cry from 'Shinny on Your Own Side' Days at Old Seminary," *Indianapolis News,* November 3, 1928.

54 *Two years later (fn.):* "Butler University Expelled from North Central Group; Athletic Plant Is Chief Factor": *Indianapolis Star,* March 20, 1930, Indiana State Library, clipping file.

55 *National Council of Church Women had canceled:* Letter, Mrs. James Smiley and Mrs. C. E. Oldham, "Discrimination in Hotels Here Brings Indianapolis Bad National Reputation," *Indianapolis Times,* February 8, 1947.

55 *pulled up at the hotel driveway:* Based on interviews with players, managers, and relatives of players and coaches. Fifty years later, Emerson Johnson told an interviewer: "The one thing I remember most is how everyone . . . said we had no business being there. They wouldn't let us stay in any of the hotels." Jim McKinney, "Champs Historic Shot," *Shelbyville News,* March 22, 1997.

Chapter 8

59 *"a state of near-insanity"*: "Whole Town Wacky, as Tourney Opens:" *Shelbyville Democrat,* March 22, 1947.

59 *A drawing was held:* "All Available Tournament Tickets Are Distributed; 100 Issued in Lottery," *Shelbyville Democrat,* March 20, 1947.

59 *a scalped one priced:* Bob Stranahan, "Four Teams Poised for Season's Final Goal Push," *Indianapolis Times,* March 21, 1947. "Scalper Selects IHSAA Head, Lands in Jail," *Indianapolis Times,* March 22, 1947.

60 *Hinkle had called:* Hoose (1986), 52. Hinkle once told IHSAA commissioner Arthur Trester that he could add five thousand seats to Butler Fieldhouse at a cost of two thousand dollars a seat, and Trester had replied, "No, Tony, five thousand would just make things worse. If you can figure out how to squeeze in another hundred thousand, let me know." Ibid.

60 *"Bookies," sports pages:* Bob Stranahan, "Terre Haute Garfield and East Chicago Washington Installed as Co-Favorites," *Indianapolis Times,* March 20, 1947; *Indianapolis Star.* March 23, 1947.

60 *"soap works, ore docks, coal piles":* Martin, 17.

60–61 *"a Slovak, a Hungarian":* Dale Burgess, "East Chicago Washington Poses Chief Threat to Garfield Five," *Connorsville News-Examiner,* March 21, 1947.

61 *sponsored a banquet:* Bob Overaker, "Title Contenders in Top Condition, Cage Coaches Say," *Indianapolis Star,* March 20, 1947.

61 *Barnes turned to Baratto:* Frank Barnes told this story often.

63 *"Whatta life":* Corky Lamm, "Kehrt and Barnes Both Still A-Tingle After Teams Post Afternoon Triumphs," *Indianapolis Star,* March 23, 1947.

63 *Sportswriters for 176 newspapers:* Bill Holtel, "Fieldhouse Packed As Garfield, Marion Square Off," *Shelbyville Democrat,* March 22, 1947.

64 *Shelbyville started tentatively:* Details of the game from Indiana Basketball Hall of Fame, Video Library; WIRE Radio broadcast of Tom Carnegie, recording courtesy of Larry Sandman.

65 *"Don't worry, Mr. Barnes":* Interview, Louis Bower, April 25, 2001; Jim McKinney, "Cold January Night Sent '47 Bears to Title," *Shelbyville News,* March 23, 1986. Frank Barnes told this story often.

66 *"Take it. I'm gettin' ":* Interview, Loren Hemingway, June 1, 2002.

66 *"Bill Garrett breaks loose:"* Luke Walton, WISH radio broadcast, March 22, 1947, heard directly by Tom Graham.

67 *"I guess if we stay within 15 points":* Norman P. Werking, "Modesty Runs Wild in Dressing Rooms," *Indianapolis News,* March 24, 1947.

67 *Doc Barnett had arranged:* Interviews, Charles Barnett, April 24, 2004; Daniel Barnett, April 3, 2004; Don Robinson, July 24, 2001. Jim McKinney, "Cold January Night. . . ."

69 *"Send 'em on out":* This and the dressing room scene generally, interviews, Bill Breck, July 7, 2001; Loren Hemingway, June 30, 2001; Don Chambers, April 1, 2001; Everett Burwell, April 2, 2001; Don Robinson, July 24, 2001; Louis Bower, April 25, 2001; Jack Worland, June 9, 2002.

70 *any sense that this was a grudge rematch:* Interviews, Clyde Lovellette, August 18, 2000; interview Gordon Neff, March 31, 2001.

70 *The starting lineups:* Details of the Shelbyville–Terre Haute game, Luke Walton's WISH radio broadcast, recording courtesy of Shelbyville High School and former athletic director Steve Drake; Tom Carnegie's WIRE radio broadcast, recording courtesy of Larry Sandman, *Indianapolis Star,* March 23, 1949.

77 *"I wondered if my skinny little kids":* Indianapolis News, March 27, 1947. *Shelbyville News,* March 24, 1987.

77 *"No school Monday":* Corky, Lamm, Bulk of Shelby County Apparently Moves into Dressing Room to Hail Champions, *Indianapolis Star,* March 23, 1947.

77 *"Man, oh man, I've wasted seventeen years":* "'It's a Wonderful Dream Come True,' Bruins Say," *Shelbyville Democrat,* March 24, 1947.

77 *"Why are they asking us?":* Interview, Loren Hemingway.

77 *"Shoulda beat 'em the last time":* Corky Lamm, Bulk of Shelby County Apparently Moves into Dressing Room to Hail Champions, *Indianapolis Star,* March 23, 1947.

77 *"I knew we could take Terre Haute":* Shelbyville Democrat, March 24, 1947.

77 *"I want to be a doctor":* Heard by Tom Graham directly, in the original WISH broadcast, March 22, 1947.

77 *Terre Haute fans:* Based on interviews with Shelbyville fans.

77 *a final-game record:* Dale Burgess, "Shelbyville, Garfield Break 11 State Tourney Records," *Indianapolis Star,* March 24, 1947.

78 *Indiana University's Branch McCracken: Shelbyville Democrat,* March 24, 1947.

78 *"would have sworn it was Adolph Rupp's":* Bill Fox Jr., "Afterthoughts," *Indianapolis News,* March 25, 1947.

78 *teams were all white until 1970:* See Fitzpatrick, 222.

79 *"Take it easy boys":* Heard directly by Kermit Graham, father and grandfather of the authors.

80 *the one following VJ Day: Shelbyville Democrat,* March 24, 1947; "Shelbyville Celebrates Victory Into Wee Hours," *Indianapolis News,* March 24, 1947.

80 *"How many Negroes": Indianapolis Recorder,* March 29, 1947.

80 *"I am deeply proud":* Ibid.

80 *"champions now, but":* "Loper Speaks at Program Honoring Team," *Shelbyville Democrat,* March 9, 1947.

81 *every Negro should be proud: Indianapolis Recorder,* April 12, 1947.

81 *"incidental to the school's idealism":* Ibid.

81 Recorder *ran:* Scotty Scott, "Salute to Shelbyville: Shelbyville, Home of Champs, An Ideal Community," *Indianapolis Recorder,* April 12, 1947.

81 *"victory dance in celebration": Shelbyville Democrat,* March 24, 1947.

81 *siblings and black classmates spurned:* Interviews, Mildred Powell, July 20, 2000; Jim Garrett, June 30, 2001; Laura Wicks, May 4, 2001.

82 *Roann Weaver, a pretty:* Interview, Roann Weaver Lewis, July 13, 2002.

Chapter 9

89 *Branch McCracken:* Video, WTIU, "Coach for Life," Indiana University Television; Byrd and Moore, 67–75; Hammel and Klingelhoffer, 84–86, 107, 112; Marquette, 69–141; Laskowski, 86–112.

91 *"Back Home Again in Indiana":* Hoose (1986), 67.

91 *"could fight over the table scraps":* Ibid., 60.

92 *wanted badly to play:* R. Dale Ogden and J. Ronald Newlin, "Race and Sport in Indiana Before And After Jackie Robinson," Hoosierisms Quarterly, Summer 1996.

92 *banquet in Mulberry Room:* "Joint Banquet Honors Teams," *Anderson Daily Bulletin,* April 24, 1946.

92 *"can Wilson play at IU?":* Interview, John Wilson, July 3, 2001. Ogden and Newlin, "Race and Sport. . . ."

92 *"gentleman's agreement":* Existence of the agreement, though publicly denied, was a very open secret. It was confirmed in writing to Indiana University president Herman Wells, by IU staff as early as 1940. Negro Folder, Wells File, Indiana University Archive. It was confirmed by Branch McCracken to Archie Chadd, basketball coach of Anderson High School, when Chadd approached McCracken in the summer of 1938 about the IU basketball program's accepting Anderson's star player, Frank Clemons (Interview, Frank Clemons, March 21, 2005). It was confirmed to Johnny Wilson's coach, Charles Cummings, when he tried to get Big Ten schools to accept Wilson. (Ogden and Newlin, "Race and Sport. . . ."). It was frequently referred to in black newspapers such as the *Pittsburgh Courier,* the *Indianapolis Recorder,* and *Chicago Defender.* Perhaps the best evidence is that, with the exception of Dick Culberson's brief stint as a reserve for Iowa during the 1943–44 season, no black played varsity basketball in the Big Ten until Bill Garrett did so in December 1948.

92 *Dick Culberson:* University of Iowa Sports Information Office.

92 *McCracken had quietly:* Archie Chadd, basketball coach at Anderson High, spoke to McCracken about taking Frank Clemons in the summer of 1938, shortly after McCracken took the IU job, and was told by McCracken that the Big Ten athletic directors had an agreement not to take black basketball players because of anticipated problems on the road (Interview, Frank Clemons, March 21, 2005). George Crowe, Indiana's 1939 Mr. Basketball, has said, "there weren't any blacks in the Big Ten, so IU and Purdue were out" (Pete Cava, "Good in a Pinch: George Crowe Made the Best of His Rare Chances in the Majors," *Johnson County Daily Journal,* June 9, 2002). IU president Herman Wells received a memo from an alum dated March 4, 1941, recommending that IU "check out" Davage Minor, saying "he is a senior at Gary Froebel High School, and while he is colored, your school might no doubt be glad to get him." (Negro Folder, Wells File, Indiana University Archives). Wells passed the memo on to McCracken, who apparently did not follow up. Minor played at the University of Toledo and UCLA and later in the NBA. For other examples, see the section of this book entitled "Eight Who Came Before."

93 *"I don't think he could":* Interview, John Wilson, July 3, 2001; Ogden and Newlin, "Race and Sport. . . ."
93 *Of all the major:* Interview, John Wilson, July 3, 2001.
93 *Wilson averaged more than twenty:* "Johnny Wilson Breaks College Cagers' Scoring Record of Ind.," *Indianapolis Recorder,* March 1, 1947.
94 *"I'm sorry, John":* Interview, John Wilson, July 3, 2001.

Chapter 10

95 *he was soon court-martialed:* Falkner, 76–86; Rampersad, 99–112; Robinson (1995), 18–23.
95 *"I learned that I was in two wars":* Hal Davis, "The Court Martial of Jackie Robinson," *National Law Journal* 17, September 19, 1994.
96 *Membership in the NAACP surged:* Patterson, 20.
96 *"Double V" campaign:* Finkle; Brooks; Martindale and Dunlap.
96 *"I spent four years":* Joseph C. Goulden, *Best Years 1945–50;* Antheneum, New York: 1976; Cf. Patterson, 23.
96 *The country did not make:* Thornbrough (2000), 95–162; Patterson, 10–81; Madison (1986), 241–47.
97 *"Fair and open sports":* W. Blaine Patton, "If So, Why?" (regular column), *Indianapolis Star,* January 10, 1948.
97 *Since the early 1930s:* Silber, 49–66.
97 *"It's my skin":* Different accounts of this story quote Thomas's words slightly differently. The words quoted here are those repeated by Clyde Sukeforth, longtime Dodger scout and colleague of Branch Rickey, in a story by Dave Anderson, "The Days that Brought the Barrier Down," *New York Times,* March 30, 1997. See also Tygiel, 51–52; Rampersad, 121–22; Robinson (1995), 26–27.
98 *At UCLA from 1939 to 1941:* Chancellor Albert Carnesale, "At the Jackie Robinson Plaque Unveiling Ceremony," Los Angeles Memorial Coliseum, April 14, 2005, online; Rampersad, 74–75.
98 *At a now-famous meeting:* Robinson (1995), 25–36; Rampersad, 125–27; Tygiel, 64–67.
99 *threatening a boycott:* Frick, 97–98.
99 *"This is America":* Ibid.
99 *"If you do this":* Stanley Woodward, "National League Averts Strike of Cardinals Against Robinson's Presence in baseball"; "Frick, Breadon Together Quash Anti-Negro Action, Quick Retribution Promised by President of Loop Even If It Wrecks Senior Circuit; General League Walkout Planned by Instigators," *New York Herald Tribune,* May 9, 1947; Stanley Woodward, "The Strike that Failed," *New York Herald Tribune,* May 10, 1947; Rampersad, 174–75.

Chapter 11

101 *Shelby County Coaches:* "All County Cage Teams Are Honored at Banquet," *Shelbyville Democrat,* April 1, 1947.

102 *"You oughtta think":* Interview, Bart Kaufman, July 18, 2003.

102 *Nate Kaufman's life:* Generally, interviews, Bart Kaufman, July 18, 2003; January 18, 2005; March 11, 2005; correspondence, July 16, 2004; January 17, 2005. Father Sam: obituary, *Shelbyville Democrat,* October 18, 1928; *Shelbyville Republican,* October 18, 1928. Paul Cross Award: 1922 Shelbyville High School *Squib.* Coach of St. Joseph's: Indiana High School Basketball Hall of Fame, website; Referee five straight state championships: Ibid.

103 *"There'll never be":* Interview, Bart Kaufman, July 18, 2003.

104 *Indiana's 1947 Mr. Basketball:* Bob Overaker, " 'Mr. Basketball' Honor Is Voted to Bill Garrett," *Indianapolis Star,* May 4, 1947.

105 *"Emmie made it":* "Johnson Named on All-Star Team," *Shelbyville Republican,* May 20, 1947.

105 *bent its whites-only:* Thornbrough (2000), 25; interview, Faburn DeFrantz Jr., June 28, 2001. According to the Senate Avenue Y's fiftieth anniversary publication, "People Are Our Business," in the early 1900s, the general secretary of the Central Avenue Y had refused to join the Senate Avenue Y in a citywide membership drive, stating, "We don't believe in hooking up success with failure."

105 *"There will have to be":* Charles Preston, " 'All-Star' Award Making Disapproved by Writer," *Indianapolis Recorder,* June 21, 1947.

105 *It became the most successful: Indianapolis Recorder,* July 5, 1947.

105 *Garrett specifically thanked:* "Bill Garrett Hails Recorder Stand for Fair Play," *Indianapolis Recorder,* October 18, 1947.

105 *"I may go to UCLA":* Charles Preston, " 'Mr. Basketball' May Spend College Days on West Coast," *Indianapolis Recorder,* June 7, 1947.

106 *"such amazing accuracy":* Bob Overaker, "Shootin' the Stars." (regular column), *Indianapolis Star,* March 24, 1947.

106 *"all just moonglow": Indianapolis Recorder,* April 12, 1947.

106 *"combination was a sober one":* Corky Lamm, "Bulk of Shelby County Apparently Moves Into Dressing Room to Hail Champions," *Indianapolis Star,* March 23, 1947.

106 *He had received a letter from UCLA:* Interview, William L. Garrett, June 5, 1970, Indiana University Oral History Project, Center for the Study of History and Memory ("CSHM") 70-16; interview, Jim Garrett, June 30, 2001; Charles Preston, "Mr. Basketball May Spend College Days on West Coast," *Indianapolis Recorder,* June 7, 1947.

107 *"I asked Tauby":* Jim McKinney, "Kaufman's Finest Legacy to Athletics," *Shelbyville News,* November 25, 1981.

107 *"the best team player":* Bob Overaker, "Star Dust," (regular column), *Indianapolis Star,* March 27, 1947.
108 *Coach Vernon McCain:* Interview, Mildred Powell, June 30, 2001.
108 *"The next time":* Interview, Bart Kaufman, July 18, 2003.

Chapter 12

109 *"I'm going down":* Faburn DeFrantz, unpublished autobiography, 10; interview, Al Spurlock, July 2, 2001.
110 *everyone else a step:* Interview, Faburn DeFrantz Jr., June 28, 2001.
110 *his father, Alonzo:* Ibid.; Painter, 116, 118, 206.
110 *When the Ku Klux Klan:* Interview, Faburn DeFrantz Jr., June 29, 2001; Gardner, 75.
110 *"I don't want this kind":* DeFrantz, 109–10.
110 *When a white fan:* Ibid., 110–11.
110 *Every Christmas Eve:* Interview, Faburn DeFrantz Jr., June 28, 2001.
111 *As the Indianapolis NAACP devolved:* Library of Congress, NAACP II:A256 (Indiana Branches, 1940–55). In December 1941, E. Frederick Morrow, national NAACP branch coordinator, wrote to Representative Robert Brokenburr, "Indianapolis is the only large city in America where there is not an active, wide-awake branch of the NAACP." A month earlier, Morrow noted, seven hundred people had attended Walter White's Monster Meeting speech at DeFrantz's Senate Avenue YMCA.
111 *"As long as I stay":* Faburn DeFrantz obituary, *Indianapolis Star,* September 25, 1964.
111 *largest black YMCA:* Gardner, 24.
111 *By the 1940s, the Y:* Stanley Warren, "The Monster Meetings at the Negro YMCA in Indianapolis," *Indiana Magazine of History,* March 1995; Gardner, 52–55.
111 *Monster Meetings:* Ibid.
112 *"have spoken by simply":* DeFrantz, 113.
112 *It was at the Monster Meetings:* DeFrantz, 107.
112 *Indianapolis had pervasive segregation:* Robert D. Lowe, *Racial Segregation in Indiana 1920–1950,* unpublished dissertation, Ball State University, 1965, 149. Thornbrough (2000), 116–137.
112 *drugstore chain had fired:* Lowe, citing Branch Report, June 11, 1948, Library of Congress, NAACP Archives, "Indianapolis, 1947–48."
112 *"My policy":* *Indianapolis Recorder,* May 24, 1947.
112 *"My administration has been":* Ibid.
113 *side by side with stories of Jackie Robinson:* See, e.g., "Indiana player breaks record," *Chicago Defender,* March 29, 1947.
113 *Both spoke regularly:* "IU Director of Athletics Alvin Bo McMillan, to

be guest speaker at Senate Avenue Banquet," *Indianapolis Recorder,*
February 15, 1947. DeFrantz, 114.

113 *"Any boy who can make":* DeFrantz, 1.

114 *Spurlock, a teacher:* Interview, Al Spurlock, July 2, 2001.

114 *They didn't say much:* Ibid.; DeFrantz, 106–7.

114 *Herman Wells was:* James Stevens, "The Tale of a Houseman," *Indiana Alumni Magazine,* Spring 1998; Wells (1980); 20, 26, 44, 46, 49.
Gallman, et al., Wells's middle name was "B," which was not an abbreviation.

115 *"You're too fat":* Karl Detzer, "This College Campus Is the Whole State," *Readers Digest* (condensed from *Kiwanis Magazine*), March 1939, 37.

115 *He had been dismissed:* Wells (1980), 90; Clark, 399–400.

115 *But Wells never considered:* Gallman, et al., 21.

115 *years of sleepy complacency:* A self-survey committee that Wells appointed upon taking office reported in 1938 that "from whatever data one draws inferences, it is clear that Indiana University does not deserve to be classed with the other state institutions in the Midwest (except Purdue), much less the leading endowed schools of the country." The report called the IU faculty "far from distinguished," noted that IU had only ten departments with doctoral programs, none of which was rated higher than "acceptable" by the American Council of Education's Committee on Graduate Instruction. The committee said "drastic steps" were needed. Jones, 316, citing Wendell W. Wright, Herman T. Briscoe, and Fowler V. Harper, "Report of the Self-Survey Committee to the Board of Trustees of Indiana University," March 21, 1939.

115 *"the privilege of the few":* Ibid.

116 *integrated the IU Union Building's:* Wells (1980), 216–17.

116 *ended segregation at the university swimming pool:* Ibid.

116 *"I want to win":* Wells (1980), 220.

116 *" 'Science' Says Kinsey":* Indianapolis Star, November 17, 1950.

116 *making sex boring:* Gallman, et al., 55.

117 *blanket diagnosis:* Wells (1980), 215.

117 *admitted no more than eighty-four black women:* Negro File, Wells Folder, Indiana University Archives.

117 *John Stewart:* Stewart, 256–303; Wells (1980), 76.

117 *"We must prepare":* Steve Kress, "Crossing the Color Line: Bias Against Black Students Inked in IU's History," *Indiana Daily Student,* March 31, 1999.

117 *"In taking the steps":* Wells (1980), 216.

117 *For years Wells had been worried:* Wells to George Henley, April 23, 1940, "Negro Students, 1939–1940," president's office records, Indiana University Archives.

117 *"No written rule":* Charles Harrell, assistant registrar to Croan Green-
bough, assistant to President Wells, May 9, 1940, "Negro Students,
1939–1940," (Harrell was writing per Henley's request.) president's
office records, Indiana University Archives.

118 *"a decent fellow":* Donal Jones to Ruby Hurley, September 6, 1946,
Library of Congress, NAACP II:A256 (Indiana Branches, 1940–55),
"Bloomington, 1946–51."

118 *Thurgood Marshall, then the top:* Watson, 58.

118 *Walter White, national:* Ruby Hurley to Willard Ransom, December
1947, Library of Congress, NAACP II:A256 (Indiana Branches,
1940–55), "Bloomington, 1946–51."

118 *"I am and shall always remain":* Wildermuth to Ward G. Biddle,
November 19, 1945, Negro File, Indiana University Archives.

118 *A founding citizen:* Wildermuth history, CRA #060—Ora Wildermuth Papers, IU Northwest, Calumet Regional Archives.

119 *"The average of the race":* Wildermuth to Wells, August 24, 1948,
Negro File, Indiana University Archives.

119 *"Why can't meddlers":* Biddle to Wildermuth, October 3, 1945, and
November 17, 1945, Indiana University Archives, Wells File; Wells
(1980), 35.

119 *"Lord God Bartley":* Interview, Peter Fraenkel, July 30, 1970, by
Thomas D. Clark, CSHM #70–13.

119 *had gone to extraordinary lengths:* "Strange Charge of Race Bias Made
at IU," *Indianapolis Recorder,* April 6, 1946.

119 *"Nothing in some time":* Bartley to Wells, Dean H. L. Shoemaker, and
J. A. Franklin, May 28, 1947, IU Archives, Wells File.

119 *"reaction personified":* Interview, Peter Fraenkel, July 30, 1970, by
Thomas D. Clark, CSHM #70–13.

119 *Wells was also going:* Ibid., 7–8; interview, Dorothy Collins, CSHM;
Wells (1980), 301–2, 318–19.

120 *"In him democracy":* DeFrantz, 113.

120 *Wells greeted them:* Interview, Al Spurlock, July 2, 2001; interview,
Dorothy Collins, July 30, 2000. Wells (1980), 217; Wells, "Indiana
University Athletic Hall of Fame Ceremonies," December 13, 1984,
president's office records.

122 *The minute his office door:* Wells (1980), 217–18; interview,
Dorothy Collins, July 30, 2000; interview, William L. Garrett,
CSHM; interview, James Roberson, August 4, 2000; interview,
Bob Cooke, July 10, 2000; interview, Bart Kaufman, July 18,
2003; DeAnna Hines, "Looking Back: IU Breaks the Color Barrier
in Basketball," *Indiana Alumni Magazine,* November-December
1986; T. J. Brown, "IU's Jackie Robinson: Hoosier Breaks Big Ten
Color Line," *Indiana Daily Student,* April 17, 1997; "Garrett Broke
Big Ten Race Barrier," *Indianapolis Star,* March 2, 1986; Jon Calla-

han, "Garrett, McCracken, Paved Way for Conference," *Inside Indiana,* online, n.d.

124 *McCracken had only met:* Interview, Al Spurlock, July 2, 2001; Wells (1980), 217. McCracken described this meeting in part in his speech at Shelbyville's "Bill Garrett Night," March 19, 1951, which was broadcast on Shelbyville's WSRK radio.

Chapter 13

127 *That evening DeFrantz reached:* Kaufman conversations with DeFrantz, Laura Garrett, McCracken, and McCain; interview, Bart Kaufman, July 18, 2003; McCracken and Nate Kaufman speeches at Shelbyville's "Bill Garrett Night," March 19, 1951, broadcast by Shelbyville's WSRK radio.

128 *amid Nashville's vibrant:* Halberstam (1998), 20–24, 51–52, 111–12.

129 *the Solid Block:* Ibid., 111.

129 *a Double V club:* "Debs Support 'DOUBLE V' Drive," *Pittsburgh Courier,* February 14, 1943.

129 *intercollegiate athletics:* George, 82–95; 1948 Tennessee A & I State College *Tennessean;* Official Encyclopedia of the National Football League, 1544–1545.

129 *"I don't know whether":* Charles Preston, " 'Mr. Basketball' May Spend College Days on West Coast," *Indianapolis Recorder,* June 7, 1947.

129 *Nate Kaufman appealed:* Interview, Bart Kaufman, July 18, 2003; interview, Betty Inskeep, July 10, 2000.

131 *He was on his own:* Interview, Betty Inskeep, July 10, 2000; interview, Jim Garrett, June 2, 2002.

131 *Seen from a shared taxi:* On the IU Campus, fall 1947: see, "From September to June, It's Been a Great Year," *Indiana Daily Student,* June 12, 1948; Gilbert Bailey, "Picture of a Postwar Campus," *New York Times Magazine,* December 21, 1947; "Students Crowd Buses, Trains to Bloomington," *Indiana Daily Student,* September 18, 1947; "That Housing Problem," *Indiana Daily Student,* September 6, 1947.

131 *Hoosier Hall, a grandly named:* Interview, Lowell Williams, March 17, 2005; 1948 Indiana University *Arbutus.*

133 *"Think I don't know":* Interview, Gene Ring, July 7, 2001.

134 *Through September and October:* Interview, Phil Buck, October 23, 2001; interview Gene Ring, July 7, 2001; interview; Bill Tosheff, October 1, 2001.

134 *"Maybe I'll be a foot doctor:* Interview, Bill Tosheff, October 1, 2001.

135 *"We seemed to group":* Interview, William L. Garrett, CSHM.

135 *Both the campus and the town:* Wells (1980), 214–20; Beck (1959); Thornbrough (2000), 5, 11, 87, 161–62; interview, Patton Hill, June

6, 1969, by Victoria Cuffel and William Pickett, CSHM #69–15; interview, John E. Stempel, November 19, 1979, by Vincent A. Giroux Jr., CSHM #79–70; Library of Congress, Manuscript Division, NAACP II: A256 (Indiana Branches, 1940–55), "Bloomington, 1946–51"; interview, William Bannon, CSHM; interview, Clarence Wood and Ezell Marrs, July 15, 2001; interview, Dorothy Collins, July 30, 2000; interview, Betty Garrett Inskeep, June 26, 2001; interview, George Taliaferro, October 27, 2000; interview, James Roberson, August 4, 2000.

135 *When Fletcher Henderson:* Interview, John Stempel, CSHM.

135 *skits in blackface:* Watson, 58; "Ubangi Prom to Have Animals and Sarongs," *Indiana Daily Student,* March 18, 1948.

135 *Bloomington restaurants did not:* Sanders; Beck (1959); Library of Congress, NAACP II:A256 (Indiana Branches, 1940–55), "Bloomington, 1946–51;" Negro File, Indiana University Archives.

136 *the storied Gables:* Interview, George Taliaferro, August 30, 2000; interview, Betty Garrett Inskeep, June 26, 2001.

136 *Bloomington's black population:* Gilliam; Watson, 53–65; interviews, Betty Garrett Inskeep, June 26, 2001; interview, James Roberson, August 4, 2000; interview, George Taliaferro, August 30, 2002; interview, Clarence Wood and Ezell Marrs, July 15, 2002.

136 *"We'd just roll up":* Interview, Betty Garrett Inskeep, June 26, 2001.

136 *"We were there":* Interview, George Taliaferro, October 27, 2000.

136 *Mays House:* Kate Barry, "Fond Memories Linger for Mays House Tenants," *Indiana Daily Student,* September 12, 1975; interview, George Taliaferro, October 29, 2000; interview, Clarence Wood and Ezell Marrs, July 15, 2002.

137 *Bill Garrett was welcomed:* Interview, William L. Garrett (1970), CSHM; Betty Garrett Inskeep, June 26, 2001; interview, James Roberson, August 4, 2000; interview, George Taliaferro, October 27, 2000; interview, Clarence Wood and Ezell Mars, July 15, 2002.

137 *joined the campus NAACP:* "Bloomington NAACP Membership List," February 1948, Library of Congress, NAACP II:A256 (Indiana Branches, 1940–55), "Bloomington, 1946–51."

138 *"Am I being treated":* Interview, George Taliaferro, August 30, 2000; interview, James Roberson, January 2001.

138 *tried out for the freshman team:* "Freshman Coach Picks 22 For Hardwood Team," *Indiana Daily Student,* December 18, 1947.

138 Recorder *had carried its first story:* Charles Preston, " 'Mr. Basketball' of 46–47, Bill Garrett, Enters I.U.," *Indianapolis Recorder,* October 4, 1947.

138 *"Race Relations Honor Roll":* "Race Relations Honor Roll," *Indianapolis Recorder,* January 1, 1948.

138 *Indianapolis chapter of the NAACP:* Deanna Hines, "Looking Back: IU Breaks the Color Barrier in Basketball," *Indiana Alumni Magazine,* November/December 1986.

138 *"never more fittingly given":* DeFrantz, 114.

138 *black newspapers around the country:* See Will Robinson, "This Hoosier Hotshot Is Called Mr. Basketball at Indiana U.," *Pittsburgh Courier,* February 4, 1950.

138 *people from as far:* Elmer O'Banion to Herman Wells, October 12, 1947, IU Archives, Wells File.

138 *Wells was not there:* Interview, Peter Fraenkel, CSHM; interview, Dorothy Collins, CSHM; Wells (1980), 318; Bill Shaw, "Man, Myth, Mystery," *Indianapolis Star,* December 6, 2000.

139 *thousands of fans began:* Interview, Clarence Wood and Ezell Marrs, July 15, 2002; interview, George Taliaferro, October 27, 2000.

139 *B-minus average:* Paul J. Harrell to M. T. Eaton, November 8, 1949, IU Archives, Athletics File.

140 *switched his major:* Interview, William L. Garrett, CSHM.

140 *had begun dating Betty Guess:* Interview, Betty Garrett Inskeep, July 10, 2000; interview, George Taliaferro, October 27, 2000. On the Guess family in Madison: Wallis, 49–56, 62–68.

140 *"I just don't have the time":* Interview, Betty Garrett Inskeep, June 26, 2001.

Chapter 14

141 *spoke with Jim Roberson:* Interview, James Roberson, August 4, 2000; interview, Frank Jones, August 2, 2001; interview, Betty Garrett Inskeep, May 4, 2001.

142 *"Freeman Mutiny":* James Warren; Ray Boomhower, "Nobody Wanted Us: Black Aviators at Freeman Field," *Traces of Indiana and Midwestern History,* summer 1993, 38; interview, Jim Roberson, August 4, 2000.

143 *"bothers me today":* Ibid.

143 *McCracken had always been obsessed:* McCracken, 52.

143 *So he pulled:* Interview, Gene Ring, July 7, 2001; interview, Bill Tosheff, October 1, 2001; interview, Phil Buck, October 23, 2001.

143 *McCracken insisted that:* McCracken, 26–31.

143 *"My boys take":* Press release, IU Athletic Archives, Branch McCracken file, n.d.

144 *held a race:* Press release, IU Athletic Archives, Branch McCracken file, n.d.; interview, Gene Ring, July 7, 2001; interview, Jim Schooley, April 3, 2004; interview, Gary Long, April 25, 2004.

144 *McCracken was always the first:* McCracken, 36–37; press release, IU Athletic Archives, Branch McCracken file, n.d.

144 *There was tension:* Based on: Interview, William Garrett, CSHM, and the following interviews: Betty Garrett Inskeep, July 10, 2000; Jim Garrett, June 30, 2001; Gene Ring, July 7, 2001; Phil Buck, October 23, 2001; Bill Tosheff, October 1, 2001; Ernie Andres, March 5, 2005; Don Ritter, November 8, 2005; Lou Watson, July 2, 2001; Ty Robbins, January 16, 2004; Bob Armstrong, April 24, 2004. See also, Irwin Boretz, "Four Sophs Among 7 Possible Starters Named by McCracken," *Bloomington Daily Herald,* December 2, 1948.

145 *"They couldn't":* Interview, William L. Garrett, CSHM.

145 *"I thought at the time":* Ibid.

146 *"There can be no":* McCracken, 9.

146 *Occasionally, in scrimmages:* Interview, William L. Garrett, CSHM; interview, George Taliaferro, October 27, 2000.

146 *"Whatever he did":* Interview, Betty Garrett Inskeep, June 26, 2001.

146 *win over DePauw:* "I.U. Squad Trips DePauw Quintet," *Bloomington Daily Herald,* December 6, 1948.

147 *the Chase Hotel had bent:* Marquette, 131 (citing Mary Jo McCracken); interview, Phil Buck, October 23, 2001; interview, Bill Tosheff, October 1, 2001; interview, Ernie Andres, March 5, 2005.

147 *"If Bill can't eat here":* Interview, Bill Tosheff, October 1, 2001; Marquette, 131 (quoting Mary Jo McCracken).

147 *One hotel manager:* Press release, IU Athletic Archives, Branch McCracken file, n.d.

147 *In Chicago to play:* Deanna Hines, "IU's Bill Garrett First Black Basketball Player in Big Ten," Indiana University, News release, February 24, 1986; IU Athletic Archives, Bill Garrett file, n.d.; interview, Marvin Christie, August 2003.

148 *"Get the nigger":* Interview, Bart Kaufman, July 18, 2003 (relating story told by Branch McCracken).

148 *"Of course, having a Negro":* Interview, William L. Garrett, CSHM.

149 *"For the next two years":* W. R. Breneman to Herman Wells, February 7, 1949, IU Archives, Athletics File.

150 *This new lineup reeled off:* Irwin Kirby, "Revamped Hoosier Lineup in First Home Unveiling," *Bloomington Daily Herald,* February 12, 1949; Steve Boda Jr., "Youth Movement Brings 2d Straight Upset Win," *Bloomington Daily Herald,* February 22, 1949; Charlie Lyons, "Buck, Stuteville and Garrett Lead Scoring," ibid.

150 *"A lot of the pressure":* George Bolinger, "Branch McCracken, Basketball Pioneer," *Lafayette Journal and Courier,* June 19, 1970.

150 *pinned the offender between them:* Based on: Interview, Gene Ring, July 7, 2001.

150 *"Bill Garrett can":* David Condon, "Chicago Writer Recalls Garrett," *Indianapolis Star,* August 18, 1974.

151 *Tosheff crossed his eyes:* Interview, Bill Tosheff, October 1, 2001.

151 *On a long flight:* Ibid.; interview, Ty Robbins, January 16, 2004.

151 *"You're gonna stay":* Interview, Bob Burton, July 9, 2000.

151 *"Our team's record":* "All-American Hopes and Victories Look Bright for 1951 Hoosiers," *Indiana Daily Student,* February 10, 1950.

152 *planning to attend the 500:* Interview, George Taliaferro, October 27, 2000. "Jerry Stuteville, Net Star, Killed," *Indianapolis Times,* May 30, 1950.

153 *Associated Press's first rankings:* "IU Given 4th Place in First Poll," *Indianapolis Star,* December 19, 1950.

153 *third in the AP national:* "Hoosiers Advance to Third in AP Poll," *Bloomington Herald Telephone,* January 30, 1951.

154 *drop a lighted:* Interview, Laskowski, 86–87.

154 *Ring and Illinois's Irv Bemoras traded punches:* Bill Libby, "Game's Waning Minutes," *Indiana Daily Student,* February 20, 1951.

154 *"from somewhere just":* Ibid.

155 *"Ladies and gentlemen":* Vic Rensberger, "Hoosiers Go Out Shooting as Illini Take Over Throne," March 6, 1951, *Indianapolis Star,* March 6, 1951.

155 *final AP Coaches' Poll:* Hoosiers 2nd in Big Ten, 7th in Nation," *Bloomington Herald Telephone,* March 6, 1951.

155 *"No one has played":* Vic Rensberger, "Hoosiers Go Out Shooting as Illini Take Over Throne," *Indianapolis Star,* March 6, 1951.

156 *"They played their":* Ibid.

156 *It was a sad:* Herb Michelson, "Victory Over Wisconsin," *Indiana Daily Student,* March 6, 1951.

156 *referees stepped in:* Ibid.

156 *"From Hammond to Hanover":* Herb Michelson, "Jordan at Flood Stage as Campus Tears Flow Free," *Indiana Daily Student,* IU Athletic Archives, n.d.

156 *Two days later:* Interview, Gene Ring, July 7, 2001; interview, Phil Buck, October 23, 2001.

Chapter 15

158 *The Washington Post announced: Washington Post,* March 8, 1951.

158 *A few weeks earlier:* "Bones' Makes It!" *Indiana Daily Student,* February 17, 1951; " 'Big Bill' Garrett Named All-American," *Shelbyville Democrat,* February 22, 1951.

158 *"Perhaps the finest":* "Our All-American," *Indiana Daily Student,* editorial, January 25, 1951.

158 *"Perhaps in this way":* "What Can Be Done," *Indiana Daily Student,* February 17, 1951.

158 *named Sherman White* (fn.): Rosen, 194–198, 219.

159 *"He's an All-American": Indianapolis Star,* March 10, 1951.

159 *no hard and fast definition:* HickokSports.com, online; Official NCAA Men's Basketball Records Book, online.

159 *a consensus second-team All-American:* Garrett was named to the All-American first team by *The Sporting News;* to the second team by United Press International, Associated Press, the National Association of Basketball Coaches, and *Look;* and to the third team by Converse and the Helms Foundation. Official NCAA Records Book, online; "Various All-American Teams," online at sportstats.com/bball/national/awards/All-American.

159–160 *IU's most valuable player:* Fred Hill, "Banquet Fetes Crimson Cagers," *Bloomington Herald,* n.d., IU Athletic Archives; Jon Callahan, "Garrett, McCracken, Paved Way for Conference," *Inside Indiana,* online, n.d.

160 *All Big Ten first team: Bloomington Herald Telephone,* March 6, 1951.

160 *Balfour Award:* Hammel and Klingelhoffer, 16, 66, 112.

160 *"as great a player":* Fred Hill, "Banquet Fetes Crimson Cagers," *Bloomington Herald,* n.d., IU Athletic Archives.

160 *"All-American Bill Garrett Night":* Deane Roberts, "Garrett Night Brings Back the Thrill for Shelbyville's Big Bill," *Shelbyville News,* March 20, 1951.

160 *"a perfect example":* Ibid.

160 *Despite his having been left off:* Garrett's name had not been on the original list of nineteen nominees for the 1951 college All-Stars that had been sent to a number of top college basketball coaches. But many coaches had written him in as one of their top picks anyway. The prospect of playing with the All-Stars in the series against the Globetrotters forced Garrett to choose between running track for IU—and maintaining his amateur status—or playing more basketball and getting paid for it. He jumped at the chance to play basketball. Jim Heyrock, "Bill Garrett Shuns Track to Join Basketball All-Stars," March 9, 1951, IU Athletic Archives.

161 *"like a professional wrestler":* Bill Libby, "Globetrotter Diary," *Indiana Daily Student,* April 18, 1951.

161 *"It's great":* Bill Libby, "A Nice Guy—That Fits Bill Garrett," *Indiana Daily Student,* March 6, 1951.

161 *For their territorial selection: Official NBA Basketball Encyclopedia,* 249; interview, Bill Tosheff, October 1, 2001. On territorial selections, see Russell and Branch, 117.

161 *finished next to last: Official NBA Basketball Encyclopedia,* 55.

161 *Olympians were player-owned:* Ibid., 50.

161 *Olympians' first three draft picks (fn.): Official NBA Basketball Encyclopedia,* 249, 395–753.

161–162 *refused to let Johnny Wilson:* Interview, John Wilson, July 3, 2001.

162 *Fort Wayne Zollner-Pistons:* Fort Wayne's first two picks were Zeke Sincola of Niagara, and Jack Kiley of Syracuse. *Official NBA Basketball Encyclopedia,* 249, 564, 687.

162 *Garrett was drafted by the Boston Celtics:* Ibid., 249; "Garrett Drafted by Boston as Olympians 'Miss,'" *Indianapolis Recorder,* May 5, 1951.

162 *"Walter, don't you know":* Thomas, 26–27; Green, 228–29.

162 *The NBA had long maintained:* Gould, 175–177; Green, 229–30; Ashe, 15; interview, Joe Rucklick, April 12, 2004.

162 *In the 1920s, Abe Saperstein:* Green; George, 41–57.

162 *Washington Capitols then drafted (fn.):* Official Basketball Encyclopedia, 52–53.

162 *Groza and Beard were arrested (fn.):* Rozen, 189–191.

163 *NBA averaged:* Association for Professional Basketball Research, website.

163 *Saperstein, who wanted to own:* Green, 232.

163 *Saperstein is reported:* Thomas, 27, citing Jerry Nason, "Globe Trotters Boss, Riled by Cooper Deal, Bars Visits to Boston," *Boston Daily Globe,* April 27, 1950.

163 *"my reps . . . tell me":* "Bill Garrett on Trotter Cage Tour," *Pittsburgh Courier,* March 31, 1951.

163 *only momentary outbursts (fn.):* Thomas, 54–55; Green, 232.

164 *Betty Guess:* Interviews, Betty Garrett Inskeep; Gray (2001), 139.

164 *Crystal Beach public:* Wallis, xi–xvi.

164 *"I thought then":* Interview, Gene Ring, July 7, 2001.

164 *Garrett spent the summer:* Interviews, Betty Garrett Inskeep; interview, Mildred Powell, June 30, 2001.

165 *shouting "Bill Garrett!":* Interview, Hallie Bryant, October 26, 2001.

165 *"All-Americans Are Just Players":* Indianapolis Recorder, August 4, 1951.

165 *Garrett worried about:* Bill Garrett letter to Gene Ring, December 27, 1952.

165 *"Every guy":* Ibid.

166 *The Celtics had released:* Interview, William L. Garrett, CSHM; interviews, Betty Garrett Inskeep; interview, Jim Garrett, June 30, 2001.

166 *Globetrotters were offering:* Interview, William L. Garrett, CSHM; interviews, Betty Garrett Inskeep; interview, Jim Garrett, June 30, 2001.

166 *NBA teams still limited:* Thomas, 132–51; interview, Joe Ruklick, April 12, 2004.

166 *Garrett had rebuffed:* Bill Libby, "'A Nice Guy'—That Fits Bill Garrett," *Indiana Daily Student,* March 6, 1951.

166 *Globetrotters, by contrast:* Green; George, 41–57; A&E Biography, "Globetrotters," 1996.

166 *the best basketball team in the world:* Green, 210.

167 *"To me the 'clown princes'"*: Library of Congress, NAACP Files, II:A239 (Indiana Branches, 1940–55), "Bloomington, 1946–51."

167 *avoided the team bus:* Interview, John Wilson, July 3, 2001.

167 *"even in vaudeville"*: David Condon, "Chicago Writer Recalls Garrett," *Indianapolis Star,* August 18, 1974.

168 *as the prospect:* Interview, Bill Tosheff, October 1, 2001.

168 *"He would never talk"*: Interview, Al Spurlock, July 2, 2001.

168 *"It was a sad time"*: Interview, Bill Tosheff, October 1, 2001.

168 *"I'm coming home"*: Interview, Betty Garrett Inskeep, June 26, 2001.

Chapter 16

169 *job in a steel foundry:* Interview, Betty Garrett Inskeep, June 26, 2001.

169 *Crispus Attucks High:* Stanley Warren (1998); Stanley Warren, "Crispus Attucks Basketball and Black Indianapolis in the 1950's," *Indianapolis Magazine of History,* March 2000; Richard Pierce, "More Than a Game: The Political Meaning of High School Basketball in Indianapolis," *Journal of Urban History,* November 2000; Roberts (1999); Aram Goudsouzian, "Baad, Ba-a-ad Tigers: Crispus Attucks Basketball and Black Indianapolis in the 1950s," *Indiana Magazine of History* 96, March 2000.

170 *"Until he thought:* Hoose (1986), 114.

170 *"salary is one of the best"*: Charles Preston, "Want Only Higher Pay: Crowe: 'Advancement' Sole Motive in Seeking New Job," *Indianapolis Recorder,* April 6, 1957.

171 *one of the lowest:* "Here's Why Crowe, Other Naptown Coaches Are Hot," *Indianapolis Recorder,* May 25, 1957.

171 *"is to pray"*: Charles Preston, "Promotion of Crown Floors Attucks Fans," *Indianapolis Recorder,* July 13, 1957.

172 *John Codwell:* Behee, 40–41; University of Michigan, Sports Information Office.

172 *Rickey Ayala:* Michigan State University, Sports Information Office.

172 *Don Eaddy:* University of Michigan, Sports Information Office.

172 *McKinley "Deacon" Davis:* University of Iowa, Sports Information Office.

172 *Ernie Hall:* Interview, Alan Karpick, author, *Boilermaker Basketball: Great Purdue Teams and Players,* Chicago: Bonus Books, 1989.

172 *Walt Moore:* Interview, Lauren Tate, *Champaign News-Gazette,* April 2, 2004.

172 *"I'd love to have"*: "Mich. Coach Denies Big Nine Discrimination," *Indianapolis Recorder,* January 21, 1950.

172 *"Bill Garrett left"*: Interview, Wally Choice, August 20, 2005.

172 *"Bill Garrett set the bar"*: Interview, Stanley Warren, July 10, 2000.

173 *"request for an athletic scholarship"*: Gibson (1994), 23–24.

174   *"No NBA team"*: *Indianapolis Recorder,* May 16, 1957.

174   *whatever any such amount* (fn.): Chamberlain, 144–45.

174   *Robertson has said* (fn.): Robertson, 74.

175   *new school versus old school:* Interview, Peter Obremskey, August 19, 2005; interview, Clarence Doninger, August 19, 2005; interview, Bill Orwig Jr., April 7, 2005; interviews, Bart Kaufman.

175   *lie detector test:* Video, "Coach for Life."

175   *"Now what would"*: Ray Marquette, "McCracken of IU Fame Dies," *Indianapolis Star,* June 5, 1970.

175   *twenty-five years in one job:* "On the Occasion of Herman B Wells' 90th Birthday," *Indiana Alumni Magazine,* March–April 1992.

175   *Wells had transformed:* Wells (1980); Bill Shaw, "Man, Myth, Mystery," *Indianapolis Star,* December 6, 2000; James Capshew, "Alma Pater: Herman B Wells and the Rise of Indiana University," *Indiana Daily Student,* March 20, 2000.

176   *"Is there anything more"*: Bill Shaw, "Man, Myth, Mystery," *Indianapolis Star,* December 6, 2000.

176   *Faburn DeFrantz turned:* Interview, Faburn DeFrantz Jr., June 28, 2001; interview, Stanley Warren, July 10, 2000; *The Y's Man,* February 10, 1951, March 3, 1951.

176   *Nate Kaufman:* Obituary, *Shelbyville News,* November 19, 1981; interviews, Bart Kaufman.

177   *"a substantial increase"*: "Barnes Accepts New Three-Year Contract Here: Coach of State Champions Will Get Substantial Increase," *Shelbyville Democrat,* April 24, 1947.

177   *Doc Barnett:* Interview, Charles Barnett, April 24, 2004; interview, Daniel Barnett, April 4, 2004; Jim McKinney, "As Coach, Barnett Shied from Limelight," *Shelbyville News,* February 13, 1987.

178   *Hank Hemingway:* Interviews, Loren Hemingway.

178   *Bill Breck:* Interviews, Bill Breck.

178   *Marshall Murray:* Bernard Sleeth, "Late Blooming Bears Surprise Team of 1947," *Shelbyville News,* n.d.

178   *Emerson Johnson:* Obituary, *Shelbyville News,* December 23, 1997; interview, Felix Megerle, April 16, 2005; Jim McKinney, "Champs Historic Shot," *Shelbyville News,* March 22, 1997. *"like trying to shoot"*: interview, Loren Hemingway, June 30, 2001; letter to NAACP: William Smith to Gloster Current, April 18, 2004, Library of Congress, NAACP Archives II: 256 (Indiana Branches, 1940–55), "Bloomington, 1946–51; Shelbyville file; interview, Jack Worland, June 9, 2002.

179   *Bill and Betty started a family:* Interviews, Betty Garrett Inskeep; Tina Garrett; Judith Garrett Shelton; Laurie Garrett Cobbini; Billy Garrett; Gray (2001), 183–203.

180 *first blacks to compete:* Interview, Laurie Garrett Cobbini; Gray (2001), 141, 195.

180 *qualified to be:* Interviews, Betty Garrett Inskeep; Gray (2001), 185 (Tina Garrett interview transcript).

180 *turned meets held out of town:* Gray (2001), 195 (Laurie Garrett interview transcript).

180 *"The only person who can":* Interview, Betty Garrett Inskeep, July 10, 2000.

180 "Compete with situations": Ibid.

180 *"Talent is what you do":* Gray (2001), 198 (Billy Garrett interview transcript).

180 *Every summer:* Interview, Laurie Garrett Cobbini; Gray (2001), 193. (Laurie Garrett interview transcript).

180 *taught the children:* Gray (2001), 187, 194 (Tina and Laurie Garrett interview transcripts).

180 *cooked the family:* Gray (2001), 184 (Tina Garrett interview transcript).

180 *He was handy:* Gray (2001), 193 (Laurie Garrett interview transcript).

180 *worked summers:* Interview, Oscar Mutz, April 18, 2004; interview, Bart Kaufman, July 18, 2002.

180 *more black referees: Indianapolis Recorder,* April 6, 1959; ibid., April 13, 1959.

181 *1959 Coach of the Year:* Jim McKinney, "175 Attend Banquet Honoring 'Coach of the Year' Bill Garrett," *Shelbyville News,* May 1, 1959.

181 *Touchdown Club:* Kaye Kessler, "TD Club Honors Stars," *Columbus Citizen Journal,* January 17, 1959.

181 *applied for the IU coaching job:* Laskowski, 6.

182 *He had smoked:* Interview, Clarence Wood, July 15, 2001.

182 *episodes of heart:* Interviews, Betty Garrett Inskeep; interview, James Roberson, August 4, 2000.

182 *had a way of teaching:* Gray (2001), 198–99 (Billy Garrett, interview transcript).

182 *One summer day:* Gray (2001), 146–7; interviews, Betty Garrett Inskeep; interview, James Roberson, August 4, 2000; obituary, *Indianapolis Star,* August 8, 1974.

182 *when the wake was held:* Gray (2001), 133, 149, 190. Interviews, Betty Garrett Inskeep.

182 *honorary pallbearers:* Gray (2001), 133.

182 *still leaving the church:* Gray (2001), 190 (Judith Garrett Shelton interview transcript).

182 *He had never spoken:* Interviews, Betty Garrett Inskeep; Tina Garrett;

Judith Garrett Shelton; Laurie Garrett Cobbini; Billy Garrett; Al Spurlock; Clarence Wood; Gray (2001), 167, 177, 191.

183 *assigned to write about:* Interview, Don Robinson, July 5, 2001.

183 *"I would be letting* him *down":* Interview, Wally Choice, August 20, 2005.

183 *"made it a pleasant situation for me":* Ibid.

183 *generation of gym-building:* Schwomeyer, 343; Indiana Basketball Hall of Fame Museum Archives.

184 *"That name should be":* Shelbyville News, August 19, 1974.

184 *dedication ceremony:* Shelbyville News, February 3, 1975.

185 *Lovellette went missing:* Interview, Clyde Lovellette, August 18, 2000.

185 *"It ate at him":* Interview, James Roberson, August 4, 2000.

186 *"I will never forget":* DeFrantz, 102.

Postscript

189 *"Truly it seems":* Wallis, xii–xiii.

190 *"like they're doing me a great favor":* Forrest Llewellen and Bruce Witwer, "Bill Garrett Unhappy in Big 10," *Ohio State News,* February 25, 1950.

Eight Who Came Before

193 *Johnny Wilson:* Indiana Basketball Hall of Fame, website; interview, John Wilson, July 3, 2001.

194 *Bobby Milton:* Indiana Basketball Hall of Fame, website.

194 *Chuck Harmon:* Ibid.; University of Toledo Varsity "T" Hall of Fame website; Victoria Sun, "Reds Honor First Black Player," *Cincinnati Post,* April 21, 2004.

194 *Davage Minor:* Indiana University Northwest, Calumet Regional Archives, CRA #403, Davage Minor Papers; Christgau.

195 *George Crowe:* Indiana Basketball Hall of Fame, website; University of Indianapolis Greyhound Club Hall of Fame, website; "Good in a Pinch: George Crowe Made the Best of His Rare Chances in the Majors," *Johnson County [Ind.] Daily Journal,* June 8–9, 2002.

195 *Frank Clemons:* Interview, Frank Clemons, March 21, 2005; University of Toledo Varsity "T" Hall of Fame, website.

196 *Dave Dejernett:* Indiana Basketball Hall of Fame, website.

196 *Jack Mann:* Indiana Basketball Hall of Fame, website.

Sources

Interviews

Ernie Andres, Bob Armstrong, Charles Barnett, Daniel Barnett, Louis Bower, Bill Breck, Peggy Yarber Breece, Jack Brown, Hallie Bryant, Phil Buck, Bob Burton, Jim Byers, Gene Byrd, Tom Carnegie, Walker Caryl, Don Chambers, Wally Choice, Marvin Christie, Frank Clemons, Peg Cliadakis, Laurie Garrett Cobbini, Dorothy Collins, Leroy "D." Compton, Bob Cooke, Joe Crosby, Ray Crowe, Jim Cummings, Faburn DeFrantz Jr., Mae Dickinson, Clarence Doninger, Bob Dro, Loretta Eckstein, Richard Fields, Jack Fix, Barbara Floyd, Billy Garrett, Jim Garrett, Tina Garrett, Mildred Giden, John Gipson, George Glass, Bob Hammel, Jack Hauk, Loren Hemingway, Bill Himmelman, Richard Hughes, Betty Garrett Inskeep, Frank Jones, Alan Karpick, Bart Kaufman, Bob King, Jack Krebs, Roann Weaver Lewis, Gary Long, Clyde Lovellette, Tom Lux, James Madison, Ezell Marrs, Bob Masters, Ken McDiffett, Mick McDuffy, Larry McIntyre, Felix Megerle, Ward Merchant, Thomas Mitchell, Norman Morris, Oscar Mutz, Gordon Neff, Peter Obremskey, Bill Orwig Jr., Charles Peters, Mildred Powell, Gene Ring, Don Ritter, Ty Robbins, James Roberson, Don Robinson, Joe Ruklick, Larry Sandman, Jim Schooley, Herb Schwomeyer, Judith Garrett Shelton, John Simpson, Eric Smithburn, Al Spurlock, Osma Spurlock, Wava Stephens, Jim Strickland, George Taliaferro, Loren Tate, Elizabeth Ivie Theobald, Bill Tosheff, Earl Townsend, Don Veller, Stanley Warren, Lou Watson, Laura Mae Wicks, Bill Wiggins, Lowell Williams, Johnny Wilson, Walt Wintin, Clarence Wood, John Wooden, Jack Worland, Patricia Haehl Wright.

Books

American Guide Series. *Indiana.* WPA: 1947.

Ashe, Arthur R. Jr. *A Hard Road to Glory: The African-American Athlete in Basketball.* New York: Amistad Press, 1988; reprint 1993.

Auerbach, Red, and John Feinstein. *Let Me Tell You a Story: A Lifetime in the Game.* New York and Boston: Little, Brown and Company, 2004.

Baker, Ronald L., ed. *Homeless, Friendless and Penniless: The WPA Interviews with Former Slaves Living in Indiana.* Bloomington: Indiana University Press, 2000.

Banta, R. E., ed. *Hoosier Caravan: A Treasury of Indiana Life and Lore.* Bloomington: Indiana University Press, 1951; reprint 1975.

Bates, Don M., *All-Star Memories: A History of the Indianapolis Star's Indiana-Kentucky All-Star Basketball Series.* Indianapolis Newspapers, Inc., 1989.

Beck, Bill. *Play On: Celebrating 100 Years of High School Sports in Indiana.* Indianapolis: Cranfill & Company for the Indiana High School Athletic Association, 2003.

Bederman, Gail. *Manliness & Civilization: A Cultural History of Gender and Race in the United States, 1880–1917.* Chicago: University of Chicago Press, 1995.

Bedford, John R., and Paul East, eds. *82 Years of JHS Wildcats: A History of Jasper High School Boys Varsity Basketball, 1913–1995.* Jasper, Ind.: Paul East, 1995.

Behee, John. *Hail to the Victors! Black Athletes at the University of Michigan.* Ann Arbor: University of Michigan Press, 1974.

Bodenhamer, David J., and Robert G. Barrows, eds. *The Encyclopedia of Indianapolis.* Bloomington: Indiana University Press, 1994.

Brooks, Maxwell. *The Negro Press Re-examined.* Boston: Christopher Publishing House, 1959.

Brown, Ward E., and Gladys L. Ward. *Indiana High School Athletic Association Membership History, 1903–1983.* Indianapolis: Indiana High School Athletic Association, 1984.

Bundles, A'lelia. *On Her Own Ground: The Life and Times of Madam C. J. Walker.* New York: Scribner, 2001.

Byrd, Cecil K., and Ward W. Moore. *Varsity Sports at Indiana University: A Pictorial History.* Bloomington: Indiana University Press, 1999.

Cameron, James. *A Time of Terror: A Survivor's Story.* Baltimore: Black Classic Press, 1994.

Carroll, Bob, Michael Gershman, David Neft, and John Thorn, eds. *Total Football II: The Official Encyclopedia of the National Football League.* New York: HarperCollins Publishers, 1997.

Cayton, Andrew R. L. *Frontier Indiana*. Bloomington: Indiana University Press, 1998.

Chamberlain, Wilt. *A View from Above*. New York: Villard Books, 1991.

Chapin, Dwight, and Jeff Prugh. *The Wizard of Westwood: Coach John Wooden and His UCLA Bruins*. New York: Warner Paperback Library, 1973.

Christgau, John. *The Origins of the Jump Shot: Eight Men Who Shook the World of Basketball*. Lincoln, Neb.: University of Nebraska Press, 1999.

Clark, Thomas D. *Indiana University: Midwestern Pioneer, Vol. II, In Mid-Passage*. Bloomington: Indiana University Press, 1973.

Crump, William L. *The Story of Kappa Alpha Psi: A History of the Beginning and Development of a College Greek Letter Organization, 1911–1991*. Philadelphia: Kappa Alpha Psi Fraternity, 1991.

Entine, John. *Taboo: Why Black Athletes Dominate Sports and Why We're Afraid to Talk About It*. New York: Public Affairs, 2000.

Erskine, Carl. *Tales From the Dodger Dugout*. Champaign, Ill.: Sports Publishing, Inc., 2000.

———. *What I Learned from Jackie Robinson: A Teammate's Reflections On and Off the Field*. New York: McGraw-Hill, 2005.

Falkner, David. *Great Time Coming: The Life of Jackie Robinson from Baseball to Birmingham*. New York: Simon & Schuster, 1995.

Finkle, Lee. *Forum for Protest: The Black Press During World War II*. Cranbury, N.J.: Associated University Presses, 1975.

Fitzpatrick, Frank. *And the Walls Came Tumbling Down: Kentucky, Texas Western, and the Game That Changed American Sports*. New York: Simon & Schuster, 1999.

Frick, Ford C. *Games, Asterisks, and People: Memoirs of a Lucky Fan*. New York: Crown Publishers, 1973.

Gallman, John, Rosann Greene, Jim Weigand, and Doug Wilson, eds. *Herman Wells Stories: As Told by His Friends on his 90th Birthday*. Bloomington: Indiana University Press, 1992.

George, Nelson. *Elevating the Game: Black Men and Basketball*. New York: HarperCollins Publishers, 1992.

Gibbs, Wilma L., ed. *Indiana's African-American Heritage: Essays from Black History News and Notes*. Indianapolis: Indiana Historical Society, 1993.

Gibson, Bob. *From Ghetto to Glory: The Story of Bob Gibson*. Englewood Cliffs, N.J.: Prentice-Hall, 1968.

———, with Lonnie Wheeler. *Stranger to the Game: The Autobiography of Bob Gibson*. New York: Viking, 1994.

Gildea, William. *Where the Game Matters Most*. Chicago: Triumph Books, 1997.

Gilliam, Frances V. Halsell. *A Time to Speak: A Brief History of the Afro-Americans of Bloomington, Indiana, 1865–1965.* Bloomington: Pinus Strobus Press, 1985.

Glenn, Dale. *The History of the Indiana High School Athletic Association.* Greenfield, Ind.: Mitchell-Fleming Publishers, 1976.

Goodman, James. *Stories of Scottsboro.* New York: Vintage Books/Random House, 1994.

Gould, Todd. *Pioneers of the Hardwood: Indiana and the Birth of Professional Basketball.* Bloomington: Indiana University Press, 1998.

Gray, Hetty. *Net Prophet: The Bill Garrett Story.* Fairland, Ind.: Sugar Creek Press, 2001.

Gray, Ralph D. *IUPUI—The Making of an Urban University.* Bloomington: Indiana University Press, 2003.

Green, Ben. *Spinning the Globe: The Rise, Fall and Return to Greatness of the Harlem Globetrotters.* New York: Amistad, 2005.

Groomes, Melvin H. *Then and Now.* Self-published, 1996.

Guffey, Greg, and Bob Hammel. *The Greatest Basketball Story Ever Told: The Milan Miracle, Then and Now.* Bloomington: Indiana University Press, 1993.

Gunther, John. *Inside U.S.A.* New York: Harper & Brothers, 1947.

Guttman, Allen. *A Whole New Ball Game: An Interpretation of American Sports.* Chapel Hill: University of North Carolina Press, 1988.

Halberstam, David. *The Children.* New York: Random House, 1998.

Hamilton, Donald. *Hoosier Temples: A Pictorial History of Indiana's High School Basketball Gyms.* St. Louis: G. Bradley, 1993.

Hammel, Bob. *Hoosiers Classified: Indiana's Love Affair with One-Class Basketball.* Indianapolis: Masters Press, 1997.

———, and Kit Klingelhoffer. *The Glory of Old IU: 100 Years of Indiana Athletics.* Champaign, Ill.: Sports Publishing, Inc., 1999.

Hartmann, Douglas. *Race, Culture and the Revolt of the Black Athlete: The 1968 Olympic Protests and Their Aftermath.* Chicago: University of Chicago Press, 2003.

Higginbotham, A. Leon. *Shades of Freedom; Racial Politics and Presumptions of the American Legal Process.* Oxford: Oxford University Press, 1996.

Higginbotham, Evelyn Brooks. *Righteous Discontent: The Women's Movement in the Black Baptist Church, 1880–1920.* Cambridge, Mass.: Harvard University Press, 1993.

Hine, Darlene Clark. *When Truth Is Told: A History of Black Women's Culture and Community in Indiana, 1875–1950.* Indianapolis: The National Council of Negro Women, Indianapolis Section, 1981.

Hiner, Jason. *Indiana University Basketball Encyclopedia.* Champaign, Ill.: Sports Publishing L.L.C., 2005.

Hollander, Zander, and Alex Sachare, eds. *The Official NBA Basketball Encyclopedia.* New York: Villard Books, 1989.

Hoose, Phillip M. *Hoosiers: The Fabulous Basketball Life of Indiana.* New York: Vintage Books, 1986; reprinted, Indianapolis: Guild Press Emmis Books, 1995.

———. *Necessities: Racial Barriers in American Sports.* New York: Random House, 1989.

Hoover, Dwight W. *A Pictorial History of Indiana.* Bloomington: Indiana University Press, 1980.

Jones, James H. *Alfred C. Kinsey.* New York: W. W. Norton, 1997.

Knight, Bob, with Bob Hammel. *Knight: My Story.* New York: Thomas Dunne Books/St. Martin's Press, 2002.

Knight, Max. *Somebody Stole the Pea out of My Whistle: The Golden Age of Hoosier Basketball Referees.* Indianapolis: Guild Press, 1995.

Kuska, Bob. *Hot Potato: How Washington and New York Gave Birth to Black Basketball and Changed America's Game Forever.* Charlottesville and London: University of Virginia Press, 2004.

Laskowski, John, with Stan Sutton. *Tales from the Hoosier Locker Room.* Champaign, Ill.: Sports Publishing L.L.C., 2003.

Lawrence, Dale. *Hoosier Hysteria Road Book: A Guide to the Byways of Indiana High School Basketball.* South Bend: Diamond Communications, Inc., 2001.

Loewen, James W. *Sundown Towns.* New York: The New Press, 2005.

Logan, Rayford. *The Negro and the Post-War World: A Primer.* Washington, D.C.: The Minorities Publishers, 1945.

Lutholtz, William M. *Grand Dragon: D. C. Stephenson and the Ku Klux Klan in Indiana.* West Lafayette: Purdue University Press, 1991.

Lyda, John W. *The Negro History of Indiana.* Terre Haute: John Lyda, 1953.

Lynd, Robert S., and Helen Merrell Lynd. *Middletown: A Study in Modern American Culture.* New York: Harcourt, Brace and World, 1929; reprint 1956.

———. *Middletown in Transition: A Study in Cultural Conflicts.* New York: Harcourt, Brace, and World, 1937.

Madison, James H. *A Lynching in the Heartland: Race and Memory in America.* New York: St. Martin's Press, 2001.

———. *Indiana Through Tradition and Change: A History of the Hoosier State and Its People, 1920–1945.* Indianapolis: Indiana Historical Society, 1982.

———. *The Indiana Way: A State History.* Bloomington: Indiana University Press, 1986.

Major, Charles. *The Bears of Blue River.* New York: Doubleday & McClure, 1901; reprinted, Bloomington: Indiana University Press, 1984.

Marquette, Ray. *Indiana University Basketball.* New York: Alpine Books for the Indiana University Alumni Association and Indiana University Athletic Department, 1975.

Martin, John Barlow. *Indiana: An Interpretation*. New York: Alfred A. Knopf, 1947.

May, Bill. *Tourney Time: The Indiana High School Athletic Association Boys Basketball Tournaments 1911–2003*. Indianapolis: Guild Press Emmis Books, 2003.

McCracken, Branch. *Indiana Basketball*. Englewood Cliffs, N.J.: Prentice-Hall, 1955.

McFadden, Marian. *Biography of a Town: Shelbyville, Indiana, 1822–1962*. Shelbyville, Ind.: Tippecanoe Press, 1968.

Mellen, Joan. *Bob Knight: His Own Man*. New York: Avon Books, 1989.

Michener, James. *Sports in America*. New York: Random House, 1976.

Moore, Leonard J. *Citizen Klansmen: The Ku Klux Klan in Indiana, 1921–1928*. Chapel Hill: University of North Carolina Press, 1991.

Myrdal, Gunnar. *An American Dilemma: The Negro Problem and Modern Democracy*. New York: Harper & Row, 1944; reprinted, New Brunswick: Transaction Publishers, 1996.

Naismith, James. *Basketball's Origins: Creative Problem Solving in the Gilded Age*. New York: Associated Press, 1941.

———. *Spalding Athletic Library: Basketball*. New York: American Sports Publishing, 1894.

Nelson, George. *Elevating the Game: Black Men and Basketball*. New York: HarperCollins Publishers, 1992.

Olsen, Jack. *The Black Athlete*. New York: Time-Life Books, 1969.

Padgett, Bob, and Bill Richardson. *Hatchets: A Comprehensive History of Washington High School Basketball, 1905–1996*. Washington, Ind.: Prep Sports Publishing, 1986.

Painter, Nell Irvin. *Exodusters: Black Migration to Kansas after Reconstruction*. New York: W.W. Norton, 1986.

Patterson, James T. *Grand Expectations: The United State, 1945–74*. Oxford: Oxford University Press, 1996.

Peterson, Robert W. *Cages to Jump Shots: Pro Basketball's Early Years*. New York: Oxford University Press, 1990.

Pieratt, Marty, and Ken Honeywell. *Bobby Plump: Last of the Small Town Heroes*. Indianapolis: Good Morning Publishing Company, 1997.

Raisor, Philip. *Outside Shooter: A Memoir*. Columbia, Mo., and London: University of Missouri Press, 2003.

Rampersad, Arnold. *Jackie Robinson: A Biography*. New York: Alfred A. Knopf, 1997.

Reese, William J., ed. *Hoosier Schools Past and Present*. Bloomington: Indiana University Press, 1998.

Reichler, Joseph L., ed. *The Baseball Encyclopedia*. New York: Macmillan, 1988.

Rickey, Branch, with Arthur Mann. *Branch Rickey: American in Action.* Boston: Houghton Mifflin, 1957.

Roberts, Randy. *But They Can't Beat Us: Oscar Robertson and the Crispus Attucks Tigers.* Champaign, Ill.: Sports Publishing, 1999.

———, and James Olson. *Winning Is the Only Thing: Sports in America Since 1945.* Baltimore: Johns Hopkins University Press, 1989.

Robertson, Oscar. *The Big O: My Life, My Times, My Game.* New York: Rodale Books, 2003.

Robinson, Jackie. *I Never Had It Made.* New York: CCC/HarperCollins Publishers, 1995.

———. *Baseball Has Done It.* Philadelphia: Lippincott, 1964; reprinted, New York: Ig Publishing, 2005.

Robison, Roger. *Everett Case and the Frankfort Hot Dogs: When Indiana Was King.* Vincennes, Ind.: Hot Dog Press, 1998.

Rosen, Charley. *Scandals of '51: How the Gamblers Almost Killed College Basketball.* New York: Seven Stories Press, 1978; reprint 1999.

Rottenberg, Dan, ed. *Middletown Jews: The Tenuous Survival of an American Jewish Community.* Bloomington: Indiana University Press, 1997.

Russell, Bill, and Taylor Branch. *Second Wind: The Memoirs of an Opinionated Man.* New York: A Fireside Book/Simon & Schuster, 1979.

Sanders, Scott Russell. *In Limestone Country.* Boston: Beacon Press, 1985.

Savage, Barbara Dianne. *Broadcasting Freedom: Radio, War and the Politics of Race, 1938–1948.* Chapel Hill: University of North Carolina Press, 1999.

Schwomeyer, Herb. *Hoosier Hysteria: A History of Indiana High School Boys Single Class Basketball,* 9th ed. Greenfield, Ind.: Mitchell-Fleming, 1997.

Shelby County Historical Society. *Shelby County, Indiana: History and Families.* Paducah, Ky.: Turner Publishing, 1992.

Silber, Irwin. *Press Box Red: The Story of Lester Rodney, the Communist Who Helped Break the Color Line in American Sports.* Philadelphia: Temple University Press, 2003.

Stewart, John. *Yesterday Was Tomorrow.* Durham, N.C.: Seeman Printing Division of Fisher-Harrison, 1976.

Thomas, Ron. *They Cleared the Lane: The NBA's Black Pioneers.* Lincoln and London: University of Nebraska Press, 2002.

Thornbrough, Emma Lou. *The Negro in Indiana Before 1900: A Study of a Minority.* Bloomington: Indiana University Press, 1993 (reprint).

———. *Indiana Blacks in the Twentieth Century.* Bloomington: Indiana University Press, 2000.

———. *Since Emancipation: A Short History of Indiana Negroes, 1863–1963.* Indianapolis: Indiana Division, American Negro Emancipation Centennial Authority, 1963.

Trogdon, Wendell. *No Harm No Foul: Referees Are People, Too.* Evanston, Ill.: Highlander Press, 1987.

Trotter, Joe William Jr. *River Jordan: African American Urban Life in the Ohio River Valley.* Lexington: University of Kentucky Press, 1998.

Tunis, John R. *Yea Wildcats!* New York: Harcourt Brace Jovanovich, 1944.

Tygiel, Jules. *Baseball's Great Experiment: Jackie Robinson and His Legacy.* New York: Oxford University Press, 1997.

Vincent, Stephen A. *Northern Seed, Southern Soil: African-American Farm Communities in the Midwest, 1765–1900.* Bloomington: Indiana University Press, 1999.

Wallis, Don. *All We Had Was Each Other: An Oral History of the Black Community of Madison, Indiana.* Bloomington: Indiana University Press, 1998.

Warren, James C. *The Tuskegee Airman Mutiny at Freeman Field.* Cincinnati: Conyers, 1998.

Warren, Stanley. *Crispus Attucks High School: "Hail to the Green, Hail to the Gold."* Virginia Beach, Va.: The Donning Company, Publishers, 1998.

Watson, Bernard C. *Colored, Negro, Black: Chasing the American Dream.* Philadelphia: JDC Books, 1997.

Wells, Herman B. *Being Lucky: Reminiscences and Reflections.* Bloomington: Indiana University Press, 1980.

Wertheim, L. Jon. *Transition Game: How Hoosiers Went Hip-Hop.* New York: Putnam, 2005.

Wetnight, John. *Shelby County, Riled Up!* Shelbyville, Ind.: Tippecanoe Press, 1976.

Wideman, John Edgar. *Hoop Roots: Basketball, Race and Love.* Boston and New York: Houghton Mifflin, 2001.

Wiggins, David K. *Glory Bound: Black Athletes in a White America.* Syracuse: Syracuse University Press, 1997.

Wilson, Kenneth L. (Tug), and Jerry Brondfield. *The Big Ten.* Englewood Cliffs, N.J.: Prentice-Hall, 1967.

Wooden, John. *They Call Me Coach.* New York: Bantam Books, 1972.

Zinkoff, Dave, with Edgar Williams. *Around the World with the Harlem Globetrotters.* Philadelphia: Macrae Smith, 1953.

Articles, Essays, and Reports

Anderson, Dave. "When Sherman White Threw It All Away." *New York Times* (March 22, 1998).

Bailey, Gilbert. "Picture of a Postwar Campus." *New York Times Magazine* (December 21, 1947).

Bell, Edward Price. "Creed of the Klansman." *Chicago Daily News* (1924) (Indiana Historical Society HS 2330.K63 Pamphlet Collection).

Bigham, Darrel E. "The Black Press in Indiana, 1879–1985." *The BlackPress in the Middle West, 1865–1985.* Ed. Henry Lewis Suggs. Westport, Conn.: Greenwood Press, 1996.

Bolinger, George. "Branch McCracken, Basketball Pioneer Who Broke Color Line and Made Fast Breaks Faster." *Lafayette Journal and Courier* (June 19, 1970).

Boomhower, Ray. "Nobody Wanted Us: Black Aviators at Freeman Field." *Traces of Indiana and Midwestern History* (Summer 1993).

Boyle, Robert. "The Private World of the Negro Ballplayer." *Sports Illustrated* (March 21, 1960).

Brooks, Jonathan. "Indianapolis: A City in the Middle of the Road." *New Republic* (November 14, 1928).

"Butler University Expelled from North Central Group." *Indianapolis Star* (March 20, 1930).

Callahan, Jon. "Garrett, McCracken Paved Way for Conference." *Inside Indiana* (online magazine, no date).

Carey, Jack. "An SEC Trailblazer Gets His Due." *USA Today* (February 20, 2004).

Carroll, J. C. "The Beginnings of Public Education for Negroes in Indiana." *Journal of Negro Education* (October 1939).

Craig, David. Numerous articles in the *Shelbyville News.*

Crichton, Kyle. "Indiana Madness." *Collier's* (February 6, 1937).

Davis, Hal. "The Court Martial of Jackie Robinson," *National Law Journal* 17, no. 3 (September 19, 1994): A12.

Floyd, Barbara L. "Chewing Tobacco, Meat Packers, Hamburger Chains, and Automobile Dealerships: Early Professional Basketball in Toledo." *Northwest Ohio History* 59 (no. 1, 2003).

Gildea, William. "A Major League Friendship: Carl Erskine Remembers Jackie Robinson and the Brooklyn Dodgers." *Traces* 9 (Winter 1997).

Goudsouzian, Aram. "Ba-ad, Ba-a-ad Tigers: Crispus Attucks Basketball and Black Indianapolis in the 1950s." *Indiana Magazine of History* 96 (March 2000).

Grundman, Adolph. "Image of the Intercollegiate Sports and the Civil Rights Movement." *Arena* 3 (Fall 1979).

Halberstam, David. "The Basket-Case State." *Esquire* (June 1985).

Hamilton, Ron. Numerous articles in the *Shelbyville News.*

Hines, DeAnna. "IU's Bill Garrett First Black Basketball Player in Big Ten." Indiana University News Release (February 24, 1986).

Jackson, Marion E. "Sports of the World." *Atlanta Daily World* (March 6, 1953).

Kelley, Brent. "Chuck Harmon: The Black Red." *Vintage & Classic Baseball Collector* 7 (July/August 1996).

Martin, Charles H. "The Color Line in Midwestern College Sports, 1890–1960." *Indiana Magazine of History* 98 (June 2002).

Martindale, Carolyn, and Lillian Rae Dunlap. "The African Americans." In *U.S. News Coverage of Racial Minorities: A Sourcebook, 1934–1996.*

Eds. Beverly Ann Deepe Keever, Carolyn Martindale, and Mary Ann Weston. Westport, Conn.: Greenwood Press, 1997.

McKinney, Jim. Numerous articles in the *Shelbyville News*.

Miller, Jack. "Speed Up! An Interview with Coach McCracken." *American Boy* (n.d.).

Mitchell, John N. "First Black to Play in the NBA Recalls High Points." *Washington Times* (February 18, 1999).

Mjagkij, Nina. "True Manhood: The YMCA and Racial Advancement, 1890–1930. Mjagkij and Margaret Spratt, ed. *Men and Women Adrift: The YMCA and the YWCA in the City*. New York: New York University Press, 1997.

Moore, Leonard. "Historical Interpretations of the 1920's Klan: The Traditional View and the Populist Revision. *Journal of Social History* 24 (Winter 1990).

Newlin, Ron. "Shooting Down the Color Barrier." *Indiana Alumni Magazine* (March/April 1998).

Ogdon, R. Dale, and J. Ronald Newlin. "Race and Sport in Indiana Before and After Jackie Robinson." *Hoosierisms Quarterly* (Summer 1996).

Olsen, Jack. "The Black Athlete." *Sports Illustrated* (five-part series, July 1–19, 1968).

Pierce, Richard. "More Than a Game: The Political Meaning of High School Basketball in Indianapolis." *Journal of Urban History* 27 (November 2000).

Preston, Charles S. Numerous articles in the *Indianapolis Recorder*.

Senate Avenue YMCA. *People Are Our Business: The 50th Year of Community Service*. Indianapolis: Senate Avenue YMCA Publications, 1950.

Spivey, Donald. "The Black Athlete in Big-Time Intercollegiate Sports, 1941–1968." *Phylon* 44 (1983).

Thornbrough, Emma Lou. "Segregation in Indiana During the Klan Era of the 1920s." *Mississippi Valley Historical Review* (March 1961).

Warren, Stanley. "The Monster Meetings at the Negro YMCA in Indianapolis." *Indiana Magazine of History* 90 (March 1995).

———. "The Other Side of Hoosier Hysteria: Segregation, Sports and the IHSAA." *Black History News and Notes* 54 (November 1993).

———. "Senator Robert L. Brokenburr: He Lived to Serve." *Black History News and Notes* 83 (February 2001).

Wiggins, David K. "Prized Performers, but Frequently Overlooked Students: The Involvement of Black Athletes in Intercollegiate Sports on Predominantly White University Campuses, 1890–1972." *Research Quarterly for Exercise and Sport* 62 (June 1991).

Wind, Herbert Warren. "The Sporting Scene: The Heart of Kokomo." *New Yorker* (April 14, 1980).

Wolff, Alexander. "Ghosts of Mississippi." *Sports Illustrated* (March 10, 2003).

Video and Audio Recordings

"Chicago's Harlem Globetrotters," WTTW Chicago.

"Coach for Life," WTIU, Indiana University Television, Bloomington, Ind., 1989.

"Globetrotters," A&E Biography, New York, 1996.

"Hoosier Hoops: A History of Indiana in the NCAA Basketball Championships," CBS Sports, 1994.

"Indiana's Game," Indiana High School Athletic Association, Indianapolis, 1986.

Zeronik, Drew, "Bill Garrett: Earning the Right to Play Big Ten Basketball," documentary video and accompanying notes.

"1947 Boys #1: Shelbyville vs. East Chicago Washington," Indiana High School Association Video Library.

"1947 Boys #2: Terre Haute Garfield vs. Marion," Indiana High School Athletic Association Video Library.

"1947 Semi-Finals: Shelbyville vs. Clinton," play-by-play radio broadcast by Tom Carnegie on Indianapolis WIRE, courtesy of Larry Sandman.

"1947 Semi-Finals: Shelbyville vs. Lawrenceburg," Indianapolis's WIRE radio broadcast, recording courtesy of Larry Sandman.

"1947 State Finals: Shelbyville vs. East Chicago Washington," Indianapolis WIRE radio broadcast, recording courtesy of Larry Sandman.

"1947 State Finals: Shelbyville vs. Terre Haute Garfield," Indianapolis WIRE radio broadcast, recording courtesy of Larry Sandman.

"1947 State Finals: Shelbyville vs. East Chicago Washington," play-by-play radio broadcast of Luke Walton on Indianapolis WISH, courtesy of Shelbyville High School Athletic Director Steve Drake.

"1947 State Finals: Shelbyville vs. Terre Haute Garfield," Indianapolis WISH radio broadcast, recording courtesy of Shelbyville High School Athletic Director Steve Drake.

Archives

Indiana Basketball Hall of Fame, New Castle, Indiana
Indiana High School Athletic Association, Indianapolis
Indiana Historical Society
Indiana State Library
Indiana University Archives
Indiana University Athletic Archives
Indiana University Center for the Study of History and Memory
Indiana University Northwest, Calumet Regional Archives
Library of Congress
NAACP Archives, Manuscript Division, Library of Congress

National Personnel Records Center
Ohio State Library
Ward M. Canaday Center for Special Collections, The University of Toledo

Newspapers and Periodicals

Anderson Daily Bulletin	*Indianapolis Star*
Bloomington Herald-Telephone	*Indianapolis Times*
Bloomington Herald-Times	*Look*
Boston Globe	*Nat Holman's Basket-Ball Annual*
Chicago Defender	*New York Herald-Tribune*
Colliers	*Pittsburgh Courier*
Connorsville News-Examiner	*Shelbyville Democrat*
Gary American	*Shelbyville News*
Hammond Times	*Shelbyville Republican*
Indiana Basketball History Magazine	*Stanley Woodward's Basketball*
Indiana Daily Student	*USA Today*
Indianapolis Freeman	*Washington Post*
Indianapolis News	*The Y's Man*
Indianapolis Recorder	

City Directories, Handbooks, and Yearbooks

Bloomington City Directory, 1947–51
Indiana High School Athletic Association Handbook, 1941, 1942, 1943,
    1947
Indiana University *Arbutus,* 1947–51
Indianapolis City Directory, 1946, 1947
Shelbyville City Directory, 1917, 1920, 1936, 1946, 1947
Shelbyville High School *Squib,* 1924, 1944–47

Unpublished Sources

Bannon, William J. Interview, conducted by Jean Freedman, March 6,
    1992, Bloomington, Indiana. Indiana University Center for the
    Study of History and Memory, #91-86.
Beck, Frank O. *Some Aspects of Race Relations at Indiana University, My Alma
    Mater* (1959).
Blocker, Jack S. Jr. "Choice and Circumstance: Destinations Sought and
    Shunned by African-American Migrants in the Lower Midwest,
    1860–1930." Meeting of the Organization of American Historians,
    Toronto, Canada (April 1999).
Chambers, Don. Scrapbook.

Clanin, Douglas E. "Anderson and the Negro." Undergraduate paper, Purdue University (1960).

Collins, Dorothy. Interview conducted by Jean Freedman, May 16, 1994, Bloomington, Indiana. Indiana University Center for the Study of History and Memory, #91-254.

Couch, Matthew M. "African-American Pioneers in Ohio Sports" (1998).

DeFrantz, Faburn E. *Autobiography.* (n.d.)

Eckstein, Loretta. Scrapbook.

Fangmeier, Julia S. *Indiana School Desegregation: A Brief Historical Overview.* Indiana Department of Public Instruction (July 1979).

Fraenkel, Peter. Interview conducted by Thomas D. Clark, July 30, 1970, Bloomington, Indiana. Indiana University Center for the Study of History and Memory, #70-13.

Gardner, Bertram Emerson. *The Negro Young Men's Christian Association in the Indianapolis Community.* M.A. thesis, Butler University (1951).

Garrett, Bill. Date Book, 1973.

Garrett, Bill. Letter to Gene Ring, December 27, 1952.

Garrett, William Leon. Interview conducted by William Picket and Barbara Benson, June 5, 1970, CSHM, #70-16.

Hill, Patton. Interview conducted by Victoria Cuffel and William Pickett, June 6, 1969, Bloomington, Indiana. Indiana University Center for the Study of History and Memory, #69-15.

Krebs, Jack. Scrapbook.

Lowe, Robert D. *Racial Segregation in Indiana, 1920–1950.* Unpublished dissertation, Ball State University (1965).

Mjagkij, Nina. "History of the Black YMCA in America, 1853–1946." Doctoral dissertation, University of Cincinnati (n.d.).

Morris, Norman. Scrapbook.

Orwig, Bill. "Acceptance Speech." James J. Corbett Awards Luncheon— NACDA Convention (June 10, 1986).

Ramsey, Andrew. "For Chief." Unpublished tribute, February 1951.

Stempel, John E. Interview conducted by Vincent A. Giroux, November 19, 1979, January 21, 1980, January 28, 1980, February 4, 1980, February 11, 1980, Bloomington, Indiana. Indiana University Center for the Study of History and Memory.

Wells, Herman B. "Acceptance Speech." IU Athletic Hall of Fame (December 13, 1984).

INDEX

TOM GRAHAM, who grew up in Bill Garrett's hometown, was an international lawyer in Geneva, Switzerland and Washington, D.C. before moving to Portland, Oregon, where he now lives and writes.

RACHEL GRAHAM CODY is a writer living with her husband and three children in Portland, Oregon.